Acknowle

This book could not have been written without the help and cooperation of some special people in my life.

My sister, Nancy Ross, kept the little brown suitcase safe for thirty years and has always encouraged me in any endeavor I have undertaken, especially this one. Some of her memories and a few of her words were used in this book. While we talked of doing this together over the years, when the time finally came that I felt inspired to do it, the same impetus was not there for her. She helped and supported my efforts in many ways and I love and appreciate her for that.

James Birklid, my Senior Partner in Life, saw that I had the proper tools to work on the project. He gave me space and time and helped with the research. He gave me constant emotional support and a calm and loving atmosphere in which to work. Thank you, Jim.

My sons and their wives were a cheerleading group, always showing interest and helping by discussing what was being done on the book. Thanks to my dear children, Martin and Laurie Caswell, Trevor and Jolene Caswell, and Daniel and Stacey Caswell. Here is a part of your heritage.

My nephew, Bryan Ross, was always interested, and assisted by providing computer-enhanced copies of some of the old pictures used in the book.

Thanks to Rick Foster, who suggested we go to the Titanic Exhibit in Seattle the summer of 2001. When I saw the black and white picture of John Jacob Astor IV seated, attired in his resplendent clothes, looking at the world with such confidence, it re-ignited my interest in the story in the little brown suitcase.

Thanks to each of the people who attended my seminar on this story at Venture Out Resort in Mesa, Arizona in February 2002. You know who you are. Your interest and enthusiasm for my talk was a prime motivator for me to begin and complete the project.

Dr. Michael Steingart of Phoenix offered me more than orthopedic advice on my sore hip. He showed a great interest in what I was doing at the time, which was preparing my seminar on the story. He thought the story sounded so interesting. He encouraged me enthusiastically to write the book.

Each of these people and others helped to arouse the passion in me to tell this story. I thank you and I appreciate you all and want you to know that your words and your actions helped and influenced me and gave me the courage I needed to write the book.

Foreword

A 1999 article on the Internet identified the fortune of John Jacob Astor I as being the fourth largest in United States history. Bill Gates's fortune is listed as the fifth largest. Astor lived in the seventeen and eighteen hundreds. How did he amass such a fortune so long ago?

The story in my grandmother's *Little Brown Suitcase* tells about her relative, John Nicholas Emerick, partner of John Jacob Astor, and how their lives intertwined to allow Astor to become the fourth most wealthy American ever.

It tells of hopes placed on a passenger on the *Titanic* who could right a great wrong and settle things once and for all.

Some say this story is myth, that little evidence remains of what actually occurred, and that the story of the great fortune is just wishful thinking on the part of the Emerick heirs.

My grandmother lived some of this story. It was real to her. Many of the events are things that actually happened. The letters quoted from John Nicholas Emerick, Dr. Lynn Emerick, Calvin Hoy and others are their own words.

The stories about John Nicholas Emerick and his partner are taken from material in my grandmother's *Little Brown Suitcase*. The only claim I lay to truth here is the truth found in the *Little Brown Suitcase*. What I have tried to do is fashion an interesting story with the best facts I have at hand. I relied primarily on the information in the *Little Brown Suitcase* and let my imagination fill in the blanks.

This story is being presented as historical fiction, allthough many of the events are true. I did not use reproductions or specific information from the many authentic newspaper stories in *The Little Brown Suitcase* because I was unable to obtain permission to do so from the various publishers.

Articles confirming the truth of this story may be found in the archives of many newspapers, especially from 1927 to 1933. Stories appeared in newspapers in New York City; Philadelphia; St. Louis, Missouri; Eau Claire, Wisconsin; Portland, Oregon; Seattle and Tacoma, Washington and many other newspapers and magazines of that era.

The photos included are from the *Little Brown Suitcase*, my family albums, and the albums of my sister, Nancy Ross.

Brief Genealogy of the Emerick Family as pertains to this story.

John Nicholas Emerick
Brothers

Christopher   Valentine

son
George Emerick

son
Warren Emerick

son
Irving Grant Emerick/m. Ella Perkins

children

Erastus Emerick
Bert Emerick

***Elsie Emerick/m. Roy Bryan**
   children
Lynn Bryan
Dorothy Bryan/m. Harold Morris
   children
Nancy Morris Ross
Carol Lynn Morris Caswell (author)

Merrill Emerick
Wilmer Emerick
Dee Emerick/ m. Grace
Mary Maureen Emerick
Hazel Emerick
Vida Emerick/m. Harry Bryan
Mabel Emerick
Myrtle Emerick
Arthur/Billy Emerick/m. Noreen

Chapter 1

I can only tell the story that is in the little brown suitcase. I can only tell that, and record the memories of stories heard when I was very young, when relatives would come to visit and late night conversations would be overheard.

Houses for the working man were small in the 1940s. Privacy was not easily achieved. A child lying in bed in the next room could easily hear conversations while drifting off to sleep.

Even as a child, I knew the tone of those conversations was different at night than it had been in the daytime. When relatives like Aunt Vida and Uncle Hank or Grandma's Uncle Lynn and his wife, Olivia, would visit, the night time conversation sometimes had an edge of anger that eddied and swirled through the words.

"If only, if only…" it seemed to whisper in my ears.

My grandfather, Roy Bryan, built the small house on five acres of land in Pierce County, Washington in the early 1930s. Before then, they had lived for a time in Tacoma on the side of a hill on Wapato Street. Shortly before their move, Grandpa had run for Tacoma town constable on the Republican ticket and lost.

He built a two-bedroom house with living room, dining room, kitchen, and because my grandmother stuck to her guns, an indoor bathroom with a bathtub. Grandpa thought a bathroom indoors was unclean and just too much of a luxury. Grandma held out and for once she prevailed.

Grandpa was what was then called a rounder. He was often in his cups. He liked whiskey. He never let his family go hungry if he could help it, but he was known to go on toots occasionally. He was known to hide his bottles in places where my grandmother might fear to go, like in the hay manger, where the cow ate.

Although married to a minister's daughter, my grandfather managed to keep his distance from anything smacking of religion. He was his own person. He was the pampered youngest child of his mother, Sarah, who watched her teenaged brothers being shot by Union soldiers in their yard near the end of the Civil War. Her mother had dressed them as girls, but it had not mattered. They died—as Sarah's first husband had—in that horrible, divisive war.

Sarah remarried a man named Bryan, who was a cousin of William Jennings Bryan, the famous orator, who ran for President against McKinley and was prominent in the Scopes Monkey Trial in 1925. My grandfather, Roy, was Sarah's last and favorite child.

When I was born in 1938, I had multiple birth defects, probably the result of my mother's admitted efforts to rid herself of an unwanted second baby. She did not want her figure to be ruined again. The doctors advised the family that I probably would not live long. My sister, Nancy, who was almost three years old, wanted to name me Charley McCarthy after the puppet made famous by Edgar Bergen on his radio show. But to her small consternation, I was named Carol Lynn. The Lynn was for my grandmother's favorite uncle and for her son, my mother's brother.

My grandfather promised God that if his only daughter's child lived he would never take another drink and he would go to church. And live I did. I was a beautiful child with a round face and huge blue eyes. When they sat me in a corner, people sometimes mistook me for a doll. I think my grandfather believed if he ever took another drink, I would die. No one in the family ever knew of him taking a drink again after his promise. He became a deacon in the church and practiced his prayers at home, where we would critique him. He wanted to sound just right.

My memories of being with my grandparents begin in the early 1940s. They had been in their home in the country for about ten years. The land was tamed by then by my grandparents and was neatly laid out.

The well-tended yard was huge in my childish eyes and was surrounded by a white picket fence. Every year Grandpa would mix milk, lime and salt to make whitewash. Whitewash was used out of necessity, as paint was too costly to use on the half acre of fence. Grandpa whitewashed the picket fence every summer. It gave the fence a nice, clean, neat appearance and it protected the wood from weathering and decay. Sometimes I helped and even talked my friends into pitching in with a Tom Sawyer approach.

There were many varieties of fruit trees, including King and Gravenstein apples, Italian prune and sweet plum, sour pie cherries, sweet yellow cherries, and peaches. There were oak trees and flowering hawthorne trees and in a part of the yard where the lawn sloped down a hill, a graceful weeping willow guarded the corner ruffling its tresses with the slightest breeze.

There was a wide cinder-covered driveway, lined on both sides by large rocks, also whitewashed every year. There was a group of roses on one side of the driveway, cuddled in their bed by masses of pink, red and white petunias in the summer. My grandmother loved flowers.

In the spring, along the back fence, peonies marched in red and white formations. Sadly, I thought, they marched off to the cemetery on Decoration Day, as Memorial Day was called then. Each year we would make a trip to the cemetery and Grandma would faithfully adorn the graves of her parents, Irving and Ella Emerick, with the vibrant blooms. It was sad to see them left alone, so brilliant and young, to nod in a vase for folks beneath the earth who could not enjoy their beauty.

Also, on the inside of the white picket fence was a grand garage with a woodshed attached. On the opposite side of the yard was an equally grand chicken house with an outhouse attached. The outhouse was left there just in case the inside plumbing clogged up and would not serve, as did happen on occasion.

I doubt that many chickens had it as good as the ones on my grandparents' property. The chicken house was a large, well-built structure. It was built on the side of a slope with tall supports underneath holding it up. It had a fenced yard that extended out into a field. The chickens had a daylight basement, so to speak. Below the chicken house, Grandpa had made a slanted walkway for them to use to come inside, where chicken feed was readily available and they could keep dry and out of the rain.

Occasionally one of them was called upon to visit the chopping block and give up its life for Sunday dinner. Except for that, they were privileged poultry.

All these things were inside the white picket fence.

Outside the picket fence, on the east facing the looming, snow-covered presence of Mount Rainier, was a large field with a creek running all the way through it, slicing the land into two areas. On the side nearest the house was a generous garden area, where Grandpa and Grandma grew vegetables of all sorts.

There were potatoes to be dug and searched for in the jet black earth and fat orange carrots and tall vines dripping with beans and early fresh peas bursting from the pods, sweet, crisp, raw and tasty, ready for a child to pick and eat in the warm sunshine. There were tall cornstalks that rustled with aliveness as they died in the fall.

Grandpa said the creek was really a drainage ditch. But I saw it as a creek with blue periwinkles and tadpoles and rushing currents, where leaf and stick boats with ants or beetles for a crew could set sail to far off places and go whooshing through the culvert under the road, and across the neighboring field—and then I could not imagine where all my boats might go.

You could not reach the other side of the field by the garden unless you went around by the road. In the summer, we would do that and climb carefully through the fence into the field because on that side of the creek black caps and blackberries grew on vines, tangled and wild and healthy without any interference by humankind the rest of the year. The vines always guarded their progeny with fierceness. We would come back with our hands scratched and ragged, happily bringing buckets of the sweet, succulent black treasures.

My childhood memories of living in my grandparents' home are rosy warm and idyllic. In reality, it was not an easy situation.

My grandparents, Elsie Emerick Bryan and Roy Bryan, willingly took me in when my parents divorced. My pretty, talented mother, Dorothy, who brought sparkle, electricity and vivid color with her when she entered a room, had decamped with a handsome, Irish prizefighter. Not that he was any prize in the end.

Pat O'Kelly brought her considerable heartache— more than a few bruises—and a surprise. Three years after their marriage, she discovered he had neglected to divorce his former wife. By then she was eager to obtain an annulment and get on with her life, which in the 1940s for a woman with an eighth-grade education, living in a small central-California town, meant she had earned the right to live in a trailer park and be a housekeeper.

She *did* have top of the heap clients: the mayor and several successful town business people. They all loved her. They loved her smile and her sunny disposition and the way she cleaned toilets and scrubbed their floors.

She had left my father, my older sister and me behind when she embarked on this new life adventure. She left us behind reeling in the wake of her departure, to struggle for years—a lifetime really—to regain some equanimity and balance to our fragmented lives.

My gentle, hardworking, good-looking, homebody father missed her most of all. But, alas, all those good qualities of his registered as boring on my mother's hunk meter. She loved to sing and dance and roller skate and party.

Sometimes on Saturday nights when I was five or six years old, before she left, my mother would take us to the Roller Bowl, my sister and me.

She would make sure my shoe skates were on properly and the laces tied in double knots so they would not come loose and trip me up. Then off she would go.

I would hang on to the bar at the side of the room and practice outside the huge oval that was the skating floor. Occasionally my mother would take my hand and lead me out on to the floor and skate me around a few times, as I wobbled and bobbled unsure of the wheels beneath my feet.

Mostly I remember watching her skate and listening to the roar of the organ music.

My mother was slim and pretty, with shoulder-length permed brown hair. She had such grace of movement it fascinated me. Men would ask her to dance and they would whirl around the floor. She crossed her feet when she turned and skated backwards as easily as forwards, always flowing to the beat of the throaty pipe organ. She was like a ballet dancer and her magical smile flashed liked a beacon when her head whizzed by.

I thought it was a marvel that anyone could skate with such skill and look so pretty. I would proudly say, "That's my mother," to the children standing next to me.

My father never went roller-skating with us. He liked to build things and work about the place. He was happy to stay at home. So the two attractive, visually stunning people who started with such high hopes and promises as so many do, were a mismatch.

But, no matter. After she left, we all three still loved her. What a spectacular heiress she would have made! She was so full of charm and had that smile that lit up her whole face like morning sunshine. She had clear blue, sparkling eyes that darted here and there like a fine sleek animal assessing the terrain of the jungle. Oh, yes, she would have made a wonderful heiress, my beautiful, spoiled, vain, lovable mother.

The talk I overheard lying in bed at my grandparents' home when relatives were there, seemed to involve items found in my grandmother's little brown suitcase.

About the size of a thick briefcase, it looked old even in those days. It was a ruddy, warm, brown leather with reddish tones, like freshly turned earth in the Arizona desert. It had lighter colored scratches and was worn along the edges. It was machine sewn but had been hand cut. The leather was folded over rather primitively at the corners.

The interior of the suitcase was lined with satin the color of burnished brass. The darker brown velvet trim made it resemble the inside of a casket, but I did not know that then.

It had two metal suitcase latches and a keyhole on each side so it could be locked to hold its secrets secure.

Actually, the contents of the little brown suitcase were not a secret. But the little brown suitcase itself always seemed to me to be touched with mystery.

One day I remember my grandmother wiping her hands on the apron which covered her flowered house dress. A freshly baked peach pie was cooling on the yellow countertop, wafting its delicious aroma throughout the house. We had picked the peaches earlier that day from the tree in the yard.

She placed the little brown suitcase on the red and white checkered oilcloth which covered the kitchen table. She sat down alone at the table looking wistfully through some of the papers in the suitcase.

"Whatcha doing, Gramma?" my childish voice queried.

I wish I had listened just a little bit more closely when she answered. Then I would have even sharper memories to augment the story the little brown suitcase has to tell.

But a little girl of eight or nine years old has a head full of dreams and activities in the here and now. Stories just a few years back seem like Greek Mythology. World War II was barely over at that time, and yet it seemed to me, as a child, to be ancient history.

So I listened to Gramma's answers to my casual questions with a light heart and fleeting interest. The worn old newspaper clippings, telegrams and letters seemed to be as dead as crumpled autumn leaves coaxed down by a frosty morning chill.

Gramma said the items in the suitcase were about our lost fortune. It had something to do with the *Titanic* and with a very important person who went down with the ship.

Running through my mind are highlights of what she said and what I heard as a child. The story spanned 200 years and involved rich merchants, an unscrupulous adventurer, a fateful fight on a New York pier, an old sea chest, a will lost for 112 years, a beautiful heiress, the *Titanic*, stolen documents, arson and, possibly, even murder.

Now, over fifty years later, the little brown suitcase calls out to me. It sits before me on the moss-green tile of my table, throbbing with the multitude of information it contains, like a small child sitting on a church pew swinging his legs waiting for the service to be over. I feel the anxiousness of its purpose.

Chapter 2

John Nicholas Emerick tossed restlessly in his bunk as the ship, the *Sea Queen*, rocked back and forth jostling his old, achy bones.

His thin face was creased on either side with a long wrinkle starting high on the cheekbones and angling down toward his chin. The straight line of his mouth neither smiled nor frowned. He still had most of his teeth, which he considered a great blessing, although some of them were beginning to feel loose and wiggly.

He had an unruly tuft of gray-white hair that insisted on standing up as if at attention on a military parade field. From the front it looked like he had a full head of hair. It was almost shoulder length when he wore it loose. The back of his head had a large bare spot that looked a bit like a lighthouse beacon on his tall angular frame.

"I must have these quarters outfitted with softer mattresses," he thought.

John Nicholas owned this ship and many others. He called his fleet the Seven Sails Sea Shipping Line. He discovered, when he first began his fur-trading business, that shipping the furs to Europe from America was a major expense. The shipping possibilities of the day were limited. The ships could not always be relied upon to depart when expected.

They could charge as they wished, knowing they were the only means available to ship large quantities of furs across the Atlantic Ocean.

John Nicholas made a very good bargain with a group of young boat builders. They were excited to receive such a fine order and built good solid ships for him. It made shipping his goods much easier. His ships were always able to find a load of freight and some passengers coming back. He charged a reasonable price. John Nicholas always prided himself on his fairness in business dealings.

He could not remember how many times he had made the trip from Europe to New York or Philadelphia.

He did remember the first time he had made the trip though. It was in 1770, over forty years ago. He and his cousin Andrew boarded a ship called the Charming Molley and bravely set sail for the new world.

He was not interested in staying at home in Hesse Castle in what is now called Hanau, Germany. Maria was dead. There was no longer any reason to stay.

John Nicholas was the first child born to John Daniel Emerick and his wife, Mary. His birth was followed by his brother Christopher two years later and his brother Valentine two years after that. Their mother died when John Nicholas was six years old.

He alone of the brothers had a vivid memory of her. He remembered sitting at her knee as she told stories. She could weave a story out of whole cloth and keep him entranced with tales of far off lands and exciting adventures. He remembered she was a happy person. He remembered her laugh.

She taught him how to read and do numbers at an early age. His memories of her were warm and pleasant. He had forgotten or blanked out the last months of her life. The younger boys, Christopher and Valentine, mostly remembered their nursemaid taking care of them. Mary was ailing when they were still babies.

She did not complain, but she became thinner and thinner and her face became gaunt and gray. She lay propped up on the window bench where she could see way down the valley to a ravine matted thick with fir trees. A waterfall plunged hundreds of feet into the bottom of the deep ravine, slicing it and spreading it apart so it looked like a dark green cake with one piece missing.

It was a view she liked very much. It was the same view from the window in the kitchen although at a lower elevation as the kitchen was downstairs. She used to like to stand at the kitchen window scrubbing fresh potatoes or carrots from their own garden while looking out on the magnificent scenery. It helped her cope with the gradual decline of her body's ability to function properly.

She would smile when the boys would be allowed to come into her room for a visit. The younger boys would clamor up on her lap for hugs and kisses. But soon she was exhausted and waved the nurse to take them away.

All the while, their father, John, sensing the inevitable, began to be away more. The young boys were unaware he was visiting a nearby widow who had as her best assets a round, happy face and a jolly mien. It happened that she was a Jewish widow, although the Emerick family was not Jewish.

Much as he loved their mother, John Daniel felt a need to be away from the house of sickness. It was terrible watching Mary fade from her lively, spirited self to a poor sick, wounded creature.

John Nicholas had a dim memory of the day his mother died. It was in the spring. A beautiful early May morning. The nurse was told to take the children out for a walk. When they came back, there were several carriages there and people milling about in the courtyard. John Nicholas knew something was wrong. He saw his father and ran to him.

"Father, what is wrong?" asked John Nicholas in his six-year-old's wonder.

"Let's go into the house, son," John Daniel replied.

His father explained that their mother had gone away.

"When is she coming back?" asked Christopher.

"She's gone to Heaven to be with God. He needs her now," said his father.

"But when will she be back?" Christopher persisted.

With great sadness of spirit John Daniel gathered his three little boys around him and said, "She will not be coming back, my sons. She is gone away and your mother will not be coming back."

John Nicholas instinctively understood what his father meant. The younger boys did not have a concept of what death was and did not really grasp the meaning. With the resilience of childhood to cushion the blow, they all accepted their father's pronouncement at their own level and went on.

There was always rivalry between the brothers. John Nicholas was the sober-sided one, tending to business and bossing his younger brothers about. He tried to make sure they minded all their manners and all the rules.

He always wondered if his younger brothers had something to do with an unlucky adventure he had one day when they were all youngsters, still gawky and green like frisky puppies.

Their cousins, Erik, Klaus and Andrew, lived nearby. The cousins had planned a day's activity riding horses in the woods. They rode into the yard leading a white plow horse and invited John Nicholas to go for a ride with them.

The name of the horse was Snowball. She was so pure white that if it had not been for her bulk and breadth she would have looked queenly pulling a golden carriage. Her back was so broad they had no saddle to fit her. John Nicholas did not especially want to go. The other boys all had horses with saddles.

"Come on, pantywaist, Baby Nicky. She isn't going to hurt you. See how gentle and calm she is," said Klaus, teasing his younger cousin, who desperately wanted to be like the older boys.

"Scaredy cat, scaredy cat," jeered Erik as he rode his bay in a circle around John Nicholas.

"Nicky, just get on the horse. It will be all right," coaxed Andrew, who was closest to John Nicholas in age.

Christopher and Valentine were nowhere to be found.

Erik led Snowball over to the big stump sometimes used for mounting. Klaus jumped down and gave John Nicholas a boost, and up on top of the huge plow horse John Nicholas slid, grasping the mane with tight fingers to keep himself from going off the other side. The horse was so wide John Nicholas's legs stuck out on either side like insect antenna ready to feel the way ahead.

Snowball was used to the rein of the plow. She did not respond to the gentle touch of a rein on her neck. A hard pull was what she expected if a change of direction was required of her. But the boys did not tell John Nicholas that secret. Considering what happened, it probably would not have mattered anyway.

It was a warm summer's day, but not so warm yet that the green had left the woods or the fields, as would happen later when the season wore on. By mid morning, the wild creatures of the area had already eaten their early repast and settled in some quiet place to remain unseen by the children on horses.

"You take your horse first, Nicky. That way you won't be left behind," said Klaus.

"But I don't know where to go," John Nicholas whined.

"It's okay," Erik replied, "Snowball knows where to go."

So John Nicholas and Snowball led out. The two older boys exchanged glances that gave nothing away yet hinted at a private knowledge.

Riding bareback on the big, broad horse, John Nicholas clung to the mane and swayed gently from side to side with each step Snowball took. This was going to be all right, he thought. He began to notice his surroundings.

They were traveling on a well-worn path which skirted the edge of the woods. Birds, annoyed by the intrusion into their territory, were showing it, with chirping and flitting from branch to branch as if to herald fear ahead of the troupe.

"Too slow, Nicky. We're falling asleep back here," cried Klaus as he rode up smartly and gave Snowball a hard slap on the rump. As big as she was, she knew how to shift gears and speed up. She began to trot and John Nicholas began to hold her mane with both hands, trying to keep a grip on the reins at the same time.

"Not fast enough!" shouted Erik. Andrew said nothing. Erik spurred his mount along side of Snowball and gave her another hard rap on the hindquarters.

Snowball's gait changed to a gallop. In some ways, it was easier now as the bump up and down of the trot changed to a rolling movement making John Nicholas' body surge backward and forward and backward and forward in a tidal motion.

It was very difficult for John Nicholas, but he realized he could do it. He could hang on and ride this horse.

He no longer saw the verdant scenery flying by. It took all of his young concentration to remain atop this Pegasus.

He could have done it, too. Only the bigger boys knew what was coming.

Suddenly the path took a right-angle turn into the woods. Snowball gave no warning. She just turned right on a dime. John Nicholas did not. He felt himself take wings and soar off her back. Before he knew what had happened, he had made a soft landing in the tall underbrush. The tall underbrush was a patch of stinging nettles.

Snowball kept right on going. So did his three cousins. With hoots and laughter, they rode on, leaving John Nicholas to find his own way back home and live with the painful results of their adventure.

John Nicholas heard laughter even after the horses were gone. He managed to catch a glimpse of Christopher and Valentine scrambling down from a nearby tree. "Now how did they happen to be there just at this time?" he thought. It was never mentioned between them, but he always wondered.

Oh, yes, his brothers would taunt and tease their older, more serious brother. The rivalry and unease between the brothers had early beginnings and life-long consequences for all of them.

By the time he was 20 years old, John Nicholas was known for his facility with numbers and his quiet way of taking charge and turning circumstances to good financial advantage for himself and his family.

He was especially good with horses, in spite of, or maybe because of, his inauspicious beginning. He loved to ride about the countryside on his favorite mount, a tall roan named Regal.

But the time came when he could not concentrate on any of his former pursuits in his usual calm and organized way.

It was a thunderbolt. More like lightning really. When one is struck, reason vanishes for a time. Life seems to go into suspended animation.

Somehow one sees in another qualities that reflect and complement one's own. Like the pull of a rushing river current, lives are swept toward their destinies.

So it was with John Nicholas when he met Maria.

Chapter 3

Little Elsie Emerick, was barely six years old when her father, Irving, decreed they were going to move out West to Washington state, a long way from their farm in Bridgeport, Illinois. Mother, Ella, was not in favor of this move. At least in Illinois she was near to her parents when Irving was off on one of his schemes and forgetting to provide for the ever-increasing family.

Irving decided they should visit Ella's Uncle Thomas in Puyallup, Washington and see what opportunities awaited them there. Shortly after arriving in Washington, the family moved to a cabin in the woods, some distance from town and from any neighbors.

Elsie Leora Emerick was born in 1888 and was the oldest girl. At this time, in 1894, she had two older brothers and two younger ones. Many more siblings would follow as years went by.

By moving out to this cabin he had bartered to obtain, Irving thought, they could become more self-sufficient and live in a less expensive manner. There was game to be found a plenty to put meat on the table. There was room for all the garden one could handle if just a few more trees were cut down. The children could play safely in the country setting. The air was better. There was room to keep a cow and a few chickens if enclosures could be built. And they would be, Irving vowed.

Although he was not as tall, he somewhat resembled President Abraham Lincoln. Irving was lanky and had a chiseled face. He had large hands that seemed perpetually to hang too far out of his sleeves. His eyes had a wildness about them. They were the fierce eyes of an adventurer and an idealist.

Irving did not really care if the experiment in the woods did not work out. He knew that in 1906 a large sum of money would be coming to him. He knew because his father, Warren Emerick, had told him what *his* father, George Emerick, had said.

The family was heir to a gigantic fortune left to them by Irving's great uncle, John Nicholas Emerick, who came from Germany in the 1700s.

The fortune was due to be paid in 1906, exactly 90 years after the death of John Nicholas Emerick. There was plenty of money for all relatives who could prove their relationship.

Irving knew this was true because as a child he had lived with other relatives after his mother had died giving birth to his youngest brother, Lynn. While living with his Aunt Martha for almost 10 years until he was 18, he had heard the stories of the fortune and the whereabouts of important papers the family would need when the time came to claim the fortune.

He actually saw the trunk of John Nicholas Emerick once when he was visiting Aunt Lucinda Jones. He was not allowed to open it, but he did see it. It was upstairs in an attic. Aunt Lucinda would not let him bother it as he was just a youngster. He remembered it was a very old-looking, leather, box-like trunk.

He also remembered hearing from several relatives, including his father, Warren Emerick, how the papers left by John Nicholas with his brother Christopher, were stolen by Irving's Uncle Will, his father's brother. Will and his brother Lynas, had a terrible fight with their parents, who would not give them the papers regarding the estate. About 1844, Will stole the papers, which included the will of John Nicholas Emerick and took his teenaged brother, Lynas, with him leaving their parents' home forever. Their parents never saw them again; such was the rift between them.

In 1849, Will and Lynas went East to the Surrogate Court of New York and filed the will of John Nicholas Emerick. They obtained a judgment which they sold for $50,000. Shortly thereafter, the courthouse with the records of the transaction was burned to the ground. It was said to be arson. Before that happened, Lynas, was said to have paid $25,000 to get back a copy of the court decree. He then vanished into Mexico and was never heard from again.

It was a strange story, but Irving had heard it from his father and his father's sisters. Nevertheless, Irving was confident that the fortune could still be claimed by the papers in the old sea chest he had seen. The family still expected to obtain their rightful inheritance in 1906.

So Irving knew that whatever he did, he and Ella would be fine.

Irving was twenty years old when he married Ella Florence Perkins on a warm autumn day at Sumner, Illinois in 1884. Ella was twenty-one.

She was a small girl with the most perfectly round face Irving had ever seen. Her face, with its bright eyes, upturned nose and smiling mouth, drew him with a powerful pull, like the tides and like the moon her face resembled. She seemed such a contrast to his rangy, rather unfinished young appearance.

He was a good catch. Ella's father, Peter Perkins, was a shoemaker in Sumner. He was known for the quality of the high-button shoes he made. It was a comfortable living. The Perkins's had a modest home, just off the main street in town.

Irving's father lived on the outskirts of Sumner. There were nine children in the family. Irving's father owned a prosperous fruit orchard. The children were all well educated and were known as having some money.

There was something about Ella that Irving did not know when he married her. She did not want to let him know this information about her. Indeed, she had been taught rather forcefully by her parents that her inclinations were inappropriate. Although almost two hundred years back, the Salem witch trials were a part of the country's history. The very fact of their occurrence made a long-lasting impression on would-be dabblers in the occult.

Not that Ella dabbled in dangerous, secret practices. What Ella had been given by her Creator was the ability to know what others were thinking without being told. She was also able on occasions to move objects with her mind.

Now mind you, Ella did not know as a child that this power she possessed was unusual. She began to learn quickly that repeating what her momma or poppa was thinking was not appreciated, no matter that she heard the words in her head as clearly as if they were spoken.

Anger was wont to erupt.

"Where did you hear that? You were listening at the door. You naughty child!" her mother would proclaim with great consternation. The stinging willow switch would come down off the wall and seek her small bare legs leaving striped red welts.

Ella's little round face convulsed in tears.

"No, Momma, no! I didn't! I didn't!" she would wail.

So little Ella learned to keep others' thoughts to herself and gradually, as she became older, the ability receded somewhat. She realized though that when she was angry with her mother, she could make a glass fall off the shelf—if she wanted to. They never suspected that, Momma and Poppa.

They did eventually recognize her mind-reading ability in a vague way. Momma would never have put a name to it or spoken of it to a neighbor. It was too embarrassing to have a child with such an oddity.

Momma would look at her with that stern evil eye before they would go into church and say, "You mind your ways in church, Missy." Ella knew what that meant. Still, sometimes it was hard to shut out the deacons' mental meanderings during the long church service. The deacons' minds wandered as deacons do.

Ella kept her latent mind-reading gift to herself after her marriage. It was a private card to be called into play as needed, she had decided.

She had a very bad feeling that day in the cabin in the woods when Irving came home from hunting, packing two live squawking and struggling bear cubs. You did not have to be clairvoyant to know this was not something a mother bear would like.

"Irv, they must have a mother out there somewhere," Ella protested.

"They were all alone, just a crying and howling to beat anything, Ella. I just couldn't leave them out there to die, could I?" asked Irving, ever the romantic woodsman wanting to tend the poor of the forest like he later tended the poor of humanity.

So Irving built the bear cubs a small wooden cage, more like a box with slats for them to peer out. He fed them warm milk from a bottle. That was the only time they ceased their incessant caterwauling.

The children played around the cage the rest of the afternoon. The small bears would suck and lick on the children's fingers if they dared to reach inside the slats. They pawed at the slats with baby bear paws that did little good. They cried for their mother. The children stroked their brown bear coats. The babies cuffed each other and rolled around as much as they could in the small enclosure.

Elsie thought the bears would make great pets and be fun to play with. Such is the six-year-old mind. She liked their furry coats and cute faces. She recognized the possibilities although the teddy bear had not yet been invented. It was eight years later, in 1902, when well-known hunter Teddy Roosevelt refused to shoot a baby bear. This resulted in the manufacture of furry, fuzzy bears called Teddy bears after the twenty-sixth president of the United States.

"Poppa, what shall we do with them?" Elsie asked. "Can we keep them for pets?"

"I don't know yet, child. Your Uncle Lynn is coming tomorrow. We'll figure out something to do with them. I don't reckon we can keep them for long," replied her father.

"Irv, I have a bad feeling about this," said Ella.

"Now, Ella, just let me handle this and stop worrying," he rebuffed her.

Ella turned and went inside the cabin and banged the door shut with a deliberate force, a fact which was not lost on the children or Irving.

It was getting late and Ella called them all in to supper. She had made a wild pheasant dish with savory gravy and light, plump dumplings for dinner that evening. Ella was a good cook. Even if they did not have much, she always made it taste good.

After supper, Elsie helped with the dishes. The boys never had to help. Poppa would not allow it. Elsie tried to understand why they could go out to play and she had to help. He did make the boys stack wood and do outside chores sometimes, but it was never a regular thing. She had to help at meals and with the cleaning early on. She was used to it by now and it gave her a special time to be with her mother. She liked that. Her mother was getting fat again. Elsie was not quite sure what that meant yet.

It was getting dark and the little bears were still crying. How could they have enough energy left to keep up that howling? Elsie finished wiping the dishes and putting them away. She went outside in the dusk to see the baby bears once more before bedtime. The boys had long since tired of the bears and were playing tag around the trees, except for the baby, Willie, who was too small and had already fallen asleep in the cabin.

Elsie edged up to the cage and the little bears stopped crying for just an instant, as if they were hoping this visit meant some kind of reprieve for them. Quickly sensing that was not the case, they continued their nasal bawling. Elsie patted the cage, told them goodnight and went into the house.

At six years old, Elsie Emerick was going to be a beauty, you could tell. She had not quite inherited her mother's round face. Hers was plumpish with sweet baby fat and clear blue eyes. She had an impishness about her that perhaps came from holding her own in rough-and-tumble games with her brothers. They never got the best of her. Of course, Ella took special care with her only daughter.

In years to come, the family would include twelve living children: six boys and six girls. But during the adventure of living in the cabin in the woods, only five of the children had been born. Too soon, Elsie, as the oldest daughter, would be expected to work hard, taking on much responsibility in the support and care of a large family.

The three oldest children slept in the loft of the cabin. It was an open loft and Irving built a railing along the opening at Ella's insistence, so the children would not accidentally fall over. The boys were forever scrapping and wrestling. Bert and Rastus slept on pallets on the bare floor. Ella had divided the loft with a temporary curtain so Elsie could have a corner of her own. They fixed up a wooden crate with a pink gingham curtain as a night stand next to Elsie's pallet of blankets. There Elsie could hide her small treasures and the few personal items she possessed.

In the crate at night she put the small collection of Indian arrowheads her Uncle Lynn had given her. Uncle Lynn was her father's youngest brother, who came to visit often. Elsie and Uncle Lynn were great pals.

Momma made her a rag doll she called Rosie. She made Elsie and Rosie matching dresses out of flour-sack material with little blue forget-me-not flowers on it. Her mother told Elsie that Rosie would be like the little blue flowers.

"Rosie is your first doll, Elsie. You will never forget her."

Momma was right. Elsie clearly remembered Rosie and could describe her in detail when she was in her eighties. Rosie had hair of bright-yellow yarn, while Elsie's hair was common brown, but Rosie had cornflower-blue embroidered eyes, the color of her owner's. She had a red-thread, always smiling mouth. It made Elsie happy just to look at her.

They went everywhere together, dirtied their flowered blue dresses with outdoor play and slept together at night.

The only thing Elsie could not remember about Rosie, when she was in her eightieth year, was what had happened to Rosie. Somewhere along the years of childhood, she disappeared into thin air. The day could not be pinpointed. Her owner no longer sought out her friend Rosie on a daily basis as she grew older and was drawn into family responsibilities. And so the doll and the little girl that Elsie was, parted company in that mysterious way of children and toys, without a mental ripple on Elsie's part.

Years later, she asked her sister, Vida, who was nine years younger, if she remembered Rosie. But Vida had no recollection of the forget-me-not doll who disappeared but was not forgotten.

That night in the cabin the three children, Rastus, Bert and Elsie, were fast asleep in the loft. Irving and Ella and the two younger boys, Merrill and Willie, were asleep on the main floor. The bear cubs were still crying, but the constant noise had a hypnotic quality that eventually lulled them all to sleep.

In the small hours of the morning, before anyone in the cabin heard or awoke, something large came racing through the woods. If they had been awake they would have heard it coming, crashing, thrashing, calling and bawling. It was the cry of a mother bear whose cubs were lost. As it was, none of them woke up until she arrived in the yard and with great screams of anger began ripping the wooden cage to kindling. Then they woke up with a terrible start, not knowing at first if the noise was in the cabin with them. When they came to their senses, they all, except for Willie, who never even stirred, scrambled out of bed and went to the windows.

There they watched in horror and fascination as the fury of the mother bear was unleashed. When the little bears were freed she stood on her hind legs looking at the cabin and roaring as if she knew whoever snatched her cubs was in there. In the moonlight they could see her great bulk and almost feel the waves of anger rolling toward the cabin. Was she going to charge the door or the windows? Would they hold? There was an instant when they all wondered, parents and children, what the huge, angry bear would do next.

Irving went for his gun. When he turned back to the window they were gone. All three had dissolved into the woods. The mother bear could still be heard scolding her offspring for their unapproved adventure.

After that the Irving Emerick family did not live in the cabin very long. Soon they were located in St. Louis in a big rental house. Elsie never really knew why. Apparently, the experiment in the woods had run its course.

Chapter 4

When Queen Anne of England, later of furniture fame, died in 1714, it presented quite a problem for the royal selection committee. Her only child had died of smallpox. There was no heir apparent to take the throne. Anne was a Stuart. So the ministers sought out a likely prospect with some Stuart blood to rule their country.

The throne was eventually offered to George of Hanover. George, who was 54 years-old, not only had Stuart blood; he also believed staunchly in the Protestant faith, so important in an English ruler at that time. There is no evidence that he even wanted to be king, but he did accept the position and the healthy stipend which came with it. He continued to speak German, never learning a word of English throughout his entire reign.

By 1770, George's grandson, George III was in power. There were close connections between Britain and Germany. For many years, the Province of Hanover had been a British sovereignty. People in Germany were drawn to explore the British Colonies in America.

The possibilities in America intrigued and interested John Nicholas Emerick. Working at his father's inn, he was exposed to people from many lands. He heard numerous exciting tales about America. It was a land rich with resources and opportunities. He determined to go.

Cousins Andrew Emerick and John Nicholas Emerick talked of making the trip together. They were both eager to set out for new shores in 1770. John Nicholas remembered the stories his late mother told of far away places when he was a young lad. Andrew was drawn by the adventure of the trip, while John Nicholas saw opportunities for increasing his station in life. He had heard fortunes were easily made in the new land.

John Nicholas and Andrew planned their trip together. John Nicholas was taking a small legacy from his mother's estate and an amount from his own accumulation with him. Andrew was taking his good spirits and a love of adventure. He looked forward to being more on his own with his favorite cousin. The world was ahead of them as the two young men in their twenties set out to conquer the new land.

John Nicholas's father had married the Jewish widow years before. John Nicholas now had a younger stepbrother named Solomon. His brothers Christopher and Valentine were not inclined to go off traveling to such a far away place. John Nicholas did not want their company. He and Andrew would do just fine.

He considered the family dynamic which existed between him and his brothers long before the term sibling rivalry was invented. The two younger men, Christopher and Valentine, were always close. John Nicholas was separate unto himself. His interests were different. He tended to business and had ideas he wanted to try. They seemed a bit feckless, but he loved them anyway. They were family, of the same mother whom he remembered so fondly.

As a last bit of business in his native land, John Nicholas Emerick visited Maria's resting place. He had had no part in selecting it, but he was pleased with the location. She was buried on her family's property, high on a hill overlooking a small quiet stream that sang constant lullabies to her. The granite stone read simply:

Maria Gretchen Klom
1743 - 1765
The Fever of Life is Over

It was five years ago, but it seemed like yesterday.

They met in the spring, two young people from prosperous families, both blessed with a restless energy that sought a spirit of equal measure. Their relationship blossomed and gradually unfolded as the spring season progressed.

She was never unsure of herself. He thought she thought like a man. He meant that in the most complimentary sense. There was nothing silly, simpering or insincere about her. He found that captivating. She was the first young woman of his acquaintance to affect him so. He felt as if he were speaking to an equal. In other girls he had noticed a streak of flirtatious whimsey he did not find appealing.

Maria was slightly taller than John Nicholas, but she stood proud and straight when they talked. She had hair the color of warm clover honey, a rather thin face, with an unusually wide mouth, which stretched happily when she smiled. Her eyes were the color of a deep amber stone in the sun.

She was not afraid to speak her mind on various subjects. What's more, she seemed to have some knowledge of the politics of the area and the value of property and would discuss the sermon they heard on Sunday at the Lutheran church. He felt her mind drawing him out into wonderful and fearful discussions like he had with no other.

The pull of the mind is a very great seduction. It fulfills an inner gnawing, hungry need to connect with another being to help calm and manage the aloneness of life. For the first time in his life, John Nicholas fell wholly and completely under the spell of this complex and interesting young woman.

If only her father had not presented her with that high-spirited horse for her birthday. She was very good with horses. John Nicholas and Maria had enjoyed many rides together. But he was not with her the day she fell. Something must have spooked her birthday mount. They found her by the pathway with her neck broken.

When the horse finally came home, Herr Klom shot him straight-away. But that did not bring his daughter back.

Sitting in his shipboard bunk and looking back some forty years, John Nicholas reminded himself that in all those years he had never found another woman who interested him as much as Maria. How different life might have been if she had lived. She would have come with him to America. He was sure of that. They talked of it a few times. The talk was speculative—it was not ready to happen then.

John Nicholas stood up adjusting his balance to the roll of the sea. He was never troubled by sea-sickness. His head felt a little light, which was a feeling he was experiencing occasionally these days.

"I just stood up too fast," he thought, and as his head cleared, he dismissed it from his mind.

He remembered boarding the Charming Molley, his first seagoing ship in 1770, carrying his sea chest on board himself. He and Andrew were tingling with excitement, both trying to outdo the other with their blasé manner, so as not to appear like country folk unused to such things.

It was a warm summer's morning when they watched the ship round the point of the harbor, its trapezoidal sails filled with a westerly breeze. Rocking peacefully with the surges of the harbor waves, she glided into port with gentle creaks and groans. The crew of a dozen sailors began scurrying about setting out the gangway, tending to the sails, cleaning the deck. Everyone knew their job and some miraculously understood the complex maze of lines that made up the ship's rigging.

Before long, the last of the passengers and cargo was loaded. The sails were unfurled and as the ship pulled away, the port began to shrink, then disappear from sight. They were on their way.

The quarters on the Charming Molley were not exactly charming. But it did not matter to John Nicholas and Andrew that they were squeezed into bunks in a tiny room below decks. They felt lucky to be traveling on such a grand adventure. Some passengers slept in one of two other separate rooms, one of which also housed the galley. The crew slept in hammocks on the lower deck. The cabin boy slept on the floor or on top of piles of gray rope or on gunny sacks of staples.

The Charming Molley was one hundred and twelve feet long and twenty-four feet at the beam. The fourteen sails she sported contained almost forty-five hundred square feet in various polygonal sizes and shapes. At most she could accommodate forty-eight passengers and a crew of twelve.

The two men loved the smell of the sea and the feel of the salt-laced breeze whipping through their hair. They rejoiced in the snap of the huge sails in the wind. They both almost lost their hats at the outset and thereafter were watchful of the wind. The young cousins were undaunted by the unfamiliar food served up in the cramped, smelly galley below decks. They ate salt beef and pork, dried fish, sauerkraut, hardtack and porridge. There was plenty of it. One could manage.

Each day brought new experiences to be savored. Because it was summertime, it was a relatively calm and easy crossing. The men spent much time at the rails, savoring the view of the endless, fascinating water and the sights to be seen. They saw huge fish and sea mammals like they never imagined. Before they knew it, New York harbor was coming into sight.

And when they landed there was such excitement. So many people were at the dock. There was such a crush of loading and unloading of different ships. It took one's breath away. New York was a busy, bustling port.

John Nicholas knew what he wanted to do. He heard there were fortunes to be made in the fur trading business if one was willing to work hard. There was a great market for fine furs from America. He had trained with a furrier in Hanover before making this trip. He knew how to scrape and treat the hides of animals to make them more marketable. He had a plan. He had the names of some people to contact. He had a goal.

Andrew's plans were not as firm. He wanted to experience the new country and see what it held for him.

Together they found lodgings at an inn in New York City. That night in a pub, they met men full of ale and exciting talk. Andrew struck up a conversation with a group discussing the violence in the New York streets a few weeks back between the Sons of Liberty and the British soldiers.

"Thought they could post those broadsheets anywhere they liked, they did," said Charley Buckridge, a fair-haired young man from Massachusetts. "But they showed 'em. The Sons of Liberty mean business."

"What do you mean, broadsheets?" asked Andrew.

"Oh, they have instructions for everything, the British do. Want to put signs up everywhere giving us rules for this and rules for that. Why, I'm surprised they haven't given us a rule for how to pull it out and pee!" said Charley. The other men around the table banged their mugs of ale and hooted with laughter.

"The Sons of Liberty. Who are they?" inquired Andrew.

"Well, nobody really knows for sure. And if they do, they'd best just forget. Why some of us sitting right here could be Sons of Liberty. Ever since the Stamp Act was passed by England five years ago, groups have formed in different towns. They all work underground for the same thing. It ain't right to tax us colonists so.   There's tax on newspapers and pamphlets, bills and legal documents, licenses, even on dice and playing cards. What kind of fairness is that, I ask you?" said Charley.

"The Sons of Liberty get their licks in when they can and they ain't above bashing some heads in if they need to," joined in another at the table.

"Here now," said the barkeeper, "That'll be enough of that kind of talk in here. We don't want no trouble. The less people know about some things, the better."

John Nicholas turned aside to another table. He and Andrew had both worked in his father's inn in Darmstadt as boys growing up. Visitors from England and France were frequent. The boys had all learned to converse in English and French as a matter of course, being exposed to the language of travelers as they were.

"Anyone here know about the fur trade?" he asked a group at the next table.

"Aye, laddie, ye best be careful goin' ta that trade," replied a Scotsman with a prickly looking red-gray beard. "Hear there's lots of money to be made if ye get back with yer skin. Me cousin, Jamie, went out on one expedition. He come back, said he'd niver seen such things. He could na' speak of it. Them savages, the Indians, they're a cruel, wicked bunch a beasts, ye ask me."

"But you say there is good money to be made?" probed John Nicholas.

"Aye, if it's money yer lookin' for it's there. 'Tis a hard way to earn it though," replied the Scotsman, shaking his head back and forth.

"There's a good market for American furs in Europe. But you need a fair amount of cash just to put a trip together. You need a good group of experienced men you can trust and trade goods and hearty provisions. Men ain't going to go out in the wilds like that without they're taken care of. A promise of the profits doesn't fill the belly, young man," said a well-dressed, middle-aged gentleman at the table.

"Now if you were so inclined and need some money to start up, I could possibly be of assistance," he continued.

"That's very kind of you, sir," said John Nicholas. "I'm not at that point right now. My cousin and I have only just arrived on the Charming Molley."

At that, congratulations were given and another round of drinks was ordered by the group.

John Nicholas was not about to reveal that under his shirt, tied around his waist was a money pouch with enough money to finance an expedition and then some. He was not so gullible that he would mention such a fact in a crowded pub—or that he had brought some trade goods with him in his baggage. Not even Andrew knew how much he had. John Nicholas kept quiet about it and kept his own counsel.

They sat in the pub room drinking ale and swapping stories with the men there until early morning. Then they went to their beds and slept a happy sleep, thankful that they had braved the terrors of the Atlantic Ocean on a small wooden vessel and had arrived safely. A good crossing was a good omen. All else would be favorable as well.

Seventy-five-year-old John Nicholas sighed at the memory of that happy time. His head cleared now, he walked out to the deck, to once again feel that rush of cold, clear sea air. It never failed to lift his spirits. He savored the sound of whipping, snapping sails when the wind was fair and the ship skimmed the water like a giant flying fish.

In two days, they would be in port and he planned to take a rest before conducting further business. As always, he carried his trunk with him. While he was in Europe, he had had a secret place made into the lid of the trunk. There he put his will, which he had updated while in New York in August, his diaries, and some other papers having to do with his estate. No one would ever guess the space was there, so well was it concealed. He must remember to tell Baltheus, and only Baltheus, of the secret hiding place. He was no longer sure his business partner could be trusted. That saddened him as he had seen such promise in the young man when they met years ago.

For many years now, John Nicholas had made his home with Baltheus Emerick in Philadelphia. Baltheus was a cousin, the youngest son of Uncle Konrad. Uncle Konrad, Andrew's father, came to the new world after John Nicholas. He was the brother of John Nicholas's father, John Daniel. Because they were so close, some people in America thought Uncle Konrad was John Nicholas's father. John Nicholas was always able to get along better with his uncle than he did with his father. They had in common the fact that they had struck out on their own in a new land and made their fortunes.

John Nicholas's fortune far surpassed anything any of his other relatives had achieved. He had dedicated his life to his business. He had never married and had no family of his own to draw his finances and his energies away. He made canny investments, buying up huge pieces of land in the country for a shilling an acre. Already these properties were becoming more and more valuable. He held on to his investments despite offers from eager buyers.

Unlike many of his wealthy contemporaries, John Nicholas did not build mansions to his own wealth or move in society's best circles. Without a wife or children to spur him on to these endeavors, he lived happily enough continuing the work he had begun as only he could, uninterested in manifesting outward achievements of his wealth.

Lately though, he had become concerned about his wealth. His partner was his concern. He wished his brothers had proved reliable, but they had not. He had come to rely on an outsider as his partner when he really wanted to keep things in the family. Christopher and Valentine would have ruined the business. They had no head nor passion for it. But now he wondered if it might have been just as well to partner with them. As it was, he feared the partner he had chosen was not to be trusted.

Chapter 5

At ten years old, Elsie Emerick had completed the fourth grade in St. Louis. She knew how to read and write cursive and could do sums. She hoped to continue in the fall when school took up again. She was not always able to go to school regularly. Sometimes Momma needed help with the little children or help with the work of running two boarding houses across the street from one another. They lived in the one on the west side of the street. In the summer the heat parched the back of the house where the kitchen was and where Elsie's small bedroom was located. It would be hot this evening at home.

Today Elsie was walking home from her job at a cracker factory. She worked eight hours every day packing crackers in cardboard boxes for 25 cents a day. Carfare on the streetcar was a nickel. Sometimes when she was really tired she took the streetcar. Mostly she walked the three miles on the city streets to save the money. Momma needed the money, especially now that Poppa had gone West.

When Irving's father died, he inherited a sizable sum, not as much as was expected in 1906 when the great fortune would be divided, but an amount large enough to allow him to pursue a dream he had. Being of a religious bent and an idealistic nature, Irving wanted to serve mankind to make the lives of others better; to heal their souls and their bodies.

Toward this end, he decided to take his part of the inheritance and go to a church-affiliated medical school in Seattle and study to become a medical doctor.

Ella was not pleased. Her mouth which had smiled so easily when they were married was now set in an almost permanent downturn at the corners. The brightness of her eyes had faded. In addition to the five children she had had during the cabin-in-the-woods adventure, she now had four more. Dee, so active and alive with curiosity at four, Mary Maureen, Hazel, and the baby, Vida, almost a year and starting to walk. In addition, she had lost twin girls. Now she was pregnant again and feeling overly heavy at five months.

"What if this is two more instead of one," she thought. "What shall I do? How will I keep up?"

How, indeed, with only Elsie old enough to help with the boarding house work and the children. True, the boys found odd jobs and contributed some, but not with the work around home. Even when he was gone, Irving would not have his boys doing housework.

Irving. Why had she ever married him? How could he leave her alone with so many mouths to feed? What's more, he had taken most of the money he had inherited with him. He felt with the two boarding houses she would have enough money coming in to manage.

She remembered why she had married him. He was a handsome young man with a long, black beard and thick, dark hair. He had a fierce dedication to the Lord. She was very drawn to his love of God and his confident way of speaking about his beliefs and the things of the Bible. When he looked at her with those deep, almost haunting eyes, she gave her heart away. She was proud of him for caring about the poor. She cared, too. But as their family increased and money was so very tight, it was harder to appreciate his bringing poor folks home to dinner and giving what money he earned away when his own family could have used it. It was difficult for Ella living with a saint.

Whatever she felt for him in the early years, and she had been pleased to be married to a person of his intellect and presence, was eroded by 1898. It would soon be the turn of the century and they still had so little and she worked so hard. She loved each of her children dearly and did not wish them gone. It was hard enough to part with the little twin girls, so finely formed, who arrived in the world too soon to take a breath. She only wished for a little rest and a husband who would be there for her.

There was too much stirring in her body. There was movement everywhere. That could only mean one thing—more than one baby again.

51

Ella sat down on the kitchen stool for just a moment. She wished Elsie would hurry home. It was almost time to serve dinner and she needed the help so badly. The cooking was done. The food was ready. She would pop the biscuits into the oven when Elsie arrived. The kitchen was an oven itself with the gas cook stove heating the already warm air in the room. Ella prided herself on her good meals. One of the things her boarders really liked was her biscuits. So, hot or not, she made biscuits.

Elsie always liked caring for the little children in the family. She liked that better than helping Momma with the boarding-house work. She was patient with the little ones and invented games to play to keep them happy and occupied. She often had a baby on her young hip as she helped with other chores. Ella relied on her oldest daughter too much. She knew that. She just did not see another way to cope.

Elsie arrived home after a long, hot walk on St. Louis city streets. She scooped up baby Vida. Dee and the little girls ran to her for a hug. She quickly set the table for the ten boarders. At least they all ate in one house. They didn't have to pack food across the street in this heat.

The ten family members would eat after the boarders were served. Sometimes it was hard for Elsie to wait after her long walk. She grabbed a bite in the kitchen if she could, to stave off her hunger and tiredness.

The older boys were working at the coalyard nearby. They had to clean up in the backyard before they were allowed in the house. Every little bit the children earned went to their mother. Or it was supposed to. But Elsie knew that sometimes the boys kept a few cents back. Once in a while, they treated her to candy they bought at the store, so she knew they didn't give all their money to Momma. At least they were generous. When they had a treat, she did too. She was not going to tell on them. They worked hard too, and little pleasures were too hard to come by.

After a year and a half, Irving came home from Seattle. His inheritance money was all spent. He was not even close to finishing a medical degree. In fact, much of his training involved classes in religion and theology, which were requirements at the school he attended.

By this time Ella had become the mother of two more girls, the twins, Mabel and Myrtle. Mabel was a thin, nervous baby and cried frequently. Myrtle had a chubby body and a placid, accepting nature.

Elsie, now almost twelve years old, doted on the twins. Yes, they were a great deal of work. Her little sisters were still too young to help much. Momma had her hands so full with the boarders to care for and with being mother and father to all the children in Irving's absence.

Just because Irving had come back from medical school in Seattle did not mean that he was present at all times. He began to travel the countryside preaching to the poor, mostly black, people. When he was home, he was a very hard taskmaster. The children were required to say Bible verses from memory at the table every day. If they forgot their Bible verse or misbehaved in any way at the table, he whacked the back of their hands with his knife.

It was not easy for Ella to get used to his taking charge of all aspects in the house when he was there, and expecting her to make all decisions on her own when he was gone. She felt that if she was good enough to run the house while he was gone for a year and a half, she should still be good enough when he was home. He did not really see it that way. He began to supervise her shopping for food and her cleaning schedule. There were shouting matches that the children tried to ignore.

He came home one day after having been gone preaching for a week. Ella asked if he had brought any money with him.

"Well, I had some, Ellie. They paid me at the Christian Church in Jeff City."

"How much did you get?" Ella asked with a measure of relief.

"It doesn't really matter. I gave it to the poor black people I met on the way home," countered Irving.

Diminutive Ella, who was already pregnant again, felt the heat of anger fill her throat. At that moment, a vase sitting on the upright piano somehow jumped off and smashed on the floor.

"I mustn't let this happen," thought Ella. "I'll destroy the furnishings."

With that she picked up a dozen eggs which were sitting in a bowl on the kitchen counter. She threw the eggs at Irving all at once. She didn't stay to clean them up either. She marched outside and went for an unaccustomed walk around the neighborhood, stopping to visit with neighbors along the way.

When she arrived back home, the egg mess was all cleaned up. She never asked. She didn't really want to know if Irving had cleaned it up himself or if he had made the children do it.

"Thank the Lord," Ella thought, when Irving announced he had located work driving a streetcar on the Page Avenue line. At least he would be busy and bringing in some regular money. Of course, she expected he would still preach on the weekends. He never seemed to be at a loss for words on how folks should behave and run their lives.

Irving still spoke of the money that would be coming their way in 1906 when the will of his relative, John Nicholas Emerick, would be honored and the great fortune distributed to all Emericks. The children had heard this story often. Like their father, they believed this would be happening and all their struggles would be behind them. Ella, on the other hand, had serious feelings that the money in question was pie in the sky. Her inner compass told her this probably would not be happening. She would, therefore, plan accordingly, as she always had, to care for her family. She often was the main breadwinner. She expected this would continue.

Chapter 6

When they awoke at the inn in New York in 1770 the day following the arrival of their ship, John Nicholas and Andrew, discussed what they would do first. John Nicholas was eager to put his plans into action. Andrew was ready to be on his own.

So they parted company early that morning, when John Nicholas headed to Philadelphia to contact relatives there. Andrew lingered as he found himself interested in the conversation in the pub the previous evening. The talk of the men there had sounded exciting. He was drawn into their concerns about the problems the Colonies were having with the king and England.

By 1770, the population of the American Colonies was 2,210,00 people. There were conflicts with Britain dating back many years. By 1763, King George III and the English Parliament had begun putting serious restrictions on the Americans' ability to trade and to move about the country as they desired. The Proclamation of 1763 forbade English settlements west of the Appalachian mountains and required people settled there to return east. This was an attempt by King George to ease tensions with the Indian tribes.

The following year,1764, the colonists were prohibited from printing their own currency and duties were increased on sugar, coffee, textiles, wines and other items coming into the Colonies. At a meeting in Boston, James Otis raised the issue of taxation without representation and published a pamphlet asserting the rights of the Colonies. Boston merchants began a boycott of British luxury goods later that year.

The following year, an especially onerous situation was foisted on the Colonies when Britain put into place the Quartering Act. It required colonists to house British troops and supply them with food.

Andrew stayed on in New York for a few days, then headed north to Boston with his new friend, Charley Buckridge. He was told that in Boston people were beginning to stand up against the continued taxation and tyranny of Great Britain. He was attracted to the conflict with the zeal of a young man ready to prove his mettle.

John Nicholas liked what he saw in Pennsylvania. He moved in with relatives in Lancaster County and set to work immediately on his plan of action for a business in fur-trading.

He knew furs could be obtained from fur trappers and from Indians. He heard the fur trappers in general were a rough and independent lot. You could not be sure where to find them. They came in at various times in the fall to sell their furs and resupply for the next season.

His first trip out to locate fur traders and do some trapping along the way was a learning experience, as most new ventures are. He had done his homework, however, and was well prepared. He located some trappers and dealt with some Indian tribes. He traded beads and silver trinkets, and coffee. He learned what the trappers wanted most was whiskey and tobacco, and some blankets would be good, too.

He realized early on that some regular meeting places for exchange of furs would be advantageous to all. He left some members of his expedition at key places in the wilderness with the promise of good money for setting up a permanent building for the purpose of trading for furs.

Later he sent provisions to the outposts, including staple goods and items like candles, flint and steel for building fire, as well as tobacco and clay pipes. Some liked the packaged tobacco for smoking and some liked the twist of tobacco for chewing. Tobacco was plentiful and easy to come by for shipping to his fur-trading centers. He provided hard cones of brown sugar which were handy to carry. It was easy to slice off a chunk of sugar whenever it was needed. And whiskey. It was important to have whiskey. Soon a network of trading posts began to emerge, opened by entrepreneurs willing to brave the beauty of the wilds for the chance of an independent life.

John Nicholas returned from that first trip tanned and hardened. He had had some narrow escapes from animals and Indians, but he had learned much. More importantly, he had furs to ship and to sell. What he bought for a dollar, he could sell for many, many times that—for as much as a hundred dollars.

The money began to roll in. Before long he established offices in New York, Philadelphia and Berlin, followed rather quickly by his own fleet of ships.

One year after arriving, in 1771, John Nicholas wrote to his father in Germany.

"My fortune is large. It grows fast. Christopher should come to me. My friend Mattson will be over in the spring and take him along."

One year later, he wrote again to his father.

"Mattson tells me Christopher will come next year with Uncle Konrad, which is very late, as I need him now, but very well, I will wait."

Another year passed and John Nicholas wrote to his cousin, Baltheus, in 1773.

"My brothers, Christopher and Valentine, have no more pleasure to go with me, but I have no other recourse."

Later that year, Christopher did indeed come. He began manning the Philadelphia office while John Nicholas continued to travel and bring back the furs himself.

In 1774, Christopher wrote to Valentine, who was still in Germany.

"I am glad you are coming. Our brother Nicholas is making large deals in the fur trading business, and has been away four months."

By 1774, Andrew was heavily involved in politics in Boston. The year before, the English Parliament had levied a three penny per pound tax on tea arriving in the colonies.

In November 1773, Andrew and Charley Buckridge attended the town meeting held in Boston in opposition to the tea tax. Philadelphia had held a meeting the previous month and summarily forced the resignations of the East India Company tea agents there. The new tax effectively gave the East India Company a monopoly on the tea trade.

"I say we do the same as Philadelphia and make the agents here resign," shouted Charley at the Boston town meeting.

There was raucous general agreement as the meeting broke into passionate talk in small groups.

Andrew, by Charley's side, exclaimed, "If we don't stand up to them now they'll have their hooks into us forever. It has to be stopped!"

There was agreement at the town meeting to try to force the tea agents in Boston to resign. It was not as easily accomplished as it had been in Philadelphia. The tea agents and the company were forewarned by the actions in Philadelphia and refused to bow to intimidation.

Shortly after that, three ships full of tea sailed into the Boston Harbor.

Charley and Andrew went to the docks to view this most recent affront. The ships were standing idle and had not been unloaded.

"You can take yer tea back where it came from. We ain't buyin'," cried Charley at some of the crew of the nearest ship.

A small crowd gathered and took up the chant. "We ain't buyin'. We ain't buyin'," yelled the crowd until muskets were hoisted by two of the sailors. The chant died down then and people began to drift away looking back over their shoulders. Some were frightened. Some were wishing they had the fortitude to stay. Some wished they had brought their guns. Some wished they were not out of tea at home.

Out of tea or not, the Bostonians held another meeting and decided to send the ships back to England without paying any import duties. It sounded like a good solution to the majority of the colonists. It was not acceptable to the Royal Governor of Massachusetts. He was opposed to such an action and loyal to the king. He ordered harbor officials not to allow the ships to sail out of the harbor unless the tea tax was paid.

On December 16, 1773, Andrew and Charley were having dinner with the Talmadge twins, Eliza Jane and Cora Ann, at the Talmadges' home in Boston.

"Well, you two seem thick as thieves these days," said Mr. Talmadge to the young men from the end of the dining room table. "Now what business is it you are in?"

"Well, we've set up a small print shop together, sir," said Andrew. "There seems to be a need for printing flyers, pamphlets, bulletins. We don't know yet if we can make a proper go of it."

"Ah, any fellow who works hard and puts his whole heart into something will make a go of it. That is the key. You must want to do it, or if not *want* to, at least perform it to the best of your ability," replied the girls' father.

Charley wondered to himself if they would have any chance at all with these comely girls if their father knew what they were going to do later tonight. The Talmadge family were Loyalists to the Crown. Charley did not care which of the girls he might have a chance to befriend. They were both real lookers, churchgoers and prim as you please. They were not identical twins. Eliza Jane was the red headed one with the freckles and a funny, playful nature. Cora Ann had jet black hair and alabaster skin. Twins could hardly have been more different looking. Cora Ann was a bit more serious and seemed partial to Andrew. That was all right with him. Eliza Jane would do just fine.

They could not turn down the invitation to dinner for the first time at the girls' home. It would be difficult, though, getting away in time for what they planned to do tonight.

"Will you be at the church supper on Sunday evening?" Eliza Jane asked Charley, bringing him out of his reverie.

"Ah, I believe we could manage that," he replied.

"Good, then we hope you and Andrew will join us at our table," said Eliza Jane.

"By Jove, this is going better than I expected," thought Charley. "I wish we didn't have to leave so early tonight."

He said, "Why, we would be honored to join you on Sunday evening."

"Don't worry about bringing a dish. We always take plenty," said Eliza Jane.

Andrew was sitting where he could see the large grandfather clock. He was watching the pendulum swing back and forth. Soon they would have to make some excuse to be on their way. It was a damn shame. He was enchanted with Cora Ann and her exotic looks. He was sure Charley and Eliza Jane were partial to each other, so the way was clear.

"Andrew, why so pensive?" asked Cora Ann.

"Oh, sorry. Just thinking about a bit of work I need to lay out tomorrow. Please forgive me."

"What a dolt I am. How could I have said that," thought Andrew. "What will she think of me, drifting off when I should be paying attention to her? It was all I could think of. This project this evening has my mind engaged. I may not be here Sunday evening. It all depends on how things go tonight."

With dessert over, they adjourned to the sitting room and after half an hour the young men exchanged a quick look that said it was time to go. They pled having much work to do the next day and the need to get up early. They promised to see the family on

Sunday evening and thanked them for the dinner and good company.

Their cart and horse was tied up outside. They leaped into it and clattered away at full speed into the cold December night. They left the conveyance and the horse tied up again. This time it was several blocks away from where they were going.

They quickly took off their good clothes and donned rough homespun for their night's adventure. Andrew patted the horse and spoke softly to her before he and Charley trotted off into the night.

They arrived at an unused warehouse at the far end of the Boston dock. They quietly slipped in a side door. Others were already there. Everyone was solemn. None of them knew what the night would bring. Certain ones had been in charge of bringing the supplies they would need.

"All right," said one man quietly, "you all know what to do."

"Let's get on with it then," said Charley.

The men began to dress in Mohawk garb. They painted each others faces with "war paint." They tied feathers in their hair and made at least a gesture of disguising their looks.

When everyone was ready, they said a prayer, wished each other godspeed, went over their strategy again and left the warehouse. They all went slowly up to the three unloaded ships rocking in the nighttime waves. At a signal, they boarded the vessels, found the tea containers and dumped all 342 of them into the harbor. As soon as that was accomplished, the men hastily left the ships. It was all done in an orderly fashion and the men took care to keep it from getting out of hand. They all dispersed in different directions, as they had planned. They doubted anyone was fooled by their disguises.

Just to be safe, Charley and Andrew ran zig zag through the streets until they were sure they were not being followed. Then they found their cart and the patiently waiting mare. They washed the war paint off with jugs of water they had in the cart. Their Mohawk paraphernalia they hid beside the road. When they looked respectable again, they drove off and went home.

It was Andrew's first participation with the Sons of Liberty.

At the church supper Sunday evening, there was much talk about the Tea Party of a few nights before. Without revealing their participation, Charley and Andrew stuck up for the action. Mr. Talmadge was concerned about relatives at home in England and about the Englishmen with whom he did business.

"By Heaven, I am confident that any action taken against the king will fail", stated Mr. Talmadge. "It is folly, I tell you."

"But, sir," countered Charley, "you cannot believe the king is making proper decisions on how to treat these colonies. People came here to escape such tyrannies. If there is no resistance, it will only get worse."

Talmadge and Charley engaged in an animated discussion of the current political situation.

Andrew found his mind uncharacteristically drifting from his first love, politics. Instead he was more interested in talking with Cora Ann.

Thereafter the relationship between Eliza Jane and Charley cooled. Eliza Jane was her father's daughter. Charley could tell she had been influenced by talk at home.

He told Andrew, "Eliza is a very nice girl. A good catch for any man, but I'll not go up against her father. There are lots of other nice girls around as well. It is clear that she takes her father's position. I could not live peaceably with a woman like that. No, I'll have no more to do with the Talmadges. If you want to continue with Cora Ann, good luck. It will be a tough row to hoe, my friend."

Andrew knew he was right. But there was something about Cora Ann—her flawless skin, so fair with just a touch of color in her cheeks. Her deep blue eyes surrounded by thick black lashes drew Andrew into them with a strong pull. He wondered how she felt. He did not have to wonder for long.

After church the next Sunday, Cora Ann managed to be beside him momentarily. With her head tucked down, she murmured, "I have some shopping to do in town on Tuesday. I expect I will be at the dry goods store around one o'clock."

Before he could answer, she drifted on and was back in her parents' circle. She did not look back. He wondered if he had really heard her say that. It had all happened so fast. Then his heart skipped a beat as he realized he had his answer. She *did* have an attraction for him as well. "Now the fat is in the fire," he thought. Right or wrong, he could not resist.

"Cora, Cora, what can we do?" Andrew opined as they met among the bolts of fabric in the back of the store. He knew they would be observed if they were together long.

"I'm committed to resisting the British. You know that. Your father. What about your father?"

"Andrew, I don't know the answers. I just know that I like being with you and I think you feel the same. Father has all but forbidden us to see you or Charley outside of church. I do respect my father's opinion on most things. I am not partial to either political belief. Oh, I know I should be. I just want to have a home and family and normal life. I hate all this talk of going to war."

He looked deeply into her eyes. "This is a great risk for you to take, Cora. I can't promise to make all that happen for you. I just know I am drawn to you like no other."

He wanted to reach out to her and take her in his arms. She would not have resisted, he knew, but they were in a public place and they had already been there too long.

"Around the back side of the church. There is a gravestone that reads "Thompson." There is a built-in stone vase for flowers, but no one ever puts any flowers there. It is always empty. Leave a note for me in there as to where we can meet. I will check it everyday and will come to you if I possibly can," said Andrew. "Now we must separate before we draw attention to ourselves."

"I am not afraid of risks. I will do that," said Cora.

As they turned away, Andrew's hand just grazed her hand, which was at her side. It sent a strong spark of electricity through them both.

Early in 1774, the English Parliament passed the first in the series of Coercive Acts. The Americans called them the Intolerable Acts. Commercial shipping from the Port of Boston was shut down until all taxes were paid on the tea dumped in the harbor. The colonists refusal to obey the Acts resulted in four regiments of British troops being moved into Massachusetts. The area was placed under British military rule.

Further Coercive Acts were enacted in the spring. They included a new version of the Quartering Act. American colonists were again required to house and feed British troops. In addition, the Quebec Act extended the southern boundary of Canada to include territories in Massachusetts, Connecticut and Virginia. Any self-rule by colonists in Massachusetts was a thing of the past. The British took over Massachusetts' arsenal of weapons at Charlestown.

In spite of these drastic measures, the First Continental Congress met in Philadelphia in the Fall of 1774. Some of those attending were Patrick Henry, George Washington, John Adams and John Hancock. The Congress acted to challenge British control of the country. By February 1775, the Congress was preparing for war. In March, in Virginia, Patrick Henry delivered his speech against British rule stating, "Give me liberty or give me death."

Throughout all these troubles of their new country, Cora Ann Talmadge and Andrew Emerick somehow managed to meet occasionally. Usually it was when

71

Cora Ann was able to go on errands by herself. It was difficult to exclude her twin sister, normally her confidant in all things. Eliza Jane could not be included in this clandestine arrangement.

There were hardships for the people of Boston. Mr. Talmadge was incensed that the colonists' rebellion was affecting his business. Tensions were running very high. Lines were drawn among families; sometimes members of families took different sides. At that time, only one-third of the colonists wanted a break with Britain. It was a difficult time for the colonists and for the new country.

Andrew continued to be in the thick of the rebellion. He openly supported the colonists' cause. He and Charley were kept busy printing and distributing bulletins, pamphlets and information about the happenings of the time. Once their shop was broken into and their equipment disabled. It took some time for repairs to allow them to be operational again. They relocated to a place that was not as public as their little shop had been. Now only those with a need to know could locate them for business.

While all of this was going on, Andrew's meetings with Cora Ann were islands of refuge. He tried not to talk to her about political concerns as she showed little interest, except where his own life was affected. She was greatly interested in that. He did not feel that his own situation was such that he could offer her the security of marriage she desired.

Cora Ann devised a new meeting place, which was a very risky business. It involved Cora Ann waiting until Eliza Jane and her parents were sleeping deeply and then creeping out of the house, careful not to make a sound. They met in the barn where the Talmadges kept their carriage horses. There was an open loft with soft hay, which tended to muffle sounds. Sometimes one of the horses would register that their presence was noticed with a snort and the stamp of a hoof. There was not much danger of that being heard from the house.

They knew they should not stay long in the loft. There was always the chance that Eliza Jane might wake and miss her sister or that Mother might need help in the night with something and come seeking one of the girls. They mostly talked in the beginning taking each other's measure; seeing if it was a good fit.

By June 1775, they had been meeting furtively for some time. Andrew longed to discuss the actions at Lexington and Concord. He told Cora Ann he could ignore the cause no longer. He signed on with a regiment and was ready to go if called to serve. His commanding officer was General William Prescott, a man Andrew much admired.

Cora Ann could not fathom his devotion to the cause of rebellion. She clung to him and cried and feared for his life. She did not tell him she feared that together they had created another life.

Andrew's call to action came on June 16, 1775. He and Charley had signed on together, both willing to put their lives on the line for the new country. They closed up the little hidden print shop, donned their new regimental coats and reported for duty.

"My god, Andy, can you believe we are at last going to be able to do something to stop those British bastards," said Charley. "They have the harbor blockaded with their warships. Do they think we will lie down for that?"

"It feels good to finally be taking some action, but these wool coats are hot and sticky. We are supposed to keep them on no matter what tomorrow. I guess it is so we can tell who is on which side, but god, they are hot," said Andrew.

"Did you tell Cora Ann?" said Charley.

"I did. She still just doesn't understand how I feel about defending this country. Some day this can be a great country. There is so much room. So many forests and rivers. Why, the land could never fill up— there is so much. She was born here. I remember living where it is not so free and where land is becoming scarce. I can't seem to make her understand. This is the best hope any of us have. We can't let it slip away because we did not stand up for it."

"There are other women, you know, Andy."

"For you, maybe. Not for me. There is no one like Cora Ann. As soon as this conflict with Britain is settled, I'll marry her. There is no one else for me," replied Andrew.

Andrew and Charley began talking with the other soldiers then. Their talk and minds were on the coming battle the next day. The British forces would not expect to see an army preventing them from securing one of the highest spots overlooking the harbor. They would think it was an easy task with no resistance. Well, they would be surprised, as in the night the colonists' army took up defensive positions, not on Bunker Hill which would go down in history as the name of the battle, but on nearby Breed's Hill, named for a family whose members had long since left the area.

The colonists' troops were ill-equipped to head into battle. They had received little training. They did not have guns which would reach as far as the warships in the harbor. What they did have in good measure was the will and the heart to be in this fight.

Andrew and Charley stuck together. They ate a hasty breakfast of dry bread and salted pork. They hunkered down in their positions. When the first British assault came, they waited as the troops marched closer and closer. They held their fire until they could see the whites of the British soldiers' eyes.

Then Andrew and Charley shot with the ragtag line of colonists and slaughtered many of the British soldiers.

The smoke from the gun powder hung in the air like a spectral presence. The acrid smell of it filled the nostrils of the two friends, who had made it through the first assault. The British were repelled, but men had fallen at their sides.

Charley took a look around him at the men who were hit. His breakfast left his stomach as he doubled over and retched in the dirt. Andrew helped to pull men to safety. The injuries were mind-numbing. Any glamour the two friends had expected to experience in this battle had fled on swift wings. It was a hellhole. And then the second assault by the British came. Again the rebel army stood its ground and fired when the British were only 150 feet away from the barricades they had hastily constructed. Again the British were held back by the fierce fighting of the American troops.

Both sides had taken terrible casualties. In Boston, ten miles away, people sat on their roof tops. The more adventurous climbed onto church steeples to watch the battle. The day was absolutely clear and still. The people in high places could see the smoke and all could hear the guns firing. It was hard to tell exactly what was happening.

By the time the third assault was mounted by the British, the American ranks were severely depleted.

The Americans were greatly outnumbered by the British and they were outgunned.

Charley and Andrew were still together and uninjured. Their faces and blue regimental coats were covered with dust and grime. Their eyes peered as if out of Halloween masks meant to scare. They were scared themselves. They had never been so scared. They each had one more ration of powder for their guns.

The British line was coming at them again. Charley gave a war whoop and stood to fire. Andrew followed suit. Then their gunpowder was gone. The British were upon them. They fought with the butts of their guns. They fought with rocks and bare hands. The regimental drum sounded Retreat.

Charley shouted, "Run, lad. Let's run for it!"

They ran together, away from the killing grounds, away from the gunpowder haze, away from the chaotic inferno of the battlefield. Charley reached a point of safety, out of gun range. He turned to look for Andrew, but Andrew was not there.

"Come on, lad. Ye've got to be there. Andy! Andy! "he called in a frenzy.

But Andrew could not hear. He had been shot in the back. The hot musket ball ripped through his blue wool regimental coat and went right through his wildly beating patriot's heart, stopping it instantly. He fell face down in the dry trampled dirt. He was one of the 800 American casualties in the bloodiest battle of the Revolutionary War, the Battle of Bunker Hill.

Cora Ann had gone to the church to hear about the battle. Her family did not know she had a special reason for caring about the outcome. She would have climbed up on top of the steeple herself if decorum had not prevented it. The men on top shouted down their observations.

"They've routed our men."

"We are in retreat."

"Our troops are running away," shouted the lookouts.

"Thank God," thought Cora Ann. "Let him be all right. Please, God."

It was the next day before lists of those wounded or killed were posted. Cora Ann and Eliza Jane went together to read the lists. Cora Ann saw his name, Andrew Emerick, on the list of those who died in battle. She began to see stars and the edges of her vision went dark. She took deep breaths and grabbed hold of Eliza's arm.

"I know," said Eliza Jane. "There are so many that we know. Look, there's that Butler boy from church. Why, he hardly seemed old enough to go. I don't blame you for being upset. Let's go home."

Cora Ann was quiet at dinner. Her mother noticed.

"Cora, dear, you look unwell. I am afraid this whole battle business has been too upsetting for you," said Mrs. Talmadge.

"You are right, Mother. It was terribly disturbing to see all the names of those we know on the list," she answered.

"Mother, that Mr. Emerick was on the list," said Eliza Jane. "Remember? He was here for dinner that time."

"Oh, how sad! He was a nice man, but see what his politics have gotten him. Thank goodness neither of you took up with those two gentlemen," said Mrs. Talmadge.

Cora Ann lay in bed quietly that night until she heard the deep breathing of her sister and knew that Eliza Jane was asleep. She crept out of bed and made her way to the barn. The horses stirred and she stopped and patted one on the nose and spoke softly to him.

Cora Ann climbed up the ladder into the loft where she and Andrew had lain together. She had known it was not right to be with him in that way. Something had compelled her. He was the love of her life and now he was gone. Cora Ann lay in the hay thinking and remembering. After a little while, she took a coiled-up rope off of its nail hanger. She threw one end up over one of the rafters and tied it there. She made a loop in the other end of the rope and tied it firmly. She slipped the rope around her neck. She whispered "Oh, Andrew." Then with a last look around she stepped off the end of the loft.

Chapter 7

Some years later, in 1781, Valentine wrote to his father, "*We have heard nothing from our brother. We are working alone and are satisfied.*"

John Nicholas found his business progressing beyond his wildest dreams. He wanted people he could trust in his offices in his absence. He was not able to interest either Christopher or Valentine in traveling with him or learning the techniques of fur-trading. They were not used to the hardships that were the unavoidable consequence of gathering animal pelts. In addition to bringing in the product, John Nicholas traveled to Europe often, to make sure the furs arrived in the right hands and to purchase trading supplies. Neither Christopher nor Valentine had the interest, the personality or the drive to supplant John Nicholas in these major duties of the business. By this time, they both had wives and children. They did not desire to be away from home.

Still, they ran the offices fairly, and John Nicholas felt he gave them fair compensation. Valentine had taken over the New York office and Christopher was well established in the Philadelphia one.

John Nicholas thought of his poor cousin Andrew, who had been killed in the War with England. Andrew had fought bravely for the Colonies. John Nicholas had arranged for his body to be brought to Philadelphia and buried in the Lutheran cemetery there.

In the years before his death, Andrew had been full of revolutionary talk. In spite of Andrew's efforts to excite them to action along with him, the three cousins had managed somehow to stay out of the fray and continue with business almost as usual. It is true shipments of the furs were held up for a time during the conflict. There were ways to avoid that by taking different routes. The business did not suffer greatly.

How often John Nicholas thought, if only they had stayed at a different inn that first night. Perhaps it would have made a difference. Perhaps not. Once Andrew's passion for the cause was ignited, it could not be extinguished. John Nicholas tried to draw him into the business, but he would not be deterred from his attachment to the colonists' cause of freedom from the oppression of England.

Seventy-five-year-old John Nicholas stood on the deck of the *Sea Queen.* He breathed in the fresh salt air in large gulps. The sails were whipping. He so loved that sound—and the creak of the riggings and the slap of the waves—as the ship cut a path through the water.

This had been a stormy trip. Today was cold with puffy little clouds as far as one could see. They were not threatening clouds. It was December though. You could not be sure in the winter months just how the sea would treat an intruder to its vast space. Here it was, almost 1817 already. Well, in all these years he had never seen a crossing like the one they had had in 1783. "Thank the heavens for that," he thought.

The Fates saw fit through that trip to bring him together with a man who would be a great asset to his business and a worry and trouble at the same time. John Nicholas had definitely made more money. His fortune had increased. He recognized that increasing his fortune was the guiding force of his life. It was not something of which he was proud. It had just happened. It happened because he had found no other passion. He always tried to be fair and honest in his business dealings. It did not turn out that way with the poor, penniless young man he had taken in and trained. Such stories were told of him that John Nicholas was fearful and embarrassed to have someone connected with himself be so notorious.

They met in 1783 when John Nicholas was returning from a European business trip on another one of his own ships, the *Maria Rose*. He always felt more comfortable when he was on one of his own ships. He knew his captain and crew could be counted upon to be sober and industrious, especially when the owner was on board. John Nicholas hired all the captains himself. He considered himself to be a good judge of character. He had standards he strictly enforced. He had heard of too many ships running amok while the captain was drunk in his quarters.

He understood life at sea wore at a man. He knew the seamen needed their grog like they needed fresh air. But he insisted that they did not overindulge to the point of insensibility. Anyone who did would not sail on his line as a crewman again. His captains had stern orders about that. As for the captains, they needed to have good experience and be known, at least as, moderate drinkers, if not teetotalers. He wanted no sots piloting his beloved ships.

It was a difficult crossing in 1783, with cold, heavy storms. It was late in the fall. He had planned to come back sooner. One never knew for sure just how long it would take to develop continuing new markets for the furs at the best possible price. It was becoming more and more difficult to deal with the manufacturers of fur items. He could give them a nice break on the price if the order was large enough. They never seemed satisfied. They wanted the same price for purchasing a small amount. He provided only the best furs at great human labor and transportation costs. He would not let his furs go cheaply.

He also bargained for the best price for trade goods, often procuring warm woolen blankets in England, beads from Italy or Czechoslovakia, and silver from Germany. Coffee and Chinese tea were also trading staples for the fur traders and the Indians. This was one of the reasons he could not trust anyone else to do the bargaining. Christopher and Valentine flatly refused to take part in what they called haggling with shopkeepers.

So this time he stayed in Europe much longer than he had anticipated. Along with the storms, they repeatedly experienced unusual bitterly cold weather on this trip. After all his years of travel, John Nicholas was not dismayed by the rocking and tossing of the ship. He had always arrived safely before. He reassured those around him in the upper class accommodations that all would be well.

The *Maria Rose* was heading for New York, but the weather was so stormy Captain Schimdt changed their course to Baltimore.

They did not know it at the time. Later, Benjamin Franklin was the first to come forth with the theory that the violent eruption of volcanoes, particularly one in Iceland called Laki, which had spewed huge chunks of ice into the sea, had affected the weather conditions in the Atlantic in 1783. That year was referred to as the Year Summer Never Came. Crops in England and America failed to ripen. There was occasional frost on the land, even in the summer. By the time late fall arrived, the Atlantic seacoast was in the grip of a cruel, cold weather pattern that refused to lift.

As the *Maria Rose* made its way around what is now Cape Charles, Virginia, and started up into Chesapeake Bay, the howling winds died down so abruptly it was noticed by the passengers on the ship, who had become accustomed to the banshee shrieking. As stillness began to reign around them, the waters in the bay froze very suddenly. One moment the ship was moving along. The next it was crunching ice and moving slowly, and the next moment it was stopped dead still by the solidity of the bay water.

This was a condition John Nicholas had never encountered before on a ship. This was something none of them on board had encountered before, not the captain and not the crew. People began to congregate on the upper deck bundled up in heavy coats, neck scarves, gloves and many in fur hats. There was laughter and joking.

"Well, doesn't this beat all."

"This will be something to tell the children."

"Imagine being stuck in the ice in Chesapeake Bay. Who will believe it?"

People were looking over the side of the ship and estimating how thick the ice was. Even as they watched, the ice began to climb up the sides of the ship like a giant vice holding it immobile and lifting it slightly.

"We may be stuck here all night," ventured one gentleman.

"Oh, surely not," one of the women replied. "How dreadful!"

Captain Schmidt came out on deck with a reassuring manner. He did not feel so sure of himself inside. He was not sure when they could free the ship from this icy trap. In his mind he was going over the food stores they had on board. It had already been a long crossing because of the storms. And to complicate matters his employer, John Nicholas Emerick, was on board. He better manage this situation smoothly if he was to keep his job. It was a good job. He loved the sea and the time away from home. Not that he did not love his family, but God, it was good to be out on the sea, in charge of his ship and away from the squalling babies and the friction which sometimes occurred between him and his wife.

Captain Schmidt was also concerned about the timbers used to build this ship. Would the sides of the ship hold against the pressure of the ice? If the wood did not hold, they all might be lost.

He knew a captain must put on a good face no matter what to keep the passengers calm.

"Oh, no, nothing to be concerned about," he said with a smile as he walked the deck. "We shall be out of this in a day or two at most. Ice doesn't hold long in this bay."

At thirty-two, Captain Josiah Schmidt was beginning to put on weight. The buttons on his uniform jacket would need to be moved over a bit when he arrived home. Ruthie was good about that. She was a good wife as wives go. He wondered if he would ever see her again. Here it was, November. He had hoped to make another trip before Christmas. He always arranged to be home at Christmas with Ruthie and the children. Emerick was good about that. He would send the unmarried captains out over Christmas if he possibly could, or sometimes he would suspend all sailings until after the holidays.

"Funny old duck," thought Captain Schmidt. "Emerick must be well into his forties. No children of his own. Not even any interest in women. Well, they were interested in him, that's a sure thing. The ones on board this trip know who he is and what he's worth."

If John Nicholas was aware of the attention he received from the few unmarried or widowed ladies on this voyage, he chose to ignore it. It was as if a spigot had been turned off when Maria died. Feelings for another woman would not flow. He was unfailingly polite but immune to their flirtatious ministrations on his behalf.

As owner, he slept in the best quarters on board. He ate his meals and hob nobbed with only a select few of the passengers and with Captain Schmidt. John Nicholas did not desire to expand his social circle on this voyage. He had many business concerns weighing on him. Each day he was absent, he wondered if Christopher and Valentine were keeping the business running smoothly at their end. Both were prone to taking time off when they chose, regardless of the work that needed doing. It was a constant nagging worry for John Nicholas. When it was time for pay, though, they were always readily available.

No one on board that ship thought they would still be there stuck in the ice after two weeks. But, stuck they were. Class distinctions had eased somewhat by this time. People from steerage were mingling on the upper deck with the upper-and middle-class passengers. After all, they had some musicians in steerage that could really play the fiddle and the flute. One young lad played the mournful sounding Irish pipes. It helped to pass the time. Everyone congregated in the large main dining room. It was too cold to be outside for long, although a brisk walk around the deck helped one to sleep better. It, also, helped the long, cold hours to pass.

Captain Schmidt feared he would be obliged to tap into the cargo of special foods they were hauling if this isolation lasted much longer. There was special salted fish and caviar meant for the tables of the very best families on the east coast of America. There were barrels of other delicacies and a whole shipment of German wines. He felt they could hold out. So far they still were managing on supplies of their own.

John Nicholas mentioned to Captain Schmidt how fortunate it was that there were people on board with musical instruments who could play for the group of weary travelers. It really did break up the monotony.

"Well, it seems there is a young man in steerage who had several flutes with him that he plans to sell when he arrives. He offered them to anyone who could play along with the piper and the fiddler," Captain Schmidt explained.

"He sounds like an enterprising fellow. I'd like to meet him," John Nicholas said.

Captain Schmidt went off in search of the young man with the flutes. He returned shortly with the fellow in tow.

"Here he is, sir," Captain Schmidt said as he pushed the young man forward. "His name's Astor. John Astor."

"John Jacob Astor at your service, sir," he said with a slight bow.

"John, you say. Well, that makes two of us. John Nicholas Emerick," he said thrusting his hand out.

"How did you come by these flutes, Mr. Astor? I have certainly enjoyed the music they have helped to provide during our imprisonment here."

"Please call me John, sir."

"Very well, we shall both be John. We are both in the same circumstances on this ship at the present time. We shall be equals," replied John Nicholas in a spirit of generosity inspired by their situation.

John Astor explained how after his mother died he had come from Germany, where his father was a butcher, to London where one of his older brothers was living. John Jacob was the youngest son of his family and used to having the hind teat as he put it. John Jacob apprenticed in a musical instrument factory in London for two years to save up enough money to buy steerage passage to America. It was a dream of his to strike out on his own and see the new land. With the last of his earnings he purchased seven flutes from the factory. He could make more himself and planned to open a shop selling musical instruments when they arrived.

John Jacob Astor was twenty-one years old. John Nicholas Emerick was forty-six. They had in common their German heritage. They began to spend much time together. None would have guessed that another month of being stuck in the ice would pass. It was getting close to Christmas. Surely, they would be free before Christmas.

John Nicholas was energized by his newfound friend. He hardly remembered his own youth and wondered if he had *ever* had that much spunk and enthusiasm.

91

He must have, he remembered, or how would he have gotten where he was today?

John Jacob made friends on board. He was sought out for his good humor and interesting conversation. He could dance a lively jig to the rustic music provided by the musicians. He seemed to grasp ideas readily. He was smart. He was a great tonic for John Nicholas.

Shortly before Christmas, John Nicholas decided to take John Jacob into his confidence about his fur-trading business. He told John Jacob about how he began the business, and how he had made a fortune. He spoke about how his brothers had worked for him for years, but had never really understood what was needed as far as dedication to business and sound decision-making were concerned. He lamented that he was tired of traveling out into the wilds to gather and trade for the furs himself. But who could one trust these days?

He found a shrewd and sympathetic ear in John Jacob Astor.

Chapter 8

"Elsie, Elsie, he's at the door again," shouted six year old Vida.

"Who's at the door?" Elsie replied nonchalantly.

"As if you didn't know. It's your boy friend, Roy Bryan," taunted her older brother, Bert.

"He's not my boy friend," Elsie answered, just a little bit too firmly to be believed.

"Well, I think he wants to be," said Vida with a grin.

Elsie was fifteen now and quite a beauty, with her almost round face, chestnut hair and cornflower-blue eyes. Roy Bryan was not the only boy who came calling. He had the distinction of being the wildest and the most unlikely for a minister's daughter though. That gave him a mysterious and special cachet that appealed to Elsie. He was twenty years old and was staying with his older brother's family in St. Louis. Roy and his brother Frank both liked to drink and carouse and hit the night spots. Roy had a reputation. And he was Irish. At least he wasn't Catholic like many of the Irish people were, thought Elsie. Poppa would never allow him near the front door if he were Catholic.

Roy had this way about him that made Elsie forget that she was not supposed to like him. He had an Irish gift for storytelling and such a smile. When he turned that smile on her and looked hard in her eyes with his, oh my!

She invited him into the front parlor. The younger children peeked around the corners of the doors. It was not as if they were ever alone. She was quiet and nervous. Roy was never at a loss for words. He made her laugh with his stories and his dramatic way of telling them. She felt her heart pounding in her chest. Her palms were sweaty. She wanted him to stay forever and talk to her. Too soon, she would be going back to the drudgery of life, helping Momma with the children and the ever present, never-ending boarding-house work. She had never really minded it until now. Now she wanted to be with Roy more than anything.

Ella understood what was going on with her oldest daughter. The boys could take care of themselves, but Elsie must be protected from herself. This Bryan boy was trouble waiting to happen. Lord knows if he could ever support a wife. He seemed so carefree and full of the devil. Ella felt she must have a talk with Elsie — a talk about men and what to look out for. Nobody had had a talk with her and she was much older than Elsie when she married. It would not have done much good she knew. She was set on marrying Irving. She had no one to blame but herself.

"Elsie," Ella began, the next day as they were finishing the dishes.

"Yes, Momma?"

"Elsie, this boy, Roy Bryan. You like him a lot, don't you." It was a statement, not a question.

"Oh Momma, don't tease me like the boys do. I feel so different with Roy. He tells such funny stories and he always treats me nice.

"I'll not tease you, child. It's just that, well, men are usually after one thing more than anything else. Promise me you will be very careful and not let him get fresh with you. It's better not to let him get mushy with you. Things could get out of hand. You understand, Elsie?"

"Yes, Momma. I understand," replied her dutiful daughter. But, she did not really understand exactly what her mother was talking about. How could she understand the needs of men or their intense desires at that young stage of her life?

Ella went away feeling she had done her duty as best she could. She had had the talk. She thought she spoke quite plainly. Elsie was a smart girl. She would be all right. Ella had many other concerns to think about.

At least Ella was not pregnant again. Arthur, whom they all called Billy for no known reason, had been born over two years ago in 1901. He was such a pleasant child and he seemed to be progressing ahead of his age. She did not remember the other children being quite as quick mentally. Maybe it was just that he was the youngest and he would be the last.

Ella decided after Billy was born that she wanted no more children. Her body and her spirit were worn out. She explained this to Irving.

"I'm moving my things to one of the upstairs bedrooms, Irv. Mrs. Cochran is moving out next week and I plan to take her room. You have been earning enough so we can get by without her board and rent money. I want to sleep by myself. I want no more babies." She was that plain with him.

"I think not, Mrs. Emerick. A wife has a duty to her husband," Irving had replied hotly.

It did him no good to disapprove and berate her in private: Ella carried out her plan and moved into Mrs. Cochran's room as soon as it was vacant. She locked the door. She could breathe easy in the quiet bedroom. Her spirits lifted and life began to look a little more hopeful.

It was October 4, 1904. Sixteen-year-old Elsie Emerick was to be married that day to Roy Bryan. He persisted and she was glad. She went out with other boys, always in a group, of course, but none touched her heart like Roy did. Poppa insisted they wait until she was sixteen and a half. He would perform the ceremony in the Baptist Church. Then they would all come back to the house for a reception.

Elsie knew that by making them wait Poppa was hoping she would change her mind or Roy would find someone else. She was Irving's oldest daughter and in that special relationship fathers have with their female offspring, he was reluctant to give her up. In fact, since Ella had withdrawn he had spent much time talking with Elsie. He spoke of the money he expected the year after next and how she would share in it, because she was an Emerick related to John Nicholas Emerick. She loved her father and believed in him, even though she knew he could be very hard at times, especially with the boys.

Momma helped her make an off-white, floor-length, lace wedding dress. It consisted of panels of lace which came to a point every few inches. The panels lapped over each other like shingles on a roof. It had a high neckline with lace and little pearls just under her chin. The skirt was bell shaped with layers of lace. There was a wide satin off-white sash, which tied around the waist with a large bow in the back. Elsie was not fond of sewing. She struggled to get the dress right. Momma helped and so did Mrs. Carlisle from next door. Working together the three of them made it look wonderful.

She wore her hair upswept and Momma gave her a pair of tiny pearl earrings. One of the boarders loaned Elsie soft white kid shoes with pearl-like buttons. She had never felt so grand.

Ella used money Irving did not know she had to make a good showing for Elsie's wedding. Ella saved the money bit by bit, hiding it under her bloomers in the drawer in her own bedroom. Irving never once came to her bedroom. That part of life was over for them. Ella did not wonder how he managed. He was still a preacher part-time. It was something he and God would have to work out. For her part, Ella was comfortable and happy with her decision.

She hoped Elsie would have a happy marriage with Roy. She worried about his wild Irish side. The young man did have a way about him. He was hard to dislike. He was obviously smitten with Elsie and she with him, but Ella knew that would pass. She hoped for an easier life for her first daughter than she had with Irving. A mother always hopes.

Ella would miss Elsie's willing help and hard work at home. Vida would have to start helping more. At seven, she was old enough.

Roy looked so nice in his new suit complete with vest and watch fob. They made a resplendent couple. Irving performed the ceremony, albeit, reluctantly. He did not approve of this fellow. For once, he gave in to please his oldest daughter, of whom he was so fond.

Irving's younger brother, Lynn, and his wife, Olivia, had traveled from Ohio for the wedding. Lynn was beginning his medical practice near Dayton. He wanted to be there for his favorite niece's wedding. Lynn had gone down to the swamps of Missouri on business for one of the relatives. He contracted malaria and had not yet completely recovered. He was small and thin, but in excellent spirits for the occasion.

The wedding went smoothly. The reception at home was a crowded and happy affair. Children went darting here and there and under the tables grabbing food like hungry little birds. Someone from the church played the organ, the food was plentiful and the wishes warm. It was a good start.

The newlyweds moved in with Frank's family temporarily. Roy's mother, Sarah, lived there as well. Roy was her youngest and most favored child. He could do no wrong in Sarah's estimation. She doted on her children, especially her baby, Roy.

It was fortunate for Sarah that Roy had married a sweet-natured girl. Elsie accepted things as they were without complaining. The only thing that ever really bothered her about her mother-in-law was something she kept to herself until long after Sarah was dead. Elsie used to take care of the laundry, which meant washing and ironing Sarah's dresses, which had long, voluminous skirts. Elsie would work so hard scrubbing them on the washboard. Later she heated the two sad irons on the wood cook stove. She took a heavy pot holder to lift the irons alternately off and on the stove. The handles were so hot. If she was not very careful she would get burned. Ironing had to be done even in the heat of summer. It took forever to finish one of Sarah's dresses. The part Elsie did not appreciate was that as soon as a dress was finished, even in the middle of the day, Sarah would put it on. Elsie never complained to Sarah or anyone about it. She simply took notice and sighed.

In a few months, Roy and Elsie managed to rent a small apartment of their own. They needed to because Elsie was expecting their first child. There just was not room at Frank's to squeeze in one more person. They found a third-level walkup with one bedroom, a living/dining room and a kitchen.

Roy was working part time driving streetcars and doing pickup labor at the flour mill or stock yards. They got by. Elsie knew it was only a short time until 1906, when the Emerick money would be realized. She was not quite sure how it would all happen. Poppa said it would happen, so she trusted that with all her heart. It would be wonderful to have fine things for her new baby.

Little Frank was born in August 1905. It was a happy occasion. Roy was thrilled to have produced a son first out of the chute. He handed out cigars and bought a round of drinks for all at his favorite pub. His vest almost burst its buttons with pride. Elsie was just happy to have the ordeal over and have a healthy baby. She had always liked caring for the little children. Now at last she had her own. And he was such a beautiful baby.

When 1906 arrived, Elsie was busy with her baby. She sometimes worried when Roy did not come straight home after work, especially when he got paid. Eventually he would come home a little tipsy and affectionate and with less money in his pocket than he should have had. Her nature was forgiving and he always joked her out of her disapproval. He went to work everyday and they did not go hungry.

Irving was now fully engaged in trying to obtain his rightful inheritance. He formed an alliance with other Emerick relatives. They hired attorneys. Irving collected documentation from close relatives as to their relationship to John Nicholas Emerick. Letters flew back and forth. It was now only a matter of time before they would all be living on easy street.

Chapter 9

It was Christmas 1783 aboard the *Maria Rose*. Captain Schmidt broke into the cargo stores some time ago to keep his passengers and crew fed. One always depended on the sea to provide provender when ill winds kept a ship off its course. The sailors climbed down and out onto the ice and chopped holes in the frozen surface. They were able to catch some fish that way. It was very slow going though to supply the food needs of the sixty souls on board.

Christmas was not very festive. They had now been stranded for six weeks in the ice. The passengers ceased telling each other things would be all right tomorrow. A lifeboat mentality had settled in. Tempers were as short as the food supplies. Captain Schmidt tried to cheer things up with the breaking open of the special German wines. It succeeded for a while, but then, when the musicians began playing favorite Christmas carols, it seemed to have the opposite affect. Tears started running down the cheeks of a few and then a general malaise set in for the rest of the afternoon.

It became a habit for John Nicholas and John Jacob to meet every day and talk. It did wonders for John Nicholas's spirits. He certainly liked this young lad who was always willing to listen and seemed to have good ideas himself.

"Had you thought about sending someone else out to do the trading?" asked John Jacob.

"I tried that once," replied John Nicholas. "The twit was not careful with the hides. He told me he knew what he was doing. Many of them were of inferior quality and some were spoiled. I lost a few customers over that."

"Perhaps your brothers?" suggested Astor.

"Ha! As if they would. They are both ruled by their women. They want the benefits of the business all right, but they are not willing to do what all it takes," countered Emerick.

John Jacob Astor filed this away in his memory. He was beginning to form a plan as to how he could be of service to this multimillionaire fur trader. Emerick obviously knew how to make money. He owned all these ships and said he had more money than he could possibly spend in a lifetime. It just keeps rolling in, Emerick had told him. But Emerick was getting tired. He was weary of the trips into the wilds.

"Perhaps before this experience is over I can persuade him to let me in on this somehow," thought Astor. "If I can, this ice will have been a lucky thing for me."

It was the second week of January 1784, when the ice finally gave way and allowed the *Maria Rose* passage on up Chesapeake Bay to Baltimore. After being marooned for two months the passengers and crew were exhausted. There was feeble jubilation upon their arrival. They all just wanted off the bloody ship.

Emerick and young Astor had by this time hatched a plan between them to bring Astor into the business. It was working out as Astor hoped. Of course, he would have to prove himself. The old man was no pushover. He could tell Emerick was lonely. His only love had died, as had his favorite cousin, Andrew. His brothers, Christopher and Valentine, seemed at times to conspire against him in their inability to grasp the complexities of the fur-trading business. Their wives and his nieces and nephews always seemed to expect financial support and were less than thankful when he extended it. They seemed to feel it their birthright as Uncle John could easily afford it. All these concerns were imparted to Astor in conversations during their long, icy exile.

Astor would remember all of these concerns and use them to his advantage as time went on.

The first action taken on their agreement was for John Jacob to learn the fur-trading business. Toward that end they traveled together to New York where Emerick introduced Astor to Robert Bowen, a furrier. It was decided that Bowen would train Astor for a period of three years. He would receive board and $2 a week. The work was hard. At first Astor spent all day just beating skins. He almost gave up, thinking such rude work was not what he had envisioned.

He probably would have quit, except for his meetings with Emerick during that time. They met together as often as they could, whenever John Nicholas was in New York. John Jacob sensed in his friend the weariness of continuing to gather the pelts himself. He knew before long someone else would be doing it. He renewed his resolve to be that person. He would pay his dues. There was a pot of gold waiting for him at the end, he was sure.

Bowen gave good reports when Emerick asked of Astor's progress.

"The lad is quick to learn, John. He tends to whatever job he is given. There is a quality about him that allows him to stay at any task—no matter what—until it is finished. Sometimes he almost frightens me with his dedication. We have given him difficult tasks, just to test his resolve. He will do well at whatever he does, I'll wager," said Bowen one afternoon when Emerick stopped by.

This was the kind of dedication which John Nicholas had been seeking. He had not found it in his brothers, Christopher and Valentine, nor in others of his acquaintance. This young man could be relied upon, John Nicholas was sure.

So when the apprenticeship was up, John Nicholas offered John Jacob a job bringing back the animal skins for a percentage of the profits of each trip. To his surprise, John Jacob said no. It was not what he had in mind. He had learned the technique of caring for furs well. He did not desire to work for anyone but himself.

This was a bold statement to make, as John Jacob had no money to fund an expedition across town, much less out into the wilderness. He counted on the fact that his friend, Emerick, would not want to lose him. Emerick relied on Astor to listen and confer on business matters already. They were the best of friends. When John Nicholas stopped sputtering and calmed down some, Astor made his proposal.

"What I want, John, is to be a full partner," stated Astor.

"A full partner! Why, you are coming to me with nothing. The risk is mine. The money is mine. Why on God's earth should I make you a partner?" puzzled John Nicholas.

"Ah, because, John. Who else do you have? You *know* you can trust me. Have I not always done what I said I would do? Have I not been a true friend to you? Name others whom you would trust with your fortune," countered John Jacob.

There was silence from John Nicholas. A silence that spoke loudly of John Nicholas's lack of other trustworthy companions.

In time, they agreed that John Jacob Astor could have one-third of the business and that he would do the traveling to gather the furs. John Nicholas would remain in the city and conduct the business and travel to Europe with the shipments.

A formal agreement was written up and filed in Superior Court in New York. It states:

Articles of Agreement Witnesseth: That we the undersigned have this day entered into a co-partnership agreement with headquarters in New York. The proceeds of said partnership to be divided two-thirds to John Nicholas Emerick and one-third to John Jacob Astor and each agrees with the other to give faithful attention to the partnership business. The agreement shall apply to all transactions made by either of the undersigned in fur trading, shipping business, merchandise, or any other business transactions in which either shall be engaged. In witness whereof we have hereunto set our hands and seals this 20th day of June 1787.

Signed: John Nicholas Emerick John Jacob Astor

At about this same time Valentine wrote in a letter to his father.

"*Brother Nicholas has arranged everything with John Jacob Astor. We do not meet anymore. Nicholas has changed and I do not know why.*"

Astor set out with a powerful zeal to traverse the wilderness and bring back furs. He charted new territory. He traded fearlessly. He became a major force in the fur-trading business.

The partnership continued successfully for many years, during which time Astor's fame as a fur trapper and trader grew to mythical proportions. Never was there a fur-trading man with more drive and ambition than John Jacob Astor. His reputation as a money-mad swindler who tried any means available, legal or not, eithical or not, to acheive his ends also grew.

In 1793, in the midst of their successful partnership, there was an odd letter from John Nicholas to his father, which may give a clue as to further happenings. It states:

"*Uncle Konrad has told me, that yourself and Christopher and Valentine have become Jews. Is that so? It is a shame to have this burden upon us. Christopher and Valentine will not answer the question, but I must know, otherwise I will not remember you, as I did not believe any of you would do that. My fortune is worth millions, but you will get nothing if this is so. My friend, John Jacob Astor, has a brother-in-law who will bring this letter to you.*"

Religious anti-Semitism had been around for hundreds of years in Europe. Jews were persecuted along with others during the Spanish Inquisition in 1540. A different feeling against the Jews arose in the 1800s. The Jews had become an economic force to be reckoned with in Europe. In addition to the religious differences which had rankled non-Jews for hundreds of years, they now were in positions of financial power. As a businessman, John Nicholas was aware of the rising competition from Jews and the companion rise of feelings of fear and hatred against them. Jews tended to deal only with Jews in business transactions. It could leave a non-Jewish businessman out in the cold if he were not careful.

John Nicholas wondered if his brothers were trying to make deals with the Jewish merchants by saying that they themselves were Jews. He would not be surprised if his brothers had done that. He would be very surprised if they had actually changed their religion.

Several years later, in 1806, John Nicholas fell very ill. It had started with a high fever. Soon he was drifting in and out of consciousness. The doctor feared he would not live. Astor was at home at this time and was sent for as the situation looked very grave indeed. He sat beside the bed, realizing that if John Nicholas should die the entire business would fall on his shoulders. It was not an entirely unhappy thought. However, Astor did revere and appreciate his friend and partner who had brought him into a very lucrative business.

John Nicholas roused briefly and spoke.

"Astor, is that you there?"

"Yes. John, I am here," replied Astor.

"That letter I wrote to my father years ago. He has never forgiven me for being so harsh with him. I must make amends. He is a very old man. I did not need to trouble him so. Please, John, write to him for me. Tell him I am sorry if he was upset by the letter. I am not sure I will make it through this illness." With that, John Nicholas lapsed back into unconsciousness without hearing Astor's affirmative response.

Astor, true to the request, wrote the father of John Nicholas stating:

"Your son, John Nicholas, is very sick, and asked me to write you, that you should not be angry on account of the harsh letter he wrote you."

In time, John Nicholas recovered from the fever.

As the partnership with Astor continued, John Nicholas saw less and less of his brothers. They continued to work for the business. He was no longer invited to be a part of family occasions. That was all right with him. He had made his home for many years in Philadelphia with Baltheus, a relative of his Uncle Konrad, and Baltheus's family. He paid a fair share of expenses and they did not expect more. The tensions so easily aroused between competing siblings were not present for him in this household. More and more, John Nicholas just wanted peace in his life and he found it with Baltheus's family.

Chapter 10

Irving could not believe it. He had waited so long for 1906 to arrive. He was ready to do battle. He was prepared to do whatever it took to obtain his rightful fortune. He expected there would be much paperwork to do and a careful check by the courts as to who was entitled. All that was merely necessary and not to be worried about.

But Irving did not expect this. The will of John Nicholas Emerick was nowhere to be found. He knew the will given to his grandfather, George, by *his* father, Christopher, many years ago, had been stolen by his Uncle Will. He also knew about the old sea chest that supposedly contained all the papers they would need. But his cousins who had the old trunk claimed it did not contain a copy of the will. He had believed it was in that chest. What had become of it? Surely, one of their cousins had it.

Could one of the family have lost it? Maybe it was thrown away accidentally? Could one of the family have sold it, too, privately, to the Astor family? Irving had no idea who might have done such a thing. Vengeance is mine, saith the Lord, he thought. I'll not accuse anyone. Surely the suit can go forward anyway. The trust is on file stating after 90 years the money held by the Astors is to be paid to heirs of Christopher and Valentine. An equal amount to each is fair. Any court should recognize that.

"Hum," said Ella when he told her the dilemma. It was lucky she never expected much from that pipe dream because now she was not disappointed. But she did not say that.

"Any court should recognize the suit is valid, Ellie," said Irving. "After all, it was the court itself said the estate could not be settled until 1906 because of the trust agreement. They said that in 1848, when old Astor himself died. Then they said it again in 1874 when the Astors tried to sell that property in New York that didn't belong to them. I reckon the courts will uphold us this time, even if there isn't any will."

Irving was destined to be disappointed. The 1906 court ruled that since no will could be found the case could not be settled. It was a bitter disappointment for Irving who had pinned his hopes on a favorable outcome.

He visited Elsie to tell her. She was let down, too. It had been a nice dream to think of having pleasant surroundings and lots of good food for her family. Still, she was not unhappy with her life. She had a charming companion who still made her heart flutter. She had the prettiest child on the block and as the year was coming to a close, she felt the stirrings of another child in her body.

Elsie, who was not fond of sewing, found her hands eager and willing to sew for Little Frank. She made him a pair of denim overalls. He looked like such a little man in them. She had already had to remove the front pocket to patch one knee. She had found a pair of tiny black socks with bright red toes and heels. He lay on his back kicking his feet in those little socks. His feet looked like small red bugs flitting here and there. He laughed and laughed.

What a beautiful, happy child, she thought. How fortunate she was. So the great fortune did not arrive as expected. Poppa still believed the family would prevail eventually. They just needed to find the will of John Nicholas Emerick. Meanwhile, she had her own small living space, she had Roy, whom she loved dearly, she had Little Frank, and she had another baby on the way. She felt content.

Little Frank awoke that morning with bright red spots on his two year old cheeks. He felt warm. He was seldom cranky, but this morning he was not quite his usual happy self.

Elsie dressed him in his little overalls and the black socks with the red toes and heels. He crawled listlessly around on the floor. Finally he just lay down and was uncharacteristically still.

He said, "Momma, me hot, hot."

He did not want to get up. He did not want to eat.

She bathed his little face with cool water. He became hotter and hotter. She held him and soothed him. They were alone, as Roy had gone to work.

About noon, she went next door to her neighbor and asked if her oldest boy could go for the doctor. The ten-year-old boy ran off as fast as he could to find the doctor.

Little Frank's eyes were rolling back up into his head. He could not or would not answer her. She was becoming very frightened.

By the time the doctor arrived, Little Frank was comatose. Dr. Carter had been there when Little Frank was born. He had seen these symptoms in children too many times. His heart grieved for the pretty young mother. He knew there was nothing he could do against spinal meningitis.

Roy was sent for and arrived home breathless after running all the way.

Dr. Carter told Roy and Elsie together as they gripped hands tightly. There was nothing he could do. There was always a chance of recovery he told them, but with a temperature so high on such a young child, it was very unlikely.

She kept bathing him with cool water and praying. They all prayed, the doctor and the neighbors. But cool water and praying did not save him.

About five o'clock that evening, Little Frank's heart stopped beating.

Elsie grabbed him in her arms shouting, "Oh, no, oh, no! Please God, no, no."

Roy was beside himself with grief. He cried and patted her arm.

"There, there, love, there will be another one soon," he said.

That did not help. Elsie knew he was trying to comfort both of them, but thinking about a new unknown life at this time did not help release the love for her first, her beautiful, beautiful boy.

She clutched Little Frank's body to her chest. She sat in the rocking chair, rocking and holding his lifeless little body. She sobbed and crooned to him.

She vaguely knew there were others in the room. Dr. Carter, who had stayed with them, was still there. Her brother-in-law, Frank, and his wife, Etta, arrived. More neighbors crowded in. Elsie was in a place of her own where she could not be comforted.

Finally Ella and Irving arrived. Then Elsie roused at her mother's urging.

"Oh, Momma. Oh, Momma. He's gone," cried Elsie, rocking back and forth in the chair.

"I know, my child. My poor, poor child," soothed Ella with tears running down her own cheeks. She cried for her daughter's pain and for her own at the loss of this grandson who was a bright light in her life.

"Come, Elsie. I'll help you care for him," said Ella softly.

"I want to lay him out myself," replied Elsie. "Momma, please make them all go away."

Ella began easing people toward the door. Irving insisted on a prayer first. He thanked God for this little life that had been shared with them for a short time. He recognized God's right to take the child back at His own will. It was a long prayer.

Elsie's heart hardened at that prayer. It hardened against God. It frightened her that she would feel so. She was trying to understand that God has His reasons. Perhaps she could understand in the future. Right now, her heart wanted to shout at God, "Why did You do this? How could You have needed him more than we? How could You bring such a cruelness on us?"

After all the people left, including Irving and Roy, who were brought together in a bond of grief, Elsie arose. She carried her precious bundle to the table. Ella brought a pan of water, a cloth and some soap. Elsie had earlier removed the little overalls and little black socks with the red heels and toes from her little boy. She began washing him. His little cheeks were pale now. The redness, which had meant life was still circulating through his body, had ebbed away.

She carefully washed all his little fingers and his little toes. Lastly, she washed and caressed his face. Ella stood by until Elsie was finished. Then together they dressed him in clean clothes for the last time. Elsie thought how strange it was to dress him without having him kick and wiggle and move. When they finished, she kissed his little face and his hands and turned away.

In all her young life, nothing like this had ever happened to Elsie. From here on to the end of her life, no other experience would equal the pain of this one. Other tragedies came, but they somehow were not as bad as this one. This was the touchstone of her life.

Roy and Frank built the small coffin. They could not afford a burial plot. It was agreed that he could be buried on top of the grave of another relative. So the grave was opened and Little Frank was laid to rest.

Chapter 11

A dizziness overcame John Nicholas. He made his way back to his cabin on the *Sea Queen*. He knew he would soon be facing the end of his life. The dizzy spells had increased. So had the throbbing pain in his head. His breath was short.

A fellow could not expect to live much beyond his present age of seventy-five. Christopher and Valentine were both still alive and they were not much younger. They had not been through the hardships he had. They had not traveled in the wilds or had the constant worry of keeping up with the business.

He kept fit for so many years by traveling and trading across the young country. How exhilarating it had been! Planning the routes, choosing men to go who were trustworthy and hardworking. Never knowing what each day would bring. There were a few brushes with the Indians. They were a calculating, evil lot. He had been fortunate. None of his men had been brutalized and chopped up by those savages. Other traders and trappers he knew of were not so lucky.

They were canny traders, the Indians. When he first began trapping and trading for furs, the Indians were in awe of the white man. Thought they were gods. That soon passed as the Indians learned what the white man would pay for animal hides. At first the

Indians were delighted to trade for beads and cheap trinkets. Later mostly what they wanted was alcohol, guns and gun powder, horses or tobacco. Whatever you gave them they always kept asking for more. You could never be sure they would not steal your horses at night. They went back on their word. An agreement with an Indian Chief did not always hold. They would enhance the value of furs to any inattentive, inexperienced trader. There were so many nuances in dealing with them. And one had to deal with them.

The ability to trap depended so much on weather conditions and finding animals in the right places. The Indians knew where to look and weather did not dismay them or inhibit their efforts. Why, some days his party might only get two or three deer or maybe a bear or an elk. The Indians provided large quantities, especially of the smaller animals. One time, he remembered, he noted in his diary the Indians brought him almost one hundred beaver pelts, so highly prized for making beaver caps. In addition, the Indians provided good quantities of other small animals such as mink, otter, fox, raccoon, rabbit and badgers, as well as, buffalo, elk, wolf, bear, deer and wildcat, all salable furs, very much desired in the European markets. Yes, you had to trade with the Indians.

John Nicholas admired Astor in those early years of their partnership. The young man was fearless. He knew how to get out there and make the best deals. He could not be faulted for that. Somehow, though, it twisted his personality until his desire for money overrode all other concerns. Astor had laughed at John Nicholas's cautions about his love of money and the ways he obtained it.

"The Indians are savages, John. They are tools to be used. I meet their cruelness and duplicity with a more than equal measure. It's the only way to deal with such creatures," countered Astor. "Besides, I don't see you refusing your share of the profits."

Astor had a way of making irrefutable statements that left John Nicholas hard pressed for a response.

Seated now on the edge of his bunk on the *Sea Queen*, John Nicholas was breathing a little easier. His thoughts returned to the previous year, 1815. He mentally chewed over the happening with his brothers again and again. As was his habit, his mind kept worrying away about how things could have been done differently. He wished that things had not turned out the way they had. Papers were signed now. There was no going back.

From his perspective, he had been extremely patient with his younger brothers. They had never worked up to his satisfaction. But they were family. He carried them and gave them a good life in America. It seemed they were never satisfied. He had been tired when he met them on the pier in New York last year. He was just arriving after a long sea voyage, for God's sake. Couldn't they let him have a few minutes? But no. There they were, waiting for him on the pier. Ready to pounce the moment he disembarked. He knew it would be about money. It was always about money. They were not coming to greet him with joy over his arrival.

By now, he decided that they and his father had not become Jews as he had been told. They steadfastly refused to discuss it with him. He could see no evidence of their changing their religion or their dress. He believed their attitude about money made people associate their grasping and conniving with those qualities thought to be the purview of the pettifogging Jews. They seemed to have gained a reputation. Of course, his father, John Daniel, had married a Jewish widow and his half brother, Solomon, was half-Jewish. Still, he could not believe his father and Christopher and Valentine would call themselves Jewish. He had no quarrel with Solomon and he had gotten along with his late stepmother. He considered them exceptions to the general ill-feeling he felt against the Jews.

Christopher and Valentine were there as he stepped from the gangway.

"Nicholas, our stepbrother has written that he has sent us some of Father's money," stated Christopher. "Before you go off with it in your own pocket, we thought we better be handy when you arrived."

John Nicholas did not answer right away. He kept his own counsel.

Valentine spoke up, "You cannot deny us what is rightfully ours! You know Solomon sold that property that was Father's. You certainly don't need a share. Your money is piling up more and more every day, you damned old miser."

Christopher, working himself into a lather, lashed out at his brother, "You have continually taken advantage of us. We should have a share of the business. But you give everything over to that young thief Astor. It's Valentine and I who have held your offices together while you were out gallivanting the world. What makes you think you can treat us this way? Give that money over!" Christopher gave his brother a shove on the shoulder.

Still, John Nicholas did not speak. He did not make a move toward his purse. He stepped back when Christopher pushed him. He formed a decision as he did so. He had not planned to deny his brothers the money sent to them from their father's estate. Suddenly he felt his resolve harden and his heart close up toward these two younger brothers. The fact that he was physically pushed was significant. The golden goose reached his limit. His brothers had not heard or remembered the old adage about not biting the hand that feeds you. They would live to regret that.

When John Nicholas finally spoke, it was with a quiet voice. Christopher and Valentine were silent. Both realized that something significant had taken place. With the physical shove, the old men knew a line had been crossed.

"Christopher, you remember four years ago when I financed the new house for your family?" began John Nicholas. "I gave you the money without strings attached. Over and above your salary. It was a goodly sum.

"Valentine, have I not paid for your granddaughters' weddings and the property on which both of them now live?" asked John Nicholas.

"I believe the money from our father's estate will almost cover what I have given you both. Not quite, but almost. I am willing to accept this money as payment for what I have advanced to you in most recent years. We will forget the many amounts before that. I tell you both now that neither you, nor your children will be remembered in my will. You have had the last money from me that you will get. There will be no more. Now please let me pass. I am tired from the trip."

With that said John Nicholas wearily picked up his sea chest and walked off the pier. His brothers stood in disbelief, unable to comprehend for the moment what had really happened. Later, when they recounted the story to their families it came out a little different. Neither of them mentioned the shove. In time, they both believed the shove had never happened; that their wealthy and notoriously stingy older brother had decided to turn against them just because he was perverse.

The day after the quarrel on the pier, John Nicholas met with John Jacob. As usual, John Nicholas shared with his friend and partner what was on his mind. He told John Jacob of the troubling incident on the pier with his brothers.

"Those two have been a drain on our business for long enough. God, what a couple of greedy dolts you have for brothers, John!" Astor was sympathetic and secretly relieved that these two were out of the picture.

"Well, I'm going to change my will now. "I have to." I'd like to leave my money to family. My mother would have wanted it so," John Nicholas was thinking aloud really.

Astor, always on the alert where money was involved, caught a whiff of a possibility that could benefit his own family.

The Little Brown Suitcase

Carol Lynn and Nancy Morris, circa 1939. "When they sat me in a corner people sometimes mistook me for a doll."

Dorothy Bryan Morris and Nancy, circa 1937. "Mother had that smile that lit up her whole face like morning sunshine."

Irving Grant Emerick, circa 1884. Ella remembered why she had married him. He was a handsome young man with a fierce dedication to the Lord.

Elsie Emerick Bryan and Roy Bryan, circa 1908.

Christopher Emerick

Little Frank, circa 1906.

Little Frank's overalls and socks. "Elsie kept Little Frank's overalls and the black socks with the red toes and heels at the bottom of *The Little Brown Suitcase*."

Ella took Billy/Arthur to a portrait studio to have a formal picture taken.

Irving and Ella are buried in different sections of Mountain View Cemetery in Tacoma, Washington. Elsie faithfully tended their graves every Decoration Day.

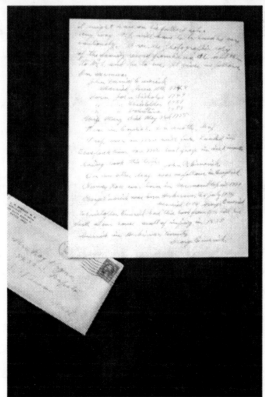

Examples of some of the many telegrams and letters in
The Little Brown Suitcase.

Chapter 12

Elsie tried to keep busy after the death of Little Frank. Sometimes she would go home to help Momma with the work of the boarding houses and with the children. She always made sure to be back at the small apartment in time to make Roy a good dinner. Cooking was a skill in which she was well schooled and one which she enjoyed.

Billy, her youngest brother, was showing remarkable musical talent. When he was four years old, he began to climb up on the organ bench at home after church and play hymns he had heard that morning.

Ella suspected early on that there was something very special about her youngest child. She did not expect his talent would be in the musical arena. There was something strange about the way her little boy looked from the back while playing the piano. His chubby little fingers looked like a child's fingers, but the rest of his little body moved with the definition and punctuation of the musical piece in such a way that from the back he looked like a grown man. Ella wondered if her long dormant fey abilities were tricking her mind into seeing what Billy would look like in the future.

By the time he was five years old Billy was playing at church services. He studied with a private music teacher. Billy was also reading books and newspapers with fine comprehension. Elsie felt so proud of her younger brother. He was not temperamental as one might expect of a gifted prodigy. Along with his extraordinary talent, Billy was blessed with a sweet spirit. Elsie enjoyed being with him, although he was not like the other ones had been at that age. He was more interested in music than in the games she played with the other children. He was never quarrelsome. Elsie found herself speaking to him almost as an equal. It was a strange feeling.

Ella had an heretical thought that Billy might be the reincarnation of one of the greats from the classical musical world. She didn't know that much about music. She wondered how he came by this great musical talent. She did used to sing before she was married and was said to have had a lovely voice, but she did not know instrumental music. She surmised it was from her family. Ella's family were all musical in some way. One or two of them made considerable reputations as concert singers or orchestra leaders. None of the other eleven Emerick children had shown any exceptional musical ability. Irving was fond of music, but had no particular talent in that area.

Irving had intellectual talent. She had always known and appreciated that. His musical ability was limited at best. He always tried to find someone else to lead the singing when he preached. He sounded off-key whenever he sang, like a crow with a sore throat. It did not diminish his stature one bit. Irving, by now, had written a number of books on natural philosophy.

He was quite well known in certain circles. The books did not bring in much additional income though. When he did sell some books after a speech or a sermon he would likely give the money away to the poor.

What Irving did receive that seemed of greater value to him was a respected place in the community. St. Louis was a big city. He was known there and as far away as Jefferson City, the Missouri state capital. He was working on the Page Avenue streetcar line and preaching and teaching whenever he could. He was writing books at home alone at night in his bedroom. Ella felt pleased that he channeled some of his energy into writing books alone in his room. She thought maybe she had given him that opportunity by moving out of their bedroom. This was something good for him that came of her defection.

Irving also continued the fight to obtain his share of John Nicholas Emerick's fortune. Irving wrote many letters to family members and to the courts to appeal the case. There was still no will to be found. Irving was undaunted. He believed that perseverance would win the day. God, who was just, would rule in their favor eventually.

Chapter 13

John Nicholas set his trunk on the edge of the bunk. His head was throbbing with pain. He opened the old sea chest that had accompanied him on so many voyages. He had brought it with him when he first came to America in 1770. It looked tired and worn after forty-six years. He always felt it best to carry his important documents with him on these trips. Of course, the most important documents were now secreted inside the lid of the trunk.

He sorted through the things that were there. His German Bible printed in 1735 was there. He opened it up. There was the wildflower he had picked on the day Maria was laid to rest. He had placed it in "The Song of Solomon."

When I am gone, he thought, no one will ever know what significance this flower had for me.

He was afraid to touch the flower. It was folded sideways instead of spread out flat. It looked like a small purple bugle. The color, though faded, was still there after all the years. After looking at it awhile, he did pick it up. It crumbled to pieces in his hand. He would liked to have thrown the pieces into the sea. But he was not feeling very well and hesitated to walk out on deck again. So he let the pieces fall through his fingers and float down to the amber floorboards in a purple mist.

He had a small very old hymn book in the trunk. His grandfather had given it to him when he was young. His grandfather had admonished him to stay close to the Lord and the church; then his life would be smooth and prosperous. He had carried the hymn book as a sort of talisman on his way through life. Well, life had not been smooth, but it had been prosperous. God could have a measure of credit for that, even though a great deal of the reason was his own hard work, he thought.

Also in the chest, were his two small notebooks, where he kept records of his life and his business dealings. They told the story of his life since coming to America. He had faithfully recorded his travels and the outcome of deals he made. When he reached home the next day he would enter the date and the results of this trip.

He had given Christopher a sealed copy of the will he had made last year following their quarrel. Astor had helped him decide what to do. John Nicholas was determined his brothers and their children should not benefit from his fortune. Still, he wanted to leave his vast estate to his own family. Family was where the money should go. There would be many children with the blood of his father and mother coursing through their veins in the future. Even though they were not directly from himself, the ties would be there. He knew his mother loved all of her boys. He could not slight those in the future who would bear the Emerick characteristics and heritage.

They devised a plan between them, he and Astor. One thing about Astor, he knew how to make and manage money. None of John Nicholas's relatives knew how to handle a great fortune. He hardly knew himself. He amassed real estate and bought bonds and gold. He was not sure exactly how much his estate was worth at the present time. He did not have current information on the real estate values. He did not spend time counting it all up. He did keep close track of what he owned. Of course, everything in the business was two-thirds his. That amounted to many millions. He had not made a bad bargain bringing Astor in with him.

Astor continued to be a bit of an enigma to John Nicholas. Whether or not he could be trusted was not always clear. Astor stated he would always be fair with John Nicholas in business and he probably had been. It was the stories that circulated about Astor that kept Emerick wondering. Maybe the wool was being pulled over his eyes and he had not noticed it. In any case, there was plenty of money and property to be left to anyone who could prove a relationship to John Nicholas Emerick in the future.

The plan they jointly came up with to preserve Emerick's fortune for his future relatives was this: John Nicholas left his entire estate in trust with Astor for a period of 90 years, after which time the estate together with the accumulation therefrom was to be divided between the descendants of Christopher and Valentine. This trust was filed in Superior Court in New York. Upon John Nicholas's death, John Jacob Astor would be in charge of all the property and money of John Nicholas Emerick. For ninety years.

After the will and the trust were signed, John Nicholas began to have second thoughts. Astor now had the whole of his estate to play around with for 90 years. Astor was still a relatively young man. There was a persuasive quality about Astor. He could talk a person into a thing. He made it seem reasonable when you were with him. Astor had often been able to convince John Nicholas of a course of action that later had been against his better judgment. Astor was often right from the standpoint of moneymaking. His moral judgments were where the rub came in.

John Nicholas reviewed his assets now as he sat on the bunk on the *Sea Queen*.

He owned the 35 acres of land in New York City; 4000 acres of choice coal and oil land in Berks County, Pennsylvania; 300 acres in South Boston in the Germantown area; 33 acres in the center of Philadelphia; and other small pieces of property.

He had 78 million in German gold coins, 47 million in United States Treasury Bonds, 21 million in other government bonds and many other assets.

His future relatives would be very well off. That is, if Astor and his descendants held up their end of the bargain.

John Nicholas had his doubts. That is why he left copies of all of the papers relating to his estate and a copy of his will and the trust at The Hague for safekeeping. Little did he know at that time that his papers would be neither safe, nor kept at The Hague.

In addition to giving Christopher and a cousin, Konrad, a copy of his will, leaving papers at The Hague and hiding papers in the lining of his sea chest, he had written a letter to his stepbrother, Solomon, in Germany, on November 15, 1816. It states in part:

"This is why I am leaving my entire holdings to my direct and indirect descendants. My brothers and their children shall receive a like amount. Christopher and Valentine and their children shall receive no more. I never married. If Astor does not treat me honest, I do not know what to do. He has my whole fortune on ninety years trust. I do not know where Astor is now. Eight months ago he went on a trip and did not say anything and I have not heard from him. He shall give up my fortune. I am seventy-five years old, very sick and will die soon. I deposited my papers in the Probate Office at The Hague, Holland last year for safe keeping (sic). Also, Christopher and Konrad have my last will and testament where I give everything to be divided. I also gave them a list of my

estate. Everything Astor has, two-thirds belongs to me and one-third to him."

John Nicholas lay his head down on the pillow for a moment. The pain in his head was almost blinding.

I have done everything I can, he thought, I will not give over my fortune to the likes of Christopher and Valentine. They have resented me all of my life. They deliberately conspired against me time and time again, they and their families. What I gave to them, I gave with a warm hand. When my hands are cold they shall have no more.

The only one John Nicholas felt he could trust was Astor. Now he was not so sure of Astor. Astor talked him into the terms of the trust and latest will made last year and now carried hidden in the sea chest. It protected the fortune from his grasping relatives, but not from Astor.

"Perhaps when we reach shore tomorrow in Philadelphia I should make a new will," he thought. "But who would I name to control the estate? I cannot name other relatives and leave out my own closest ones, my surviving brothers and their families. Who but Astor would even know how to handle such a fortune?"

He could not think clearly with his head hurting so. He thought of this so many times before and no answer had come. He would reconsider what to do when he arrived home the next day. He would not bother Baltheus with his concerns. That was never part of their relationship, although he had lived with Baltheus' family for more years than he could easily recall. Oh, naturally they discussed John Nicholas's trips and business in a surface manner, but Baltheus was never a part of decision-making. John Nicholas always kept his own counsel.

Yes, he would think about it some more tomorrow. Right now some sleep would probably help relieve the stabbing pain in his head. The rhythmic roll of the ship felt familiar and comforting. He drifted off to sleep.

Chapter 14

Elsie was now eight months pregnant with her second child. It was getting to be a bit of a struggle to reach the third floor of their apartment building. She had gone over to Momma's helping again today. She liked being around a large family. It was lonesome for her being alone all day while Roy worked at whatever jobs he could find. She wanted to have a large family, too. It would be good to have a baby again. It still would not ease her heartache about Little Frank, but it would be such a pleasure to hold another child of her own.

She saved Little Frank's overalls and the black socks with the red toes and heels. She left them over at Momma's. She could not bear to part with them, but she did not know if she could put them on another baby. Best to wait and see. They did not have money to buy new things for this child. She could find plenty of hand-me-downs at Momma's. Still, she would like new things for a new baby. Just another month and it would be there. All signs were good for a normal birth, just like last time.

Momma gave Elsie a good piece of salt pork that day. She planned to make a large pot of navy beans the next day. With that in mind, she pulled the sack of beans out of the cupboard and put some beans to soak overnight. Tonight she would make biscuits and milk gravy. Roy liked that.

She was not sure if the flour mill was going to pay today. Roy was still working part time for the streetcar company, too. On his days off he did pickup work. The flour mill usually had something available and Roy had worked there for the past three days. If they paid tonight, Roy might be late. Elsie accepted that her husband liked to drink. At least he did not drink alone. He just liked to cut loose with his friends after work sometimes, especially on pay days.

The biscuits were cold. The gravy was congealed. Elsie sat in the rocking chair reading her Bible and nodding almost asleep. She was so sleepy lately. She wanted to be awake when Roy finally came home. She knew he would want to eat. She could reheat the gravy and he would not notice the biscuits were cold. He would bring news of the world to her and laugh and make her forget his transgressions like he always did. He was a good man. She smiled just thinking of him.

Soon she heard his footsteps coming down the hall. The door opened and there he was, happy and tipsy. She guessed by now that it was pay day at the flour mill. He swept her up with a hug and kiss, even though that required leaning over her enormous belly. He told her all the news. He had seen Frank at the Pub. Etta was pregnant again.

"Goodness, what will they do with more children?" Elsie exclaimed.

Roy and Elsie had spoken before about the way Frank and Etta let their children run loose. At least they had a house and a yard. The yard was often littered with the children's play things. Wagons and balls and buckets and mud pies and forts they made of scrap lumber covered the yard. There was no grass in the small yard anymore as it was trampled to dust by so many little feet. The children were always running and screaming and slamming doors. When they had lived there, Elsie had tried to help watch them. Etta was not much for watching the children. Somehow, in spite of their parents' lackadaisical attitude, they did all seem to thrive. It was a happy household.

"Aw, you know Etta, she might not even notice she has another after it gets here," replied Roy with a grin.

It was late when Roy had arrived home. By the time he had eaten his meal and Elsie had cleaned up, they were both ready for bed.

They quickly fell into a deep sleep, Roy, from the liquor and the hard work, and Elsie, from the weariness of being eight months with child.

What first woke them up was a pounding on the door. Elsie reluctantly came awake first. She heard people screaming. She thought maybe she was dreaming. It was not as dark in the room as usual. She could see light out the window. But it was not early morning as she thought at first. The light was flickering. Now she heard cries of, "Fire! Fire!"

Roy was waking up. He got up and pulled on his pants, slipping his suspenders over his shoulders.

"Stay back, Elsie. I'll go check."

He cautiously opened the door. People were filling the hall in their nightclothes. Smoke was invading the space like a ghostly presence flowing above the heads of the fleeing tenants.

"Hurry, Hurry, Bryan! We need to get down the other stairs! Get the Missus and c'mon!" shouted the man from next door.

Elsie had crept out of the bedroom wearing her white nightgown with the long sleeves. Her brown hair, undone for the night hung almost to her waist. Her feet were bare on the wooden floor. Roy took her arm and steered her out the door. She was not moving very fast. It was all so confusing and noisy.

"C'mon, love," said Roy, "We'll go down the middle stairs. The building had stairs on the outside at one end that could be used in case of fire. But not this time. That end of the building was on fire. They could see the bright tongues of flame shooting through the now dense gray smoke.

They moved toward the stairs in the center of the building. Others were fleeing as well. Mothers were shushing their children and urging them to move more quickly. There was a bit of a crush at the first landing. Roy tried to shelter her from the pressure of the other people. They were both mindful of her condition. They reached the second floor and could go no further.

Choking smoke was billowing up the stairwell. About a dozen of them turned back. They ran to one of the apartments that was left with the door standing open. Everyone made their way through the apartment to the bedroom window. It faced the street where people were gathered in bunches standing to watch the spectacle. Some of them had just escaped and were looking forlornly at the destruction of their homes.

A fire wagon came clanging into view, the horses galloping hooves slipping on the cobblestones of the street. People began easing over the windowsill. It was only a one-story drop to the sidewalk. Parents held their children over the edge as far as they could. Others came to help and catch them.

At last, only Roy and Elsie were left.

"We'll have to jump, Elsie. It's not so far," Roy said breathlessly.

"I can't, Roy. What about the baby? I can't hurt our baby," Elsie gasped, coughing from the smoke.

"I can't get her to come" Roy shouted down. "Somebody get a ladder up here quick!"

In short order the firemen put a ladder up to the window. Roy helped Elsie as she clumsily climbed over the edge of the sill onto the ladder. Willing hands grabbed her from below. She was in her bare feet. So was Roy. Neither noticed the metal rungs cutting into the bottoms of their feet. It was an insignificant price to pay for rescue. They made it safely to the bottom of the ladder. It was March and very cold in St. Louis. Someone put a blanket around Elsie's shoulders. They hurried across the street and sat on the steps of a neighboring building. Elsie was trying to catch her breath. Her heart was pounding hard in her chest. People were rushing everywhere. They heard the roar of the fire and the shouting of the firemen.

Looking up they could see an old woman in a window in the middle of the building on the third floor. They did not know who she was. In fact, they had not seen an old woman on the third floor. She must have kept to herself or was visiting someone. She stood at the window, now framed in yellow and orange darting flames, like a phoenix about to rise from the ashes. The firemen called to her. They spread a large canvas between six of them.

"Jump! We'll catch you. Jump!" the firemen called separately and as a group in a sort of chant that echoed through the night.

"Jump! Jump!" joined a chorus of people on the ground.

She either would not or could not jump. As the flames ate away the supports of the building it began to fall inward from the sides.

Roy and Elsie were watching in horror and fascination. Roy reached over and turned Elsie's face into his shoulder. She should not be watching this, he knew. Elsie buried her face in his chest and began to shake uncontrollably.

After a while Frank and Etta appeared. They had heard about the fire and had come to help. Etta put her arms around Elsie and stroked her back.

"There, there, lovey. It will be all right. You are coming home with us," soothed Etta. "Frank, we need a cart," she continued, "Elsie can't walk all that way."

"C'mon, Roy. She'll be okay. Etta will see to that. Let's go find a cart," said Frank.

Soon they were back with a borrowed horse and cart. Elsie and Etta got in the cart. Etta was chatting in a comforting way to keep Elsie's mind off what she had just been through.

Roy helped Elsie out of the cart when they reached Frank and Etta's house. He was helping her down the walk when his mother, Sarah, ran down the steps and flung her arms around Roy.

150

"Oh, son, when I heard it was your apartment house on fire I was beside myself with worry. Thank the Lord you are safe."

"We're okay, Ma. I got to get Elsie into bed though," said Roy as he continued assisting Elsie.

Suddenly Elsie felt a stabbing, intense pain that almost knocked her to her knees. She doubled over and realized it was a labor pain.

"Oh, not yet. It is too early," she thought.

They put her to bed in Sarah's room. It had the softest mattress. One of the children went to find Dr. Carter.

The doctor could not be found at first. He was busy tending to people hurt in the fire. When he was located, he promised to come as soon as he could. He did not like the sound of it. Labor pains already. He knew young Mrs. Bryan was not due for another month.

Elsie was deep in labor by now. Roy was bathing her face with a cool washcloth. Sarah and Etta were preparing things and doing what they could to comfort her. Finally Etta told Roy to leave the room. His agitation and worry were not helping. She ushered him to the door and told him she would be sure to call him in case he was needed. He felt some guilt that he was relieved to be away from Elsie's anguish.

By the time Dr. Carter had arrived, Sarah and Etta had delivered Elsie of a baby boy. They had cleaned him, wrapped him and handed him over to Elsie. He was whimpering and seemed to be having trouble breathing. His little fingernails were blue. Dr. Carter's heart sank again at the sight. He knew as he had known before, that this child had very little chance of surviving the night. He was just born too soon. He looked like a perfect little specimen of manhood. His lungs had not developed to the point he could breathe properly. Again, there was little the good doctor could do but stand by and wait for the end.

Elsie was not totally aware of the concerns for her new baby. Exhaustion overtook her and she fell asleep holding him in her arms. They took him out of her arms and the doctor told Roy there was little hope. Indeed, before Elsie awoke her second baby had died, unable to breathe with lungs not well enough formed for the task.

When she awoke in the late afternoon, they told her. Silent tears crept down her cheeks. She was too tired to weep. She had only seen him briefly. Like the flames that had devoured her home and were now dead ashes, his little light was put out -…forever.

If the little one had a name, it was never spoken. Ever after on the rare occasions when she did speak of him, she called him "my second baby."

Chapter 15

The next morning John Nicholas roused in his bunk on the *Sea Queen*. The cabin boy was knocking on the door bringing fresh water and hot tea and biscuits.

"We're almost there now, sir," said Jonathan, the young lad assigned to him for the voyage. "Cap'n says we should dock before noon."

"Well, you've done a good job, lad. Here's a gold piece for you. Work hard and save your money. You will do fine in life," said John Nicholas.

"Oh, sir! Thank ye very much! I didn't expect -..."

"Nonsense, lad. You earned it. You gave me very good service and you deserve to be rewarded," said John Nicholas.

The young lad left him alone and went off to brag about his good fortune.

The pain in John Nicholas's head *had* calmed down.

"The sleep was good for me," he thought. "That's all I needed."

Still, he thought he would remain in his cabin until the docking. He just did not quite feel up to the gaiety which would be occurring on deck. It was always a thrill to arrive at one's destination after a long trip. People would be getting restive and joking with each other while the crew made the necessary preparations for their disembarking. John Nicholas was not up to that.

First, when he arrived home, after a rest, he would make his notes and write up the trip as he always did. One never knew what was going to happen on a trip until it was over. Then he would see about redoing his will and revoking that trust.

"By God, if Astor thinks he can go away for eight months without any kind of word and still have control over the estate of his partner, well, he is wrong. I may be a sick old man, but I am not a stupid one. That Astor, he needs to be reined in. Ever since he's thought he's gained control of my estate he has not bothered to keep in touch. I still own two-thirds of this business and I am not dead yet," thought Emerick.

He heard the shoutings of arrival as the ship slowed and snuggled into the dock at Philadelphia.

The cabin boy, Jonathan, appeared again ready to take his baggage.

"No, no, I'll take the small trunk myself," he said as Jonathan reached for the old sea chest.

"Right, sir," said Jonathan.

He waited a little while and then ambled out on to the deck. Most of the other passengers had filed off. The crew was tending to the riggings and tying down the sails. There was always work for the crew when the ship arrived in port.

John Nicholas was not expecting anyone to meet him. As was his custom, he traveled on his own schedule and would be home when he arrived.

John Nicholas congratulated the captain on a good trip. They shook hands. He knew it was always important to recognize his employees for their good work. If he had not spoken to the captain, it would have been quite an affront to the good man.

John Nicholas stepped up over the edge of the ship and made his way down the gangway carrying his own sea chest. He set foot on the planks of the dock, when the world around him became very, very light. The pain in his head slashed a cruel, ruthless swath all through his consciousness. Then he knew no more.

John Nicholas Emerick's knees buckled and he crumpled down on the boards of the Philadelphia pier. His sea chest lay beneath him, his fingers wound tightly around the handles as if he had grasped it as tight as he could with his last bit of strength when he fell. The fever of life was over for John Nicholas Emerick.

Jonathan ran to his side.

"Sir! Sir!" he shouted shaking John Nicholas's shoulder.

"Cap'n, Cap'n. It's Mr. Emerick. Come quick," called Jonathan.

A crowd had gathered. Nobody made a move to touch John Nicholas.

"That's old man Emerick," commented a male voice in the crowd.

The captain came quickly and took charge. He checked the body. He knew when life was over, and life had departed from John Nicholas.

"I'm afraid he's gone," said the captain with regret, at the same time wondering how his own status would change as a result.

"Someone should go get his relatives. They'll know what to do," suggested a voice in the crowd.

A young lad said, "I'll go. I know where he lives— down on High Street." He leapt off like a gazelle on the Savanna, anxious to be the first bearer of such astounding news.

"Well, we can't leave him here," said the captain.

"Aye, Cap'n," said one of the sailors who had gathered around. "Where shall we take him?"

"Take him into the dock master's area for now," replied the captain.

Some unwilling hands among the crew hoisted John Nicholas's body. It was bad luck to touch death just after arriving safely from a long voyage. It was also bad luck to disobey one's captain if you wanted your fair wages and wanted to sail with him again.

As his body was lifted, John Nicholas's hands released the tight grip they had on the sea chest. It fell free and was left sitting on the dock until Jonathan saw it. He knew it had been important to the old man.

He picked it up and followed along behind as John Nicholas's body was carried inside to the dock master's area.

"Here, you can't go in there, lad." He was stopped at the door by a tall dark-suited man with gold braid on his shoulders.

"But I've got his trunk, sir. The dead man's. Mr. Emerick's," said Jonathan.

"I'll take that. Don't you worry," replied the big man guarding the door.

"It was awful important to him," said Jonathan. "I'd rather take it in meself, alls the same to you. He was powerful good to me on the trip. Didn't he give me a right grand tip? I owe it to him."

"A cheeky lad," thought the tall guard. "Shows some spirit though."

Aloud he said, "Well, all right, lad. I'll give you just two minutes. Go along with you."

Jonathan hurried down the dimly lit hall to a room at the end. John Nicholas's body lay on a cot and was covered with a blanket. He was glad he did not have to look on the old man's face again. He was determined to do his duty, but he did not like being close to the dead. He was young and he felt he would live forever. Yet being in the presence of death sent a chill over his young soul. A cold feeling flittered by like the swiftly moving shadow of a large bird against the white face of a cliff. Jonathan shivered and the feeling passed.

"Here's his trunk," said Jonathan to the men grouped around the body. "I brung it. He allus wanted to have it with him."

The men parted and the dock master came forward.

"Why, thank you, lad. Just set it there by the cot. I will be sure his family receives it," the dock master said reassuringly, giving Jonathan's shoulder a pat.

Jonathan had no way of knowing what a service he had done. He had no idea of the value of the contents of the sea chest. He could not have imagined that over one hundred years would pass before this chest would give up its secrets, or how it would be a focal point in one of the most contested fortune fights in the twentieth century.

His task accomplished, and glad to be out of the room of death, Jonathan fairly raced back to the door. The tall guard looked slightly surprised as he rushed by.

Jonathan remembered his manners and turned back with a, "Thank ye, sir," tossed over his shoulder.

Baltheus was notified by a breathless boy that John Nicholas had fallen dead at the dock. Arrangements were made. Hired men were sent for John Nicholas's body, which was loaded into a wagon for his last trip home. The sea chest was placed beside him.

Baltheus recognized John Nicholas's sea chest and picked it up from the wagon himself. He would see that it got to George, one of the old man's nephews. His brothers were such old men, there was no use giving it to them. They would be joining John Nicholas before long themselves.

Baltheus wrote to George Emerick, Christopher's son:

George Emerick
Lysander, New York

I am sending John's trunk and things to you, I do not think the heirs will get any of his money. He came from the boat and died suddenly. He was a rich man, you know, and John J. knew just how to manage him to get his hands on everything. He had his trunk on this trip with him and they brought it home. He is buried by the side of Andrew.

Baltheus Emerick
December 28, 1816

Baltheus was a rather prominent citizen. He was one of the trustees of the old St. John's Lutheran Church and owned property at 234 High Street. Baltheus also wrote the following:

John Nicholas Emerick died December 16, 1816. Buried from my house, which had been his home for many years. Laid to rest in the Lutheran Cemetery, Philadelphia. I am sending his trunk and papers to George Emerick, New York, his nephew, as directed. His partner, John Jacob Astor, who gave both sweet and sour wine—mostly sour—is an unscrupulous man.

LIFE

He was generous to a fault, John Nicholas Emerick, son of John Daniel Emerick was born in Germany.

Came to this country a poor man. Made his fortune. Took a young German, John Jacob Astor, from Baltimore to New York, who was penniless in 1784. Took him to Bowen. Later in 1787 made him a one-third partner, and has left his estate in trust with him to the descendants of Christopher and Valentine. He was much of his time in New York, the headquarters of his business. In later years he stayed at the office and John J. worked outside. This is taken from his papers and records left with me and is a true copy. And I am sending this record with his trunk, as it was left here, where he made his home.

B. Emerick
Philadelphia, Penn.
December 28, 1816

The death certificate of John Nicholas Emerick was signed by the sexton and the minister, which was the custom of the day. There was no undertaker. It read as follows:

Philadelphia, Pennsylvania
December 16, 1816

John Nicholas Emerick, 234 High Street, Philadelphia came from his boat, died suddenly from apoloxy (sic), December 16, 1816, at age 75 years.

(Signed)

C. R. Hagen
W. A. Walsh

A certificate of the minister officiating at his burial, reads as follows:

John Nicholas Emerick, died December 16, 1816 and was buried December 18, 1816, from the home of Baltheus Emerick, 234 High Street Philadelphia, Pa., where he had made his home and lived for many years. He was laid to rest in the Lutheran Cemetery in Philadelphia.

(Signed)

Rev. W. *A. Walsh*

Chapter 16

By 1908 Billy (Arthur, as he was known professionally) Emerick had become quite a well-known musical prodigy.

Ella took him to a portrait studio to have a formal picture taken. She bought him a fine suit of navy blue with rows of seven gold buttons up the sleeves and eight gold buttons up the front of the jacket and more gold buttons on the knickers. He wore long black stockings up to his knees and high-topped shoes with raised heels making him look taller than he was. He had a white collared shirt and a red bow tie. Ella combed his fair hair back and made sure the part on the left side was straight. They had him stand on a little raised platform, which made an elegant backdrop for the picture.

Ella wrote her sister, Minnie, in Ohio, about her youngest son's achievements.

"Minnie, he really is such an unusual child and I should know because I have had so many. I first noticed Arthur's love of music when he was just a baby. He has always loved music, and noticed and sat as still as a mouse, when anyone played or sang. In fact, I could not sing him to sleep as I did the other children. It would just make him more wide awake. He would laugh and squirm in my arms whenever he heard music of any kind.

"He absolutely loved the band concerts in the park when he was a baby. I enjoyed taking him because it gave him such delight. He swayed and cooed in my arms.

"Irving and I thought this was unusual, and took notice of it, but did not consider it exceptional, until I discovered him playing the organ.

"I tell you, Minnie, it was the strangest thing. It was about two years ago, just before his fifth birthday, in fact. I heard the organ playing softly. I could not imagine who it was. The notes were very tenative. The song I could tell was "Brighten the Corner Where You Are." You know the hymn that mother liked so much. I was so bewildered I left my work and went to find out who was playing the organ.

"Well, I cannot tell you, Sister, how astonished I was when I found it was little Arthur. There he was standing on one pedal. He worked the pedal by pulling himself up and down with one hand hanging on to the edge of the keyboard. He was using the other hand to strike the notes. His little head barely reached the keyboard.

"Why, I was so proud of him I put out my arms and he ran right over and gave me a hug. I do not know who was more pleased Arthur or me.

"Now, Minnie, he plays whatever instrument he sees. In fact, it is difficult to keep him away from any instrument he sets his eyes on. He can play anything he hears. I do wish you and Horace could see him and hear him play. We finally have found someone well qualified to teach him. He says Arthur is the most remarkable pupil he has ever had.

"Sometimes he plays his own tunes and sometimes those he has heard. He loves to play the new ragtime. Sometimes he switches into it. I have to reprimand him rather sharply as his teacher does not want him playing that kind of music. Whatever he plays, he plays so far beyond his age.

"I wish you could have seen him at his first recital. Irving promised him ice cream if he would go up on stage and play his piano piece. He marched right up on the stage and played his piece right through and then was asked by the clapping of the audience to perform an encore. He began to play an encore and then stopped abruptly and called out, "Poppa, can I have my ice cream now?"

"The crowd roared with laughter and they made such a commotion over him. Afterwards, so many people offered him ice creams he certainly would have had a terrible tummy ache if he had eaten them all.

"There are many times, when he seems just like one of the other children, wanting ice cream or making faces at himself in the mirror. Then other times, when he is involved in his music, he seems like a different child, all grown up somehow.

"I do not know how we all began calling him Billy. His sisters started it, I think. But now, I am endeavoring to call him by his rightful name of Arthur because he is becoming so well-known. It is a strange feeling, Minnie, having a child who is already a celebrity. I wish our parents could have known him.

"He sneaks into the house after dark when we are all cooling off on the porch and plays the piano softly to himself and is all wrapped up in the music. In the dark. Can you imagine that? He will be a great pianist some day, I am sure.

"The Lord gave Arthur a great musical talent. Irving and I are trying our best to allow him to make the most of it. Where it came from, I am not sure. While we have had some musical talent in our family, I mean, Aunt Harriet sang opera and cousin Douglas directs the symphony, no one in either my family or Irving's has ever shown as much talent as Arthur. Certainly, no one ever took such an interest in music at such an early age.

"Arthur really is a wonderful child though, in other respects as well as music. We have not sent him to school, so he has never had lessons in reading or spelling, and yet he can read as well as some of the older children and can write better than most as well.

"Arthur does take a great deal of my time with his everlasting questions. He is the most inquistive child. Irving and I wonder how he will turn out. Will he be a great man to make us proud or is his genius a childhood attribute which will disappear as he becomes older?

"I am sending you a copy of the newspaper story they did on Arthur recently. The reporter was here for two hours and wrote a very nice story.

"Well, Minnie, I hope you and your family are all well. I must get on with my household chores. Tell all of the family hello for us and write soon.

"Your loving sister,
Ella"

Ella was aware of the dual personality of her youngest child. One moment he was a genius performing near impossible musical feats, next he was a small child wanting a treat. "He will be a dreamer," she thought. She hoped his love of fun would continue and act as a balance to his character in years to come.

Ella thought Billy was as talented and creative as one of the great masters. She thought he might be like Mozart. Only Billy was strong and vigorous at seven years old, not sickly as Mozart had been.

Elsie and Roy came to visit on Sunday. Elsie missed being around her large family with all the hustle-bustle and chatter that regularly occurred. They had seen the newspaper story about Billy.

Ella saved a picture of Billy in his formal studio portrait for her oldest daughter. Elsie was thrilled to have the picture and so proud of her youngest brother. She kept his picture and the newspaper story about Billy all of her life. Eventually, they made their way into the little brown suitcase, where she kept the most important things of her life.

Roy and Elsie stayed to Sunday dinner. Elsie helped her mother in the kitchen, just like old times.

"Momma," Elsie began, "I'm with child again."

"That's wonderful," exclaimed Ella. She would not let Elsie see the least hesitation about this expected event. She knew how much her daughter wanted another child. She knew how Elsie loved children. She could only hope that this time the child would survive and bring joy to her daughter and son-in-law who had suffered too much tragedy in so short a time.

Roy and Elsie were now living in a very small house, not too far from Frank and Etta's. They had had to start over after the fire wiped out all they had. Friends and family had helped get furnishing together for the small house. They managed to make the rent each month, but Roy still did not have a good steady job.

Irving was convinced the money from the John Nicholas Emerick estate was still going to be settled in their favor. He brought it up at dinner.

"I've drafted a new letter to the Astors that I'm sending off the first of the week. They can't continue to ignore what they know is the right course of action. Will or no will, the trust agreement has been honored in court before. Why, in 1849 the court issued papers that the estate would be settled in 1906 according to the trust. Even if the family doesn't have those papers, that is, the court decree, the Astors know what they should do. They have to settle eventually. It would help if we had the will, but we can settle without it," Irving said.

"It seems like you are the only person working on this anymore," said Roy.

He was as anxious as any of them to have the estate settled. He did not know about it when he and Elsie married, but he had become quite interested in it in the past four years. It sounded too good to be true, but Elsie believed in it and her father believed in it. Roy wanted to believe, too.

"Well, the rest of the family think I'm a bit daft," said Irving. "They'll eat their words when things are settled. I'll just keep on working until the Lord sees fit to allow us to succeed. What is right is right. Then watch all the family jump on the bandwagon."

Such unshakable faith served to convince them all—all except Ella, that is. No, she would not pin her hopes on money she did not have. If it ever happened, it would happen. One could not predict what the Lord would do. If they were meant to be wealthy, they would be. They had been doing much better the past few years. Irving was revered for his stirring messages in church and his books. The children were doing well and were healthy, and now little Billy, her baby, was a huge celebrity. Asking for more might just be tempting fate. Ella thought she was managing just fine where she was in life, thank the Lord.

Chapter 17

Many originally envisioned the New World as a classless society, but by the mid-nineteenth century, lines between the classes were clearly drawn. It was a uniqueness of the American democratic system that one was not born to a particular class to languish there forever. The social ladder could be climbed. It was truly possible for penniless upstarts to become scions of industry and society. The key was then, as it is now, the ability to generate an enormous amount of money. And if, in that stroke of luck and good fortune, one could not be separated from one's former odious condition and inferior company, who had not gained similar financial heights, then *what* really was the point?

Financial snobbery was well entrenched in American society in the mid-1800s. People measured and remeasured their lives, the meaning of their lives, and the power they possessed, against all others. It was a way of sorting people into groups, to afford a certain level of comfort.

Caroline Schermerhorn Astor brought financial snobbery to a fine art. She was from Dutch-American heritage and was from a very wealthy family herself. Like royalty, the very wealthy tend to marry within ranks of the chosen gilded circle. Therefore, it was not unusual and entirely appropriate that Caroline Schermerhorn would link her life with an Astor, the heir to one of the largest fortunes in America at that time. William Backhouse Astor, Jr. was the grandson of John Jacob Astor I.

Caroline and William were married in 1853. Were it not for her favorable financial situation in life, Caroline might have been considered plain-looking. Her flair for style and dress, her regal bearing and her forceful personality overcame any lack she may have had in the good looks department. She brought with her, long lines of flawless social background to join with the Astor millions.

William's father, also named William Backhouse Astor, was known as "the landlord New York." In addition to his real estate holdings, part of which were from the John Nicholas Emerick estate, he added to his family's fortune by shrewd investments in railroads and telegraph. Caroline and William B., as she called him, made even better investments and also increased the Astor wealth.

Caroline, the Queen of New York and Newport society, insisted upon being called "*The* Mrs. Astor" by friends. Caroline was responsible for creating the first social register. It was she, who had the idea to devise the famous 400, a list of people whose ancestry could be traced back three generations.

Caroline and William's only son was born in Rhinebeck, New York on July 13th, 1864. He was named for his great grandfather, John Jacob Astor IV.

When he was seventeen, his parents bought an ocean front estate in Newport, Rhode Island. The mansion was thirty years old when they purchased it. It was a finely crafted, imposing structure with clean lines. The second story arched windows complement the three archways in the covered carriage area at the front, making an impressive visual statement as one came up the curved drive.

The Astors hired a well-known architect to create an atmosphere that was worthy of their status. The family invested millions in renovations, but it was Caroline whose vision and impeccable taste allowed the home to be completed in a magnificent way. With her formidable, forceful personality she supervised all aspects of the remodeling.

Caroline Astor presided over numerous social activities each summer when the family visited their summer palace. Every summer, people in her society set looked forward eagerly to an invitation to Mrs. Astor's Summer Ball.

The Summer Ball took place in the sparkling ballroom inspired by the Hall of Mirrors at Versailles. The arched French windows of the ballroom looked out on the rose garden and lawn sweeping down to the ocean.

Wealthy ladies purchased the most gorgeous gowns of the day especially for Mrs. Astor's Ball. They wore intricate hairdos with gold and silver woven into their tresses or diamond tiaras gracing their heads. The ladies stepped carefully and elegantly in satin shoes making them appear as graceful as the multitude of potted palms that swayed gently with the ebb and flow of dancing people. The palms looked as if they, too, were keeping time with the romantic music of the orchestra.

Black tuxedos with black satin lapels, adorned by a red or white rosebud, white ties and top hats were the gentlemen's attire.

Deals were made in the side rooms over brandy and cigars. The unmarried eligibles of society were herded together at the balls and encouraged to find a life partner befitting their rank and position. Finery and ever elegant manners were on display. Popular music, played by a small orchestra, enhanced the occasion. The food and drink was simply superb.

Those lucky enough to be invited to Mrs. Astor's ball knew they had an assured place in upper-class society.

It was amidst this privilege and sheltered refinement that John Jacob Astor IV was raised.

As time passed, he experienced private school education and attended Harvard. By all accounts, he was a fine, upstanding, intelligent man. He was a person with wide ranging interests and abilities. He could not be accused of being merely a wealthy dabbler in life. He was a patron of the arts. His interested extended to scientific and governmental pursuits.

After Harvard, he made the grand tour of Europe for two years, returning home in 1891 to take over managing the family fortune. When his father died in 1892, the bulk of the Astor fortune, which contained the Emerick fortune, became his responsibility.

He was the richest man in the world.

And quite a catch he was for the lovely daughter of Edward Shippen Willing of Philadelphia. Ava Lowle Willing and John Jacob Astor IV married on May 1, 1891 in Philadelphia. They soon became the parents of two children, William Vincent Astor, known as Vincent, and Ava Alice Muriel Astor.

Astor had a home and kept offices in New York City. From there he managed the family fortune.

In 1894, Astor authored a semi-scientific novel, *A Journey in Other Worlds*, about life on Jupiter and Saturn.

One of his many accomplishments was to build the Astoria Hotel in New York City in 1897. It was the epitome of luxury at the time. After completion it was joined together with the Waldorf Hotel, built by his cousin William Waldorf Astor. The resulting hotel became known as the Waldorf Astoria.

It is built on land belonging to John Nicholas Emerick.

Apparently, it was possible to *build* on Emerick land, but not to sell it. In 1874, the Astors tried to sell some of John Nicholas Emerick's property. The court ruled the Astors did not own it and could not sell it. It was a minor victory for the Emericks. In the large scheme of things, it had little impact on the eventual outcome of the Emericks' ability to obtain their piece of the fortune.

During the Spanish-American War, Astor was commissioned as a lieutenant colonel in the United States Volunteers. He allowed his yacht to be used for government service. After the war was over, he continued to be addressed as Colonel Astor.

The marriage of Astor and Ava, although a good match for alliteration, was not such a good match for longevity. After the death of his mother, Caroline, in 1908, it was easier for Astor and Ava to seek an end to their incompatible situation. They divorced in 1909, after nineteen years of marriage.

With this uncoupling, Colonel John Jacob Astor easily became the most desirable bachelor in New York. And New York, along with its surrounding summer playground cities, was the center of the universe for wealthy society.

Astor was no longer a young man. He was forty-six. He sported a handlebar mustache which was starting to show signs of distinguished gray speckled throughout. He was an impeccable dresser, due in part to his stylish mother's influence. He was not a large man. However, his incredible wealth, which felt comfortable to him because he had grown up with it, gave him an unequaled air of confidence.

The upper strata of society were abuzz with talk of possibilities. Mothers of eligible daughters considered how they might best bring their progeny to the attention of Mr. Astor. Divorced and widowed women in his circle of friends and acquaintances considered their options. One must not be too forward or pushy. Opportunities for casual meetings were hatched and rehatched. Amateur matchmakers saw occasions to engage in their favorite hobby.

The object of all this speculation went about his business as usual. He was not unaware of the intense interest in his love life. How could he not be aware? Cards were left at his door. Party invitations increased ten fold. Did they think he had nothing to do but attend soirees and cocktail parties? Really, they did get to be such a bore. The same set of people. The same vacuous chat.

So when an invitation for a different kind of party arrived one day, he determined to go. It was a fad at the time to have little informal parties in the Bohemian fashion.   At these parties, disparity in bluebook standing did not matter. A cross section of people were invited. The most patrician of the four hundred could mingle comfortably with those who wanted to reach the charmed circle, but who were not yet there.

There would be new people he had not met before. Astor was intrigued.

The night of the party, he took special care with his dress. He asked Victor, his valet, which vest might look the best for a lighthearted evening. They chose a cream and navy striped vest and a navy suit. He was almost excited about going to this affair. He wondered why. He had seen much in his lifetime. It was, after all, just another party. Still, there would, no doubt, be new people to meet. It was a change. And that was always an invigorating prospect.

He arrived at the party fashionably late, as was his custom. He liked everyone else to be there so he could survey the room and be free to choose his own company. He tried to enter unobtrusively. That was not possible. Lookouts were posted. The signal went out. Approaches were made casually, but hearts were a flutter.

"My dear, Colonel Astor, do come join our table. We have such a nice little mix. We have been having a perfectly grand discussion about the new motor cars." That last comment was a little bait to whet his attention by a matronly lady who gestured to a nearby table.

"Why, thank you. So kind of you. I shall make my way there shortly, I'm sure. If you will excuse me I have a few obligations to attend to first."

He might have gone with her. He was there for the fun of it and why not? But something had attracted his attention. Not something. Someone.

She was across the room, standing a little to herself for the moment looking pensive. She had a cloud of thick, dark hair swept up and billowing out so that her face was surrounded by a beautiful dark frame. She had the sweetest face he had ever seen. It was a small face with delicate pink lips and, sapphire-blue eyes with finely arched brows attesting to her beauty and importance. High around her neck was a lace-like collar of gems with two strands of pearls lingering on her exquisite chest, which was exposed by a V-neckline. Her satin dress was the color of blue sky on the fairest day imaginable.

"God, what a beauty!" Astor thought.

Madeleine Talmadge Force was born in Brooklyn. She and her family had recently moved to Manhattan. Her father had made quite a success of his trucking business. The two teenaged Force beauties, Madeleine, and her sister Katherine, desired to join the sparkling whirl of Manhattan society.

For pedigree, they could point to their great grandfather, a Talmadge, who had been Mayor of Brooklyn. There was, also, a small family fortune, amounting to a few hundred thousand dollars. They were not in the league of the Astors and their ilk.

The Force family was at first unable to find an avenue into the higher levels of society. But once they moved to the heart of Murray Hill, then the most aristocratic residential area in America, things began to look up.

At about the same time, another family moved to Manhattan from Brooklyn. The Dick family, like the Forces, sought to elevate their position in life as their recently acquired wealth entitled them to do. The family had made a fortune in sugar. The heir to this fortune was a young man in his twenties named William K. Dick.

It was natural that the two families would meet often in the following year. Both families were entering society at the same time and in a similar financial position. It was also natural that Madeleine and Willie Dick would become acquainted and even take quite a liking to each other.

In fact, it was thought by their friends that Madeleine and Willie were about to make an announcement of their intentions toward each other.

"My dear," said the charming Mrs. Force. "You would never have to worry if you married young Mr. Dick. They say he stands to inherit a considerable fortune."

"I know, Mother," replied Madeleine. "I do like Willie so much. He is pleasant company, and he is ever so courteous."

"Well, what is it then?"

"I can't identify it for you, Mother. I'm just not sure I want to spend my entire life with him. I've plenty of time yet. I'm only eighteen."

"Beauty is a fading thing, my dear. You want to make the best match you can make while yours is still in flower. The important thing is to choose wisely and be well taken care of. It is best to have someone you like and enjoy. Love changes as time goes on. It becomes less important as you grow older and financial security becomes more so. I do not want either of my daughters lacking for the finer things of life. You have not been raised that way. So if you are looking for someone to fall madly in love with, make sure he has the means to take care of you well."

"Oh, Mother. I don't know what I am looking for."

They were sipping tea in a tiny garden cafe. They were on an expedition to locate just the right dress for Madeleine to wear to attend a different kind of party that was coming up. It was to be a party with a cross-section of people invited. There would be some artists and musicians and some of the créme de la créme of society if the hostess could be believed.

So far they had been unsuccessful in their search for a dress. Madeleine took her mother's arm as they strolled down the street to the next exclusive shop.

"I don't know, Mother. Perhaps, I shall just wear my green taffeta."

"No, no! No daughter of mine is going to wear a dress already seen by the majority of her friends. What would people think? I'll tell you what they would think. They would think your father had fallen on hard times and could not afford a new frock for his daughter. I'll not have them thinking that."

"Yes, Mother. Well, let's try in here."

With that they walked into a little shop that featured one-of-a-kind dresses by the well-known designer "Lucile."

Madeleine saw it immediately, the dress that was the color of blue sky on the fairest day imaginable. It almost took her breath away.

"Oh, Mother, look at this! Did you ever see a more beautiful color? And look at the neckline. Do you think it is too daring? I must try it on."

"Of course you must try it on. That is a striking color. I think it looks too large for you, but they can take it in. We'll see how the neckline looks when you have it on."

"Colonel Astor, may I present Madeleine Force," said their hostess.

"Madeleine, this is Colonel Astor".

Astor had sought out their hostess with the request that he be introduced to the young lady near the wall who was wearing the striking blue dress.

"That's a lovely shade of blue you are wearing, if I may make such a comment to you. It gained my attention when I first entered the room tonight. The dress drew my attention as did the beautiful lady who is wearing it."

Madeleine tried to hide her pleasure at being noticed and remain calm. She knew who he was. She did not expect to meet him here tonight.

"Oh, thank you," blushed Madeleine demurely. "Do you like it? It is one of the dresses designed by 'Lucile'."

"Ah, Lady Duff-Gordon."

"Who?" said Madeleine.

"My friend, Lady Duff-Gordon. She designs under the name 'Lucile'."

"Oh, I didn't know that. You must know everyone, Colonel Astor."

"Please, call me John."

Chapter 18

One evening in 1907, Mrs. J. Bruce Ismay stepped carefully up into the carriage, which would convey her and her husband to dinner at the London home of Lord and Lady Pirrie. Ismay was the president of the White Star Line. Lord Pirrie was at the helm of the great shipbuilding firm of Harland and Wolff.

"I suppose you gentlemen will be discussing business all evening," said Mrs. Ismay with a sigh.

"I suppose so, my dear. That is the purpose of this meeting. So much more friendly to make it a dinner meeting, don't you know. Do make an effort with Lady Pirrie, Vera. I know she is not your favorite dinner companion. This is important to me and to the company. Promise me, you will do your best," replied her nattily dressed husband, smoothing his dark, well-trimmed moustache with his gloved hand.

"Well, of course, dear. Please, do not trouble yourself further about it. I shall charm Lady Pirrie by smiling as she recounts her latest adventures at court, and feign fantastic interest in her newest grandchildren. And, oh yes, I shall show polite envy of her fashionable attire. You need not worry," she answered with a slight smile.

It was dusk when they arrived and disembarked from the carriage at the home of Lord and Lady Pirrie.

They were shown into the drawing room by a stiff dark-suited butler. Soon, their hosts joined them and preliminary refreshments were offered by a sober maid in black and white attire.

As the ladies began their verbal dance toward common conversational ground, the gentlemen began discussing the need for the White Star Line to compete with the swift new Cunard ships and the German liners.

The year before, in 1906, the Cunard Line launched two great ships, named the *Mauretania* and the *Luisitania*. The discussion over caviar centered on what could be done to gain an edge on the competition. The conversation continued during dinner.

"What if we built ships like no one has ever seen before?" said Ismay, "What if we build three ships each grander than the last. The largest ships anyone has ever seen. Does the technology exist to do that?"

"Of course, it does," replied Lord Pirrie. "What it takes to accomplish that is vision, commitment, and dedication of funds."

"We'll hire the best designers we can find. The ships will be elegantly outfitted. They will be luxurious, floating palaces. We will lure the trade of the wealthiest patrons. We will make them the finest and fastest ships afloat," said Ismay enthusiastically.

Over coffee and cigars the gentlemen talked about how large they could build a ship. Like modern day Noahs, they planned and postulated possible lengths, widths and depths until their minds were churning with ideas like froth on the sea.

Ismay drew an envelope out of his inside breast pocket. On the back, he made rough sketches of the kinds of ships he imagined. He invented names for each ship. The *Olympic*, the *Titanic* and, perhaps, they would call the third one, the *Gigantic*. These three ships would be the fastest and the most lavish ships ever created.

Because these were men with wealth, substance, position and drive, to whom all things seemed possible, their talk was not idle. They were ultimately able to create the ships they had dreamed of that night.

The first ship they built was the *Olympic*, but its sister ship, larger and even more extravagantly appointed, the *Titanic*, was the one that made the name White Star Line remain in the minds of people almost 100 years after that fateful dinner meeting.

And so events began which would change the lives of so many and resonate in the world for decades to come.

"My dear, my dear. Do you know what this means? They say he is the richest man in the world! My goodness, Madeleine, he is obviously smitten with you. He has called on you almost everyday. You must be vigilant, my child. A man like that. He is quite out of our class. You must insist on marriage. He must be used to having what he wants. Well, *we* must be sure he does not get it unless he is willing to marry you," said Mrs. Force.

Madeleine was gazing out of the window. She was very aware of Astor's interest in her. She knew the talk was he would never marry someone not of his own class. Still, he had been a perfect gentleman so far. She wondered what he *did* want.

"He is so much older, Mother. He has children older than I am. Can you imagine me a stepmother to Vincent and Ava Astor?"

"Age does not matter in these things, my dear. He is a handsome, virile man yet. I might fancy him myself if...well, never mind. He could do so very well for you, Maddy. Actually, for all of us. For the family. What does he say?"

"It has only been two weeks since I met him. We talk of his travels, his interests. He *has* mentioned, well, how lonely it is to travel alone."

"Yes?"

"That's it, Mother. There is nothing to report yet. Chances are he will move on to someone else soon," she said wistfully.

"Not if you play your cards right, my girl. I know a man who is besotted when I see one. But you must hold out for marriage at all costs."

John Astor and his cousin William were seated in brown leather chairs in their gentlemen's club in New York City. The attendant had just brought them drinks and lighted their cigarettes. It was quite private in their corner of the room. The heavy deep green velvet draperies and thick brown carpet tended to muffle conversations.

"Surely you cannot be serious, John," said his cousin William. "The little tart is just looking for a leg up, so to speak."

"Don't speak of her that way. She is not like that."

"Why not just bed her and give her a stipend for her trouble? People like that…"

"Stop it, I tell you! She is too fine to even consider such reprehensible behavior. I tell you she is a jewel. A beautiful, delicate, fragile, unequaled, sweet-tempered gem of a girl. I'll not find another like her."

"Oh, God," groaned William, "I can see it is too late. You have gone over the edge. So you are going to propose marriage?"

"If she will have me," replied the richest man in the world.

"John, at least promise me this. You must protect yourself and the family. Make sure your will and papers are in order before you marry. Make sure she does not benefit greatly from your death.

"By the way are you still hearing from that Emerick clan? My God, will they never quit?" continued cousin William.

"Our attorneys tell me we receive regular letters from them, especially from one persistent fellow named Irving. They do have a case, you know. Eventually we will probably have to settle with them. As long as there is no will they can produce, I suppose we can put it off. I, for one, would like to reach an equitable agreement with them and be done with the whole affair. None of them is very well-off. They will settle for pennies on the dollar, mark my words," said Astor.

Chapter 19

"He cannot seriously be thinking of marrying the girl..."

"They say he is entirely obsessed with the little creature..."

"She is just a gold digger. He will be very sorry if he falls for *that*..."

"I was hoping my Polly might have a chance..."

"I was hoping *I* might have a chance. It has been so lonely since Edward died..."

"She is younger than his son. Can you imagine..."

"Well, I do not know what the world is coming to..."

Nothing was quite so offensive to the blue-blooded ladies of the 400 as someone breaching their ranks without the proper credentials. No one would go so far as to shun Colonel Astor. After all, the Astors were the epitome of high society. It did present quite a problem. How could they not offend a charter member of their group, yet refuse entry to the beautiful, but financially lacking Madeleine?

"If he brings her to my party next week we will all be civil to her, but cool, agreed?..."

"Who does she think she is? Her parents should have more common sense than to let her consort with a man her father's age…"

"I tell you it will come to nothing. He will soon have had enough of her and come to his senses…"

"Thank God Caroline is not alive to see this. I hate to think…"

So the talk went swirling through the upper crust community. At least where the ladies were concerned. The gentlemen's reactions were quite different. While in the company of their wives they shook their heads and tut-tutted with appropriate phrases of condemnation. When they gathered together over drinks and cigars they were not so incensed and much more forgiving.

"She is a fine looking woman, isn't she?…"

"That old rascal. We should all be so lucky…"

"I wouldn't turn that down if I was free and it was offered…"

"Of course, he should try to control himself, but he is unattached…"

"What's the harm? I know John. No young woman is going to take him for a ride…"

To John himself, when their wives were not looking, the gentlemen patted him on the back and made subtle jokes about his ability "to keep up with" such a young woman.

Truth be told, many of the gentlemen of the 400 set were more than a little envious.

Knowing his fortune was great enough to support a new young wife of little means, Astor could not fathom why marriage to Madeleine was unacceptable to his friends. He, by all accounts, was so taken with the beautiful girl in the dress the color of blue sky on the fairest day imaginable, that reason flew out the window. He began to press his suit by speaking with her parents.

While the highest society set abhorred the possibility of marriage between these two monetarily unequal people, the next set down felt it was a coup of the finest order. Mr. and Mrs. Force were honored beyond measure to find that their oldest daughter, the first product of their union, more than met the standards of the richest, most eligible bachelor in the world. Their friends were pleasantly astounded and envious. And that, of course, made it even sweeter.

Madeleine's parents were assured by Astor that their daughter would be greatly loved and provided for extremely well. It remained for Madeleine to give her consent and marriage would be arranged.

Madeleine was a little afraid to think that marriage to Astor was a real possibility. She found him to be a charming, handsome gentleman. One that would be easy to like even if he were not so rich. Still, she knew it would anger and annoy his set if they married.

She thought of Willie Dick and knew she had possibilities there. He was so much younger and such fun to be with. It would not be hard to love Astor though. She enjoyed his attentions and the look of total involvement in his eyes. She did not doubt that he adored her. She did not doubt that she was worthy. As a beautiful woman on whom much admiration had been showered her entire life, Madeleine knew her power over men.

Her mind darted back and forth, here and there. It only remained for her to make a selection.

Astor invited her family to dinner at his splendid home in Newport.

As they drove up in the curved driveway to the mansion, Madeleine imagined herself as the queen of this elegant castle. When she saw the interior, she fell in love with the glamorous home. She pictured herself as mistress of this appallingly regal splendor.

After dinner, Astor took her into the great ballroom alone. The lush seductiveness of the room surrounded them. He pressed for her hand in marriage. She could not think of a reason to resist.

She did not resist, but a tiny bit of her heart held back. She did not know why. She was going to be the fairy princess. Cinderella, well not exactly, and Snow White all rolled into one. And they would live happily ever after.

Their wedding was held in the ballroom of Astor's Newport home. The sparkling hall of mirrors reflected the huge bouquets of soft pastel flowers in pinks and yellows and pale blue, which were placed around the room on tall white pedestals and on the mantel of the marble fireplace. The multiple mirrors reflected the beautiful bouquets over and over, so the guests felt immersed in a sea of flowers.

The large, arched French doors and windows looked out on a smooth lawn sweeping down to the sea. The crystal chandeliers reflected their light into infinity in opposing mirrors. The gold filigree around the ceiling set the tone of the room. A small five-piece orchestra played subdued selections as the crowd gathered and found seats.

Friends of the Force family were eager to attend. They wanted to see the great house as well as experience a great occasion. Astor's friends did not desert him. However, only the closest friends and family on both sides were invited to this celebration.

Madeleine was flushed and rosy from pleasure that it was actually happening to her. Astor considered himself the luckiest man in the world to have captured the heart of this beautiful young woman.

Not wanting anything to diminish their happiness, Astor planned a lengthy trip to Europe for their honeymoon. They left immediately. He did not want Madeleine to be upset by snubs from his supposed friends. If they were gone long enough, talk would die down or move on to someone else, he reasoned. Eventually, he had no doubt, she would be accepted into the societal fold. They would not be able to resist her beauty and charm and she would be sanctioned by marriage to him. They would get used to it. And those who did not could jolly well take their friendship elsewhere.

Chapter 20

Astor and Madeleine came across Margaret "Maggie" Brown while touring Egypt. Maggie was traveling by herself. She was the colorful wife of J.J. Brown, mining magnate from Denver, Colorado. J.J. had discovered the richest vein of gold in the United States up until that time. Maggie and J.J. separated in 1909 after a stormy 23 years and two children. In later years, she became known as the Unsinkable Molly Brown. She was called Maggie by friends and family. Somehow the Press and Hollywood later called her Molly.

Colorful was used to describe Maggie because she was different. She was high-spirited, hot-tempered and very strong-willed. She had a flamboyant way of dressing. She and her husband made the financial cut. She had enough money to be considered among the very wealthy. But that was not entirely it. Maggie had presence. She always stood upright and held herself in a regal manner. She was attractive, but not what would be called a beauty. She was someone to be reckoned with who commanded attention wherever she went. She was admitted to the places the very wealthy habituated.

Maggie was known for speaking her mind. That did not always fit with polite upper-society conversation. Somehow, though, Maggie did her speaking out with a warm heart and a generous spirit, so, although there were those who did not wish to be in her company, it was not always held against her.

In fact, Astor and Madeleine not only did not hold it against her; they felt comforted and warmed by her presence. They received no censure from Maggie. Traveling alone, she was delighted to join up with the couple. They were delighted to feel completely accepted in her presence.

Madeleine was pleased to have at last found someone in her husband's financial category who was friendly to her.

The trio of friends met while visiting in Cairo. They visited the great pyramids and the sphinx at Giza. They shopped in the bustling and colorful bazaars. Then they took a boat down the Nile River to Luxor.

They booked rooms for two weeks in the Winter Palace Hotel. The Winter Palace was built in 1886 primarily to accommodate wealthy European travelers. It was a winter destination for oriental royalty as well. Visitors liked the warm, dry climate in Luxor. The hotel was known for its friendly service and hospitality.

The Winter Palace is on the east bank of the Nile, amid large, lush tropical gardens. The three-story pinkish-tan structure is reminiscent of British architecture. There are long, colorful, curved stone steps leading up an incline to a covered entrance portico. The facade reminded Astor of his own home in Newport. The interior decor of the hotel had a British colonial charm.

There are several areas near Luxor with temples from bygone days that are popular places for tourists to visit. No one knew in 1912 that the tomb of Tutankhamen, or King Tut as he became known, was near by. That remained for Howard Carter to discover ten years later. When he did, he posted his discovery on the notice board at the Winter Palace. In that way, it was first announced to the world.

"So what do you think, John? Shall we take in some of the temples tomorrow? Are you up for another outing in the sun and sand?" asked Maggie smiling.

The Astors and Maggie had spent the day exploring the town of Luxor and Madeleine looked tired.

"What do you think, Maddy, my dear?"

"Yes, John, I would like to see the temples tomorrow. Of course, we must go."

"We're for it, Maggie," said Astor. "Shall we meet at eight for dinner tonight?"

"Sounds good to me," replied Maggie.

"John, I shall be right along. You go on up to change for dinner. I just want to speak with Maggie for a moment," said Madeleine.

"Of course, my pet." He kissed her cheek. "Don't be long."

"I won't be long."

With that he left for their room.

Madeleine and Maggie remained in the opulent lobby of the Winter Palace with its high ceiling and sparkling chandelier looming overhead. During the daylight hours, light streamed into the lobby from huge second-level windows. The detailed ironworks railing on the stairways and the balcony framed the high windows. Tall, white, square columns in the lobby gave a solid, old-world appearance. Palms and fresh flowers warmed the area.

Astor felt quite at home at the Winter Palace. He particularly liked the bar with its library of old books. It had an upper-class, homey feeling.

As soon as he was out of sight Madeleine said, "Oh, Maggie, I am so glad we are traveling with you. I must tell someone. I have written Mother, but I must *tell* someone."

"Well, tell away, child. Your secret will be safe with me."

"It isn't really a secret, Maggie. It is just that I did not want to mention it in front of John. Oh, he knows, naturally."

"Naturally," said Maggie and waited for the information to come as her friend was ready.

"It's just, you see, I'm going to have a child," said Madeleine. "There has been no one to tell whom I could be sure would be really glad for me."

"Why that is just grand, Maddy. Your first child. It is such an exciting time for you. Bless your heart and you alone over here with only your husband for company."

"John is wonderful company. But I miss my mother and my sister, especially now."

"Well, now, that is not hard to understand. Of course, you miss them," sympathized Maggie.

"I am ready to go home. We both want the baby to be born at home. We have been traveling for nearly a year. I am just ready to go home," said Madeleine.

"Say, I have an idea. Let me talk to that husband of yours at dinner. I'll see you then, honey," Maggie gave her a reassuring hug as they parted company to dress for dinner.

The Astors' suite of rooms was on the west side. The walls were painted a bright golden yellow as if to emphasize the sunny climate even more. The elegant furnishings were in complementary colors. There were two huge armoires, which gave the sunny room a Victorian look. Potted palms around the rooms gently waved their long, green fingers when the windows were open. Their suite overlooked the ever interesting Nile River. They enjoyed a natural light show early each evening before they went to dinner as the sun set in a blaze of winter colors over the Nile.

Maggie's suite was on the opposite side facing the gardens. Bright red bougainvillea flowers adorned the sturdy branches which wound around the railing on her first floor terrace. She was not always up early enough to see the sunrise over the misty, shimmering gardens. It, too, was a sight to behold. She did enjoy having morning coffee on the terrace in the midst of brilliant tropical flowers and tall graceful greenery. It started her day off just right.

The three friends sat in the Winter Palace dining room on red velvet covered chairs at a round table suitable for seating six. The table was covered with a white linen tablecloth. There were matching napkins folded to crisp peaks, fresh flowers and candles on the table. The walls of the dining room were a sunny yellow by day, but cloaked in shadows for romantic dining by candlelight this time of the evening.

"They say it is the largest ship ever built and the most elegant," said Maggie at the dinner table that evening. "The first-class accommodations are the best you can ever imagine. It's like a floating palace. I'm going to book passage on her tomorrow. I've received word that my grandson is ill and I am ready to go home. There is plenty of time to travel to France before she leaves from Cherbourg. What do you say you join me? Someday we can say we traveled on the *Titanic* on her maiden voyage."

Madeleine looked at John expectantly. He had not yet decided just when they would return home. He saw the hope in her eyes.

"Well, dearie, is that what you would like?" he asked her.

"Yes, I would like that, John. I do so miss my family and it sounds like a wonderful adventure to travel on such a ship."

"Well, it is settled then. I have business at home that needs attention. I have put it off too long as it is. I will notify my office we are coming home on the *Titanic*."

Chapter 21

On April 12, 1912, as the *Titanic* was steaming its way across the Atlantic, ignoring ice warnings, Elsie Bryan was about to have her fourth and last child.

In 1908, Roy and Elsie became the parents of another son whom they named Lynn after Elsie's beloved uncle, Dr. Lynn Emerick. Little Lynn was of a strong and hearty constitution. Elsie pampered him and kept him a baby as long as she could. He had such a fair face he could have been a girl. Elsie let his hair grow into long natural curls as long as Roy would allow it. Sometimes he was mistaken for a girl when they went to the park.

A few days previously, Roy had come home from Frank's, carrying a mantel clock under his arm. It was black, hard plastic with tan and green splotched designs. It had black Arabic numbers encased in a lustrous metal snowflake face. The hands were black.

"Where did you get that, Roy?" Elsie inquired.

"Frank picked it up at an auction. The kids had it out in the front yard riding it for a horse," said Roy. "Don't that beat all? It's a Seth Thomas. Says 1884 on the back. It's too good a clock to let kids play with it. I asked Frank if I could have it. He gave it to me. He didn't care."

"Will we have room to take it with us?" Elsie asked.

"Sure, we'll find room for it somewhere," said Roy.

They wound it up and listened to the stentorian *bong, bong* of the chime. They thought it had a pleasing, friendly tone. They never did have a mantel to put it on, but after that the clock had a place of honor wherever they lived. It always resided in a prominent corner like a benevolent spirit, reminding all of the hours passing in its melodious and ever consistent way. It came to symbolize home. All was well once the clock was installed and running.

They were already packing for their expected move to Montana. Roy had the promise of a job with the railroad in Billings. It would be steady work with benefits. It would be better than trying to just get by, as they had been in St. Louis.

Elsie was very near her time. She did not want to leave until after this baby came. She wanted to be near Momma a little longer. She did not want to be having this baby in wild and wooly Montana without family or friends.

Irving came by that same afternoon they reclaimed the clock from Frank and Etta's young hooligans. He admired the clock and kept his opinions about Frank's children to himself. He was too excited about the news he had received to think of much else.

"It won't be long now," he said.

"What's that, Poppa?"

Elsie continued folding the fresh laundry she had just brought in from the clothesline in their tiny back yard. She held some of the pieces up to her face. She loved the smell of fresh, clean clothes whipped dry by the wind.

"This came today. It's from the Astors' attorneys," said Irving, waving a letter in his hand. "They say old J. J. the Fourth is coming back from Europe with his new wife. They say he's going to settle with us. Settle the Emerick estate. They finally answered me with some information that matters. He's coming back on that new ship—the *Titanic*. They'll be in New York in a few days."

"Why do you suppose he's decided to settle?" commented Elsie. "Did the will turn up?"

"I don't believe so," said Irving. "I've been thinking about just that. Why at this time after all these years would he decide to settle? I think the Lord smote his heart and he can't rest easy anymore until he does what he knows is the right thing. He's a good man. Always has been. It's those around him, advising him, that have kept him back."

"Maybe he's just happy with his new wife and has mellowed," said Roy with a smile.

"Well, whatever it is, it is about time. The Lord has seen fit to allow our family to prevail. You needn't go to Montana now. We'll all be taken care of," said Irving.

"These things take time," said Roy. "I can't see the Astors letting loose easy, even if Astor himself wants to. I got a good job waiting. We can always come back."

Elsie served her father and Roy some oatmeal spice cake and a glass of tea. It was getting hard for her to get around. She did not mind. She was so glad to be welcoming another baby. She wished for a girl, but a healthy baby was most important to her.

Irving's visit had been five days ago. Now here it was, Friday, April 12, 1912. Elsie cleaned the house and made sure there was food prepared ahead. They had a small ice box and a cooler, which was a cabinet built into an outside wall with open louvres to the outside. This time of the year the cooler was still cool, not cold. She could store butter, jam and pies there among other things.

Elsie's twenty-fourth birthday was just a few days away, on April 17th.

"It would be nice if the baby was born on my birthday," she thought. In any case, it would not be born far from her birthday. She knew it would be soon. Maybe they could give this baby fine things like they had been unable to afford before, now that the Astors were willing to give them their inheritance.

She sat in her rocker watching Lynn play. He was so lively and healthy. He was building a fine house with his blocks. She sighed and relaxed at the thought of having plenty of money. What would that be like?

They could have a bigger house with a yard of smooth green grass, where the children could play, and a fence to keep them safe. Perhaps she would have a maid or a hired girl to help with the housework. There would be no nanny to take care of *her* children. She wanted to do that herself. She would supervise the cooking because she knew how things should be done. It would be grand to have a carriage or a motor car. Which would it be? And a few new dresses for herself. Someone to do the ironing. A pony for Lynn. A nice watch for Roy to keep in his vest pocket...

Just then her reverie was interrupted. She felt her first labor pain.

"Mother," she called to Sarah, her mother-in-law, who was staying with them temporarily. "Will you take Lynn over to Etta's and send for Dr. Carter for me, please? I think it's time."

"Of course, child," answered her stern-faced, elderly mother-in-law. "Will you be all right for a little while?"

"I think so. Roy will be home in about an hour. But do hurry."

Dr. Carter had been there for several hours now. Elsie was in deep pain, drifting in and out of consciousness. The baby would not come. Apparently it was lying the wrong way. No matter how hard the young mother pushed, it did not come. Dr. Carter could not get a grip on it. He knew Elsie was becoming weak. He was so hoping that this baby would be healthy like the last. That had been a normal birth. He had been glad to present this couple with a large healthy son over three years ago. Now here he was again, attending the fourth birth for Mrs. Bryan and he was very worried they would not only lose the baby, but maybe the mother as well.

He was having a hard time seeing what was going on as the bed was so low and the footboard so high.

"We're going to have to move her," he said to Roy.

"Move her? Where to?"

"I need to have her someplace higher so I can see what's going on and reach better. How about the kitchen table?"

"Doc, just do what you need to do. You got to save her. You got to."

Ella had been sent for and had arrived. After giving birth to fourteen children, she still had a tiny waist and always dressed with a certain style and flair. Today she had a row of little blue bows down the slit in her long white dress. Her waist was nipped in with a matching blue belt. She was washing her daughter's face with a cool cloth and speaking to her softly. She could not tell if Elsie heard her or not anymore. She was lying so still, only moaning occasionally now.

Ella said, "Roy, put the side leaves up on the table and make sure they are in tight. Where are your extra blankets?"

They padded the tabletop as best they could with the blankets. Then the three of them lifted Elsie and the sheet and carried her to the kitchen table.

Dr. Carter worked over her for a few minutes. Then he called Roy to come over to the side of the room.

"I need your permission to use ether. She is fading and so is the baby. We need to get the baby out fast. I don't believe she can survive what I need to do if she feels the pain. I am afraid we will lose her this time if I don't do something fast."

Ether was not unknown as an anesthetic in 1912. It had been used since the 1840s. However, using ether remained an inexact science, as frequent deaths occurred due to overdosing or the effects on breathing.

Roy found himself considering what might happen. If they did not use it, she might die. If they *did* use it, she might die.

"Oh, God, help me!" he thought suddenly becoming religious. "God help me. Help her. I got to do the right thing. I can't live without her."

He turned to Dr. Carter: "Let's give it a try, Doc. You got my permission."

Dr. Carter administered the anesthetic. He was not entirely sure how much to give her. Elsie was a small woman. He had to be careful. He had to save her. Soon she was breathing easier. Ella and the doctor both spoke to her. She made no response. Her breathing was shallow, but regular.

Dr. Carter was swift and skillful. Soon he extracted a baby from Elsie's womb and began repairing the collateral damage to her body.

Ella took the baby and said, "It's a fine girl, Roy. Just what Elsie wanted. Isn't she beautiful?"

Roy was sitting on the sidelines in a chair with his head in his hands trying to get on good terms with a God he did not know very well. He looked up at the baby briefly. His mind could not shift gears that fast. His thoughts were with Elsie. He looked at Elsie and then at the baby.

"Thank, God it's over. The baby looks okay. Is she okay, Ella?"

"She's okay, Roy."

Roy then turned his attention to his wife. She was lying there so still. He went to her side. He stroked her cheeks and held her hands. She made no move. Her hands felt cold and clammy. Roy felt a hard knot rise up in his throat. His heart started pounding. There was a noise in his head like someone beating a large kettle drum.

"Doc! Doc!" he shouted. "I think we've killed her!"

Chapter 22

The White Star Line was a British company. However, it was owned by the American, J. P. Morgan. The seven-and-a-half million dollars it took to build the *Titanic* was Morgan's money.

On the last day of March, 1909, hundreds of workers streamed into the shipyard of Harland and Wolff in Belfast, Ireland, to begin work on the largest and greatest ship ever to be built. They were thrilled and proud to begin work on the *Titanic*.

Plans for the second ship, in the trio developed by Pirrie and Ismay over dinner, were crafted by Thomas Andrews. Lord Pirrie, a much involved company chairman, monitored and oversaw the entire project.

The *Titanic* was built with a double hull for safety reasons. There were sixteen watertight compartments. It could stay afloat if any two of the middle compartments or any four of the first compartments flooded. The builders could not imagine a collision which would produce worse damage than that.

When the *Titanic* was ready to leave the shipyard, two years after it was begun, Mr. & Mrs. Ismay and Lord and Lady Pirrie were seated together in the front of the stands, to witness the launch of the largest moving object ever built. J. P. Morgan arrived to be seated with them.

It was an exciting occasion. A band played. Speeches were made. Townsfolks, shipyard employees, and other interested people, crowded into the stands built especially for this auspicious event. Thousands watched as the *Titanic* slipped into the water for the first time.

Work on the *Titanic* was not finished after the launch. Next, was the fitting out. That meant adding the decks, delineating rooms, painting, installing furniture, putting the funnels in place, and completing everything necessary to make the ship ready for passengers.

When all the work on the interior and exterior of the ship was complete, the *Titanic* set out into the Irish Sea, on April 2, 1912, to perform sea trials. After one day of tests, she was pronounced seaworthy. A departure date of, April 10, 1912, was announced.

The *Titanic* then sailed for Southhampton, where more of the crew was hired and cargo loaded.

On the morning of April 10, Captain Edward Smith prepared to leave his home in Southampton. He kissed his wife lightly on the cheek.

"Do have a grand time, Edward. Such an honor for you to captain the largest ship in the world," she said with enthusiasm. "Just think of it. After this trip you may retire with great honor, and we can enjoy a leisurely trip on the continent without hurrying back for once."

"Oh, Father, do bring me some souvenirs from the *Titanic*," said his twelve-year-old daughter. "I will just be here plodding away with my studies while you are off on another exciting adventure."

Captain Smith ruffled his daughter's hair. "There, there, my little cherub. Your time will come in life. Take care of your momma for me, and mind what she says. Yes, your time will come," he said as he fondly kissed the top of her head.

He had many things on his mind this morning. "Yes," he thought, "I believe I will make this my last trip. I am not feeling as young as I used to. My lumbago is bothersome. A nice quiet villa in Italy for the winter would suit me just fine. I must remember to check all our supplies. I hope all those hired for the crew will show up this time. This will be a trip of a lifetime for us all."

His taxi pulled up in front of the house. He picked up his valise and stepped out the door.

Turning back he said, "Take care of each other, my loves. I shall be back before you know it."

He boarded the taxi for transport to the White Star dock. His wife and daughter waved until he was out of sight.

Captain Smith was a favorite of the wealthy patrons of the White Star Line. Some booked passage on his ships specifically because they enjoyed his company. He was unfailingly cheerful and very popular as the stalwart and trusted master of the ship. Although he had been the captain of the *Olympic* when it had been involved two minor mishaps, his salary was twice that of any other captain on the White Star Line. As he was a very experienced seaman, it was thought he could handle any emergency.

Some of his crew had spent the night on board. Others arrived that morning as he did. There were almost 900 crewmembers on the Titanic. A very few of them were women attendants.

It was almost time for the ship to leave the dock, when First Officer Murdoch was approached by the head stoker, or fireman.

"Several of our stokers have not shown up this morning. We need a full crew to run this monster. What do you want me to do?" he said.

"I would say those who have not reported for duty, no longer have a job here. Go out on the docks and see if you can find replacements. And hurry!" answered Murdoch with a scowl. "We gave them their chance."

"Yes, sir," said the head stoker.

He hurried out on the docks, where he found men ready and waiting for just such an occurrence. They quickly agreed to hire on and followed him back to the ship, slapping each other on the back at their good fortune to sail on such a ship.

Just as the ship began to pull away from the dock, the missing stokers, who had lingered too long in a nearby pub, arrived. They stood on the dock shaking their fists and swearing at the loss of a good job. Their shouts were drowned out by the ship's band and the cheering of the people.

It took about four hours to cross the English Channel to reach Cherbourg, France. It was near sunset when the *Titanic* arrived in the harbor. Because of her size, the *Titanic* could not pull up to the dock at Cherbourg.

The White Star Line had two small steamships built, just to carry passengers, luggage, and mail, to and from the docks and their large liners at Cherbourg.

"Well. Here we go," said Maggie.

The small steamship was pulling out of the Cherbourg dock. It was only for first and second-class passengers.

Maggie and the Astors were standing on the upper deck for the short ride to the big ship they would travel on to go home. In the Astor party were his valet, Victor Robbins, Madeleine's maid, Rosalie Bidois, and her private nurse, whom they had hired to watch over her pregnancy, Caroline Louise Endres. Also with them was their pet Airedale, incongruously called Kitty.

The servants placed the bright red and white White Star luggage stickers on all items. The ones which were not needed during the trip had a red and white sticker which said "Not Wanted." The items needed on board had a sticker which said "Wanted."

Victor monitored the loading of the luggage making sure each piece went in the proper direction. If not marked, "Wanted," items went to the hold and could not be accessed during the trip. Rosalie and Caroline remained below decks away from the wind. Caroline made sure Madeleine had a scarf around her neck and a hat that tied on. Although it was a short trip to the *Titanic*, the evening was cool and gray. A rather stiff breeze blew off the salt water.

"I shall hate putting Kitty in that awful kennel on the ship. Really, I do think we should be allowed to have her in our room," complained Madeleine, who dearly loved the happy dog they adopted along the way. Kitty was a tan, medium-sized Airedale who always seemed to be smiling. She was a comfort and good companion to her mistress. Now they must be parted for the five days of this trip.

"I would rather have the better suite, my dear. You will be most comfortable. They simply would not allow larger pets in the better suites. You will be glad for the extra room and amenities, I am sure. At any rate we can go take Kitty for a walk everyday if we wish. And if we don't have the inclination, she will be walked by the kennel keeper. I dare say, she will hardly miss us."

Madeleine sighed and reached down to hug her canine friend, whose leash she held.

"If she were just a little smaller they would have let us have her in the better suite," said Madeleine.

"We can't very well shrink her, can we?" smiled Astor.

He indulged his young wife as much as possible. She was such a treasure. He hoped she would not change with the birth of this child and the return home to some household responsibilities. His mother had enjoyed the social routines and handled her household with confidence. He was not sure Madeleine would take to such things. But she had certainly not disappointed him. She was a fine companion and that compatibility was of utmost importance to him. The difference in their ages did not matter to him. He did feel a need to look out for her in a way he had not felt with his previous wife. She was, after all, still a child in her teens.

"Boy, oh, boy. Did you ever see a ship like that? It makes this little tender look pretty puny, doesn't it?" marveled Maggie.

"It should give us a good, comfortable crossing," said Astor. "I doubt we will even feel the sway of the water."

"I am glad I am over my morning sickness," thought Madeleine.

Maggie saw a friend, Mrs. Brucknell, across the deck. She made her way over to her.

"Edith, what a treat to see you here! Isn't this going to be an adventure? Look at the size of the ship!"

"Oh, Maggie, I have a bad feeling about this ship."

"What ever do you mean, Edith?"

"I cannot explain it to you. I just know that not all is well with this ship."

"Colonel Astor thinks it will give us a good, comfortable crossing. What could possibly go wrong on a ship like this? It is much too big to sink. And it is only a few days. We shall be just fine," Maggie encouraged her friend.

Later she, Astor and Maddy laughed about Mrs. Brucknell's premonitions, thinking them ridiculous.

As they made their way on to the huge vessel, they surrendered their boarding cards and were greeted by the chief steward. The crew was made aware of the rich and famous personages who would be traveling on the ship. Foremost among them was John Jacob Astor IV. At that time, the year before Federal Income Tax was instituted in the United States, he was still the richest man in the world. The orders were to treat him and his party, as well as the other well-to-do people on board, with the greatest care.

The Astors and Maggie were personally escorted to the first-class reception room by the chief steward. Astor was given a white rosebud for his lapel. They were then shown to their rooms. They did not have one of the two deluxe suites. One of those was occupied by a family from Philadelphia and the other by J. Bruce Ismay.

The White Star Line knew it was going to lose money on its first-class passengers. The magnificently appointed staterooms and suites, the amenities and the special meals in first-class were beyond what could be charged for the trip. The Line would make it up on the volume of third-class passengers and mail. The result would be that everyone would want to travel with the rich and famous. It would pay off.

When the passengers, luggage and cargo were loaded the ship weighed anchor and was underway.

"Oh, how lovely," said Madeleine as they were settling into their ornately decorated rooms.

She picked up one of the booklets provided for first-class passengers. It told of recreation available and when meals were served.

"It sounds as if we will not lack for activities, here on the ship. I believe I shall enjoy lounging in a deck chair and having hot drinks brought to me. Do you think it will be very cold this time of year on the sea, John?"

"The first-class promenades are well protected, my dear. However, I think we shall need our wraps and maybe a blanket to sit out on the deck."

"With a hot drink and a blanket I am sure I should fall asleep. I am so sleepy these days," answered Madeleine.

Astor was thinking that he had seen a number of his friends and acquaintances in the reception area. He saw Sir Cosmo and Lady Duff-Gordon and nodded at them from across the room. He looked forward to introducing Madeleine to Lady Duff. As he would later discover they were traveling under assumed names, as Lady Duff was so famous for her fashion designs, she was a minor celebrity. Many of the wealthy women packed gowns designed by "Lucile" to wear for the special occasions on board. He must remember to tell Lady Duff of his first meeting with Madeleine when she was wearing a "Lucile" creation.

"I wonder what Maggie's room is like. They are all supposed to be decorated in different styles. She was right about these rooms being elegant. Well, we shall see her tomorrow. I am very tired, John."

Madeleine was reclining on the four poster bed with the velvet draperies pulled back. As she rested, she looked up at the intricately decorated ceiling and elaborate light fixture. The head and footboards on the bed had carved patterns in the dark wood. Multiple mirrors made the room look larger than it was. A small roll-top desk and chair were near the fireplace. In the adjoining room, a table and chairs and another desk sat on a beautiful floral carpet. There was another bedroom, two wardrobe rooms for clothes and a private bath.

"Well, my darling, you rest. I'll summon Rosalie to help you get ready for bed. I believe I'll take a walk around the deck and have a smoke." He leaned over and kissed her forehead. "I shall look in on you before I retire."

Madeleine slept well and did not feel the sway of the huge ship.

"Rosalie, I believe I shall eat a good breakfast today. For a while I did not think breakfast would ever sound good to me again. But I am quite hungry this morning. It must be the sea air from last evening."

"Yes, ma'am. Would you be going to the dining room or should I have the light breakfast brought here?"

"Please send word to my husband that I should very much like to attend breakfast in the dining room. I have not yet seen much of the ship."

"Yes, ma'am. Right away."

As hungry as she was, Madeleine found the breakfast choices a bit overwhelming. There was a variety of fresh fruit, cereal, fish and meats of many kinds. There were eggs, potatoes, pancakes, and biscuits with butter and jam.

"Will this cornucopia of food assuage your hunger, my dear?"

"I'm sure it will take care of it very nicely."

"I am so pleased to see you have regained an appetite. You must try to eat well now and stay healthy," said Astor.

"It is so thoughtful of you to be concerned for me. Don't worry I shall take care of myself and our son."

"So you think it is a boy, do you?"

"Yes, John, I am convinced it is a boy. We will name him after you, John Jacob Astor V. Doesn't that sound wonderful?"

"Yes, my dear, it does. Now eat something and we will take a walk about the ship. We will be stopping in Queenstown later and there will be a small market on the promenade deck after lunch. Boats from the mainland are bringing some Irish shopkeepers out. Perhaps we can find a souvenir for you this afternoon," said Astor.

The *Titanic* anchored off shore at Queenstown. As at Cherbourg, small boats transported additional passengers, luggage and mail bound for America out to the huge ship. The new passengers were mostly Irish emigrants seeking a new life in America. This was the last stop before the *Titanic* set out across the ocean. It is unknown for sure just how many people were aboard. Some people were unable to go at the last minute. Others were waiting to find an opening for the trip and purchased their tickets as they became available. There were about 2200 people on board.

Other small boats were used to ferry provisions out to ships which could not enter the harbor. That day they brought sellers of Irish wares, such as lace, teapots, blankets, sweaters, plates, cups, and other souvenirs, out to the ship. A small market appeared on the deck.

At lunch Madeleine and Astor saw Maggie. They were assigned to the same table in the huge first-class dining saloon. Table-seating assignments lasted for the entire trip—unless some enterprising matron conspired with the maitre-d' to have her marriageable age daughter be seated by a desirable, eligible bachelor. For a certain consideration, seats could be adjusted.

Meals were considered to be a highlight of the trip on the Atlantic liners. The first class menu on the *Titanic* was designed to appeal to both British and American travelers who frequented the Atlantic sea lanes. The lunch menu on April 11 was no exception. It offered superb fare.

"So what do you think? Isn't this the Taj Mahal of ships?" said Maggie as they enjoyed the scrumptious luncheon set before them.

"It's lovely," said Madeleine. "Do you like your rooms?"

"The Queen herself doesn't have better rooms at the palace, I'll bet," replied her friend.

"We're going to the market on the promenade deck right after lunch. There should be just enough time. Would you like to come with us?" said Madeleine.

"Let's do it!" said Maggie with her usual over-the-top enthusiasm.

They hurried off to the market as soon as lunch was finished. They knew the stop at Queenstown would be less than two hours and they had already been stopped over one hour.

Maggie was in high spirits. She bargained for prices just like she had in the bazaars in Cairo. The sellers were not so eager to reduce the prices here. Even so, she managed to find some treasures she could have for less than the stated price. It warmed her heart. She had been poor once.

"What a beautiful lace shawl!" exclaimed Madeleine.

"Try it on, my dear. Here, let's put it around your shoulders," said Astor.

"It really is exquisite. Such fine stitching and beautiful lace! I am quite taken with it."

"Then you shall have it, Maddy."

"It's very dear. She wants a great deal for it."

"I believe I can pay whatever it costs," said Astor as he pulled out his pocketbook and counted out the amount.

"Thank you, John. You do spoil me so. Maggie, look, what he has bought for me."

"Well now, that's just about the finest shawl I've ever seen. Won't you look swell wearing that!" Maggie joined in the appreciation.

The trio of friends were all still on deck as the *Titanic* pulled away from Queenstown harbor and set forth on the voyage to New York.

On April 11, another ship left port. This one left from New York harbor. The *Carpathia,* a Cunard liner, began her eastbound trip across the Atlantic. Because it was a smaller, less significant ship, there was little fanfare at her leaving. The *Carpathia* was transporting many of its passengers to vacations in southern parts of France or Italy. There the warmth of the Mediterranean climate and the old world atmosphere, lured those of financial means to enjoy a spring holiday. The mood on the ship was festive. The passengers would experience a few days of acquaintance on board ship, and then scatter to various locales, perhaps, never to meet again.

The next afternoon, April 12, while Elsie Emerick Bryan was beginning the ordeal of the birth of her only daughter, Madeleine and Astor set out to explore the ship. Astor had already explored the ship while his wife was resting.

She had descended the Grand Staircase on her way to meals already. In the first-class section, the stairway was its most ornate. It served seven of the eleven decks, but on the other decks it was not nearly so grand as it was in first-class. The large overhead dome functioned as a skylight in first-class. It was a circular dome made of wrought iron and glass. The wood of the walls and balustrades was of warm oak,

228

connoting a richness appropriate to the wealthy passengers inhabiting the area. Descending those stairs, dressed in finery for the evening meal, made the ladies of the first-class section feel like princesses about to greet their subjects. It made them feel exactly as it was designed to do.

Madeleine was no exception. She liked looking down and seeing John waiting for her. It made coming down the stairs all the more impressive.

The couple went into the first-class lounge, which was decorated to look like a room from the palace at Versailles. So elaborately was it decorated that one could easily believe that Marie Antoinette would appear at any moment.

Benjamin Guggenheim and Madame Aubert, his Parisian mistress, were seated next to the fireplace. While some of Astor's contemporaries on board were cool toward Madeleine, Guggenheim, not having any room to be critical of the Astors, was cordial. They exchanged pleasantries in a civilized manner. Astor did not wish to expose Madeleine to that kind of company for any length of time. Legitimate as the Astors were, there were still prejudices to overcome regarding their generationally and financially unequal union. They did not need the additional baggage of consorting with Guggenheim and his paramour.

Madeleine and Astor stopped by the gymnasium. There were mechanical horses, stationary bicycles, and rowing machines, as well as, other exercise equipment. The gym boasted the latest types of devices for exercising one's body while confined to a ship.

They peeked into the swimming pool. It was filled with sea water. A few people were enjoying a swim.

"How is the water?" called Astor to one young man, who was just climbing out.

"It's damn cold. Colder than a well digger's butt," he shouted.

Just then the man noticed Madeleine in the background.

"Oh, ma'am, I am sorry. I didn't see you there. Please forgive me," he continued, embarrassed at his language.

Madeleine nodded an acknowledgement and eased back out the door.

They walked a bit on the covered promenade deck that was specifically for first-class passengers. Then they decided to lounge in deck chairs swaddled in White Star blankets while stewards brought them hot drinks. They glanced through the Atlantic Daily Bulletin, an on board newspaper which gave the menus for the day, stock prices, results from the race tracks and items of interest about society members.

As Madeleine had expected she soon became pleasantly drowsy.

Madeleine and Astor were unaware, as were the other passengers, that the ship was receiving warnings of ice in the sea lanes. Numerous ice warnings were received on April 12.

Jack Phillips and his assistant, Harold Bride, worked in the small wireless room. Together they took care of all the wireless messages sent and received by the *Titanic*. They were hired and trained in Morse Code, by the Marconi company, but their paychecks came from the White Star Line.

They even slept in the same small room. It was good it was small, because there were few distractions. Great concentration was required to hear and to send messages consisting of dots and dashes for letters of the alphabet and numbers. They wore headphones and had the unique ability to decipher words snatched out of the air from other ships or stations on land. They were the only ones who could send messages, as well. They were very important people on this ship. Communication with others during the voyage depended on these two young men.

The second day out at sea, they began receiving warnings of ice in the shipping lanes from other ships. When they received a message warning of ice, they immediately took it to the officer in charge on the bridge. While it was a concern to Jack and Harold that ice warnings were being received, it was not their concern to worry about. They had enough to do just sending and receiving so many messages. Many of the first class passengers invoked their right to send and receive messages from friends and family while on this trip. It kept the young men very busy.

"Listen to this one," said Jack. "'Having a grand time on board the largest ship in the world. Will see you soon.' With all we have to do, you would think some of these passengers could just wait until they arrive. I hardly think messages like this are worth our time."

"Well," said Harold. "Just think about it. If you were traveling as a passenger on a fancy ship like this some day, wouldn't you want to send your mum a wire, just for the fun of it, Jackson, my friend?"

"It would knock her knickers off, I guess," said Jack. "But these are rich folks. Their families would have the butler bring the message in on a silver tray. They probably would not flick a whisker when they read it. They don't think about us poor blokes having too much work to do. Still and all it's a good job."

"It's a great job!" said Harold with enthusiasm. "We are lucky to have a job on the greatest ship afloat. On the first trip, too. We can tell our grandchildren about it."

Jack did not hear the last part of Harold's comment. He had slipped his headphones back on, as a new message began peppering in his ear.

On April 13, numerous ice-warnings were received from other ships.

On Sunday afternoon, April 14, Madeleine and Maggie were seated at the Cafe Parisien, a charming little restaurant on board that served coffee and little sandwiches in-between meals. The small tables, delicate white wicker chairs and general ambiance made patrons feel as if they were sitting in a sidewalk cafe in Paris.

"I have been so hungry lately," said Madeleine. "I cannot believe I am so hungry. It has only been an hour and a half since we had that huge lunch. John is pleased I finally have an appetite."

"Well, you're eating for two now, honey. Don't you worry a bit," said Maggie sipping her coffee.

"I am just so excited to be almost home," said Madeleine. "It will be good to see my parents and Katherine and to be in a real home—just for us—for the first time. Really, it is difficult not having had a home for the past year. We plan to live in the city, and spend the summer in Newport. You *must* come to visit this summer. The house in Newport is truly spectacular. You will be enchanted, I am sure."

"Why sure, I'll come, but first I want to go back to Colorado for a spell. See my kids and grand kids. Traveling sure is nice, but going home is nice, too," replied Maggie.

Just then Astor arrived leading Kitty.

"What do you say to a walk around the decks, Maddy? Kitty is ready to go."

Kitty smiled up at her mistress with that unconditional love found only between dogs and people. Bidding Maggie adieux they started off for a tour around the decks to exercise their penned-up pet, as well as themselves. After this, Madeleine found herself almost hungry again and eager to attend the lavish Sunday-night dinner which was to be the fanciest and most elaborate meal of the trip.

Rosalie had helped Madeleine to dress in one of her finest new Paris gowns. It was a pale cream taffeta with a generous gathered skirt flowing from just under her breasts. It hid her growing girth and allowed her to feel beautiful and elegant.

The tables that evening were decorated with fresh flowers and baskets of fruit. The eleven course meal began with a variety of choices for hors d'oeuvres. There was a delicate soup and choices of smoked salmon and oysters.

Waiters went throughout the huge first-class dining saloon, with serving trays balanced on their shoulders, offering diners something from each tray. It was typical of the time to prepare high-calorie and fat-laden dishes.

The filet mignon was slathered in a butter wine sauce. The chicken was stuffed with truffles and served with butter topped potatoes. There was roast duckling and squab, as well as, beef dishes, an assortment of vegetables, and desserts.

If the chefs had been planning a last meal for the diners they could hardly have done a better job. The cloth napkins were stiff and white. The china table service spotless. The five-member orchestra played popular songs of the day during the meal. The food was prepared and served with style and flair.

The first class diners had been seated together now for three days. They were experiencing a trip on the most luxious ship ever built. They knew this was going to be the trip of a lifetime. They knew they would fondly remember the elegance and the service available to them for years to come. This would definitely be a trip to remember. They collectively felt a certain air of comraderie. One person at the Astors' table expressed that the feeling was just too good to last.

During the elaborate dinner on Sunday evening, Captain Smith ordered a slight directional adjustment for the ship, but did not decrease speed. He had said earlier he could not imagine anything that would cause the *Titanic* to founder. It was his belief that modern shipbuilding had gone beyond that.

He had received several ice warnings earlier in the day. Harold Bride had delivered one of them himself.

"Thank you, Bride," said the captain accepting the message. Harold noticed he placed the message in his pocket, hardly looking at it.

When he returned to the wireless room, Jack was very busy sending greeting messages for the first-class passengers. They had piled up during the night. The wireless had been down and Jack had worked all night to fix it.

"Here's another ice warning," said Jack. This one's from the *Amerika*." It said that the *Amerika* had passed two large icebergs and gave the location.

"Do you think we are in any danger from all these icebergs floating around?" said Harold.

"Not a chance," replied Jack. "This ship is so big nothing could hurt it. They say it is completely unsinkable."

Bruce Ismay was seated at his assigned table in the first-class dining saloon that night. Captain Smith had shared the ice-warning message he received from

Harold earlier in the day with Ismay, who had come to the bridge.

"She is running smoothly, Mr. Ismay. There is no doubt you have produced the finest ship afloat," said Captain Smith.

"She is a beauty isn't, she?" replied the president of the White Star Line.

"Oh, here is something which may interest you," said the captain, as he pulled the ice-warning from his pocket.

"An ice-warning," said Ismay.

"Oh, nothing to be concerned about. I have been receiving these regularly. We are keeping the locations in mind. Our path is charted, and it is free of obstacles, I can assure you."

So the ice-warning made its way into the pocket of Ismay.

He brought it out at dinner to show his companions.

"Listen to this," said Ismay. He read the wireless message, which said the ship sending it was surrounded by icebergs.

"Of course, we have nothing to fear," he continued. "Captain Smith is keeping a close watch on our location. I doubt icebergs could do much damage to this ship in any case."

There was general mild amusement at the suggestion that ice in the sea could harm a ship the size of the *Titanic.* It was, after all, unsinkable.

A journal, widely read by those in the shipbuilding trade, had called the *Titanic* "practically unsinkable." The label stuck. It was not a condition put forth by the White Star Line. They, of course, did nothing to discourage the notion. The word "practically" gradually fell away. The word "unsinkable" became inexorably linked with the ship's name. So by the time of *Titanic's* sailing the two words were fixed together like Tweedle Dum and Tweedle Dee in everyone's minds. Not only that. A belief system had grown from the pairing. Soon it was known for sure that the *Titanic* was unsinkable.

Jack Phillips was exhausted that evening. He received a message from a ship that they were in an ice field. It gave their location. He did not realize that it was directly in their path. Jack put the message aside, as he was so busy. He intended to give it to the officers, as soon as he had time.

Later that evening another ship notified the *Titanic* that they were stopping and were surrounded by ice. By this time, Jack was even more tired. He had no patience with the operator sending the message.

Jack rudely told him to get off the line. He did not notify the bridge.

The two seamen on watch that night observed a calm ocean with their naked eyes, on a clear, cold, moonless night. By the time they saw it, it was too late. One seaman rang the warning bell three times to sound the alert. He called the bridge on the phone shouting, "Iceberg right ahead!"

They had only seconds to avoid the iceberg. It was not enough time. Although Officer Murdoch took quick measures to avoid a collision, the huge ship struck the iceberg. Steel plates buckled. Steel rivets gave way. The iceberg tore a huge gash through the hull allowing water to pour into six front compartments of the ship. It was the disaster none of the designers and builders of the *Titanic* thought could happen.

It was near midnight. The Astors were preparing to go to bed after a leisurely dinner and pleasant evening. They felt the jolt. It seemed more like a shudder really. Still, the engines had quieted. Astor left the suite to investigate the cause.

"Not a thing to worry about, my dear. The ship has struck an iceberg. I have been assured there is no danger whatsoever. The damage does not appear serious," stated Astor when he returned.

"Well, I am glad for that," said Madeleine, somewhat relieved. "Just the same, let's not go to bed just yet."

To amuse themselves they played a game of dominoes. It was hard for Madeleine to concentrate. After a while, it was impossible. The noise coming from the hallway increased. There was shouting.

There was a knock on the door. Astor opened the door. People were careening down the hallway in both directions.

"Get your life jackets, sir," said a steward, "And hurry! The ship's going down!"

As calmly as he could Astor told her they would take their life jackets and go have a look for themselves to see what all the fuss was about. It would soon be explained away.

"People tend to panic in these situations, don't you know," he imparted to his wife.

"Yes, of course, John," said Madeleine, gathering up her coat and her recently purchased shawl. Astor brought both of their life jackets.

They went to the boat deck, where confusion and pandemonium was beginning to reign. Astor did not want his wife to be upset in her condition.

"Come, Maddy, let's go into the gymnasium to get away from all this hubbub."

A frightened Madeleine was willing to follow him docilely. He would surely be able to sort all this out. He was so much older and a man of the world. He had shepherded them safely all through Europe and part of Africa for a year. He was a person of importance who was respected by all. He would know what to do.

Astor guided them to the gymnasium. They sat on the mechanical horses.

They both slipped their life jackets over their heads.

"Let me fasten your life jacket, my dear," said Astor.

"John, what are these made of? Will they hold one up in the water? God forbid we should have to find out," said Madeleine.

"You stay here, Maddy. I will be right back," said Astor.

When he returned, he had another life jacket with him. He took out his knife and cut a slit in the jacket.

"This is what is inside, Maddy. They are proper life jackets. I want you to feel sure yours will hold you up. Mind you, we are not going to have to test these out. This is a huge ship. She cannot possibly sink."

Madeleine felt her heart go cold at the thought of possibly ending up in the frigid Atlantic waters. She kept up a brave face to her husband. He was trying so hard to keep a cool head.

Eventually, they went back to A deck. Lifeboats were being loaded. Astor ridiculed the idea of trusting their lives to those little boats.

"We are safer here than in that little boat," he told Madeleine.

All the same, it became time to make a decision. The Astors were informed the ship was sinking. There was no possibility of it not.

They sent Victor to the kennels to get Kitty. She was at their side reacting to the panic of the humans around her. She was pacing and barking and swinging her head back and forth. Her always smiling face was reflecting the terror of the people who surrounded her.

Officer Lightoller was in charge of loading life boats on the Astor's side of the ship. There was room for Madeleine in Lifeboat #4. She clung to her husband.

"The ladies have to go first, Maddy. Get in the lifeboat to please me," said Astor.

Then he helped her climb through the window of the enclosed promenade into the lifeboat. Officer Lightoller commanded her to step aboard quickly. Astor asked Lightoller if he could board also as his wife was in "a delicate condition." Lightoller said that no men could enter the boats until all the women were loaded.

Astor threw his gloves to his wife and said, "Here, take these. Goodbye, dearie. I will see you later."

Just before the order was given to lower the boat, several young men jumped into Lifeboat #4. Officer Lightoller would have none of that.

"Here, you men get out, I tell you. Men are not allowed. There are still some ladies here," shouted Lightoller above the din.

One young Irish man, seated himself next to Madeleine. Faced with exiting the lifeboat, he began to cry.

When Officer Lightoller turned away momentarily Madeleine pushed the young man down.

"Hush!" she said and threw her expensive Irish shawl over his head. The boat was lowered with the young man on board.

Astor stood back and asked Lightoller which boat his wife was in. He was told Lifeboat #4. Astor then lit a cigarette and stood alone. He watched as others worked to lower the remaining collapsible lifeboats, which were the last boats available for use.

Astor's fate may have been very different if they had gone to the other side of the ship where Officer Murdoch was in charge of loading lifeboats. Officer Murdoch was allowing men to enter the lifeboats after all the ladies standing nearby were loaded. Many of the lifeboats were lowered in a great hurry with many empty seats, especially when they first started to load and leaving the ship was a more difficult decision. Later, there was a clamor to get aboard.

As it was, Astor stood smoking on the deck with Kitty nearby running back and forth, frantic at being separated from her mistress. He noticed Benjamin Guggenheim and his valet come on deck. He overheard Guggenheim say, "We have dressed in our best and are prepared to go down like gentlemen."

J. Bruce Ismay, president of the White Star Line, boarded the last collapsible lifeboat.

Maggie, who claimed she was thrown out of bed by the collision, made it to Lifeboat #6, where she eventually took charge and earned her sobriquet of the "Unsinkable Molly Brown."

At 2:10 am, Captain Smith released Jack and Harold from their duties. Jack remained to send one last SOS.

At about the same time, the *Titanic's* bridge plunged underwater. Astor, standing on the upper deck, was swept into the sea. He bobbed under the water briefly, but was brought to the surface by his life jacket. Gasping for air in the 28 degree water, he clung to the hope of reaching one of the lifeboats and somehow being rescued.

He looked up into the clear, dark night sky with stars calmly twinkling over all the chaos below them. Astor did not see the dark sky or the twinkling stars. In his mind's eye, he saw Madeleine as he had first seen her wrapped in stunning satin the color of blue sky on the fairest day imaginable.

"Maddy. Oh, Maddy," he thought, just as the number one funnel on the *Titanic* snapped off and came crashing down upon him.

In one of life's strange ironies, sea ice played a large role in providing John Jacob Astor I with an avenue to great success, and sea ice claimed the life of his great grandson, John Jacob Astor IV.

Chapter 22

On the *Carpathia,* by 12:15 am the morning of April 15, the captain had gone to bed for the night. The radio operator, although not quite as tired from his duties as Jack was, prepared to go to bed. He unbuttoned his shirt and stretched out his arms as a yawn overtook him. As he bent down, to untie his boots, he remembered he still wore his headphones. As he reached up to take them off, he heard a message in his ears. It was the unmistakable signal that help was required. It was the *Titanic* calling.

"The *Titanic!*" he thought. "It can't be the *Titanic.* Everyone knows it is an unsinkable ship. What could have happened?"

The wireless operator quickly awoke the captain, who immediately ascertained the position of both ships and knew he must respond.

Several other ships also heard the SOS from the *Titanic.* Only the *Carpathia* followed the law of the sea and was close enough to be of help.

The captain of the *Carpathia* gave hurried orders and off they sped. He hoped he could reach the *Titanic* in time.

Just before 2 am, a last message was received from the *Titanic.*

Shortly thereafter, the lights of the *Titanic* blinked once, and then went out forever. The ship split in two. The bow section slipped quietly into the water, followed momentarily by the stern. The great ship was gone.

Within four hours the *Carpathia* reached the site and began to pick up survivors in the lifeboats. By early the next morning, all survivors had been rescued. Nothing more could be done. The survivors huddled quietly on the crowded the decks of the *Carpathia*. They drank hot coffee and soup in almost stunned silence. Some of the women went to the ship's rails and searched the water with tear dampened eyes for their husbands, fathers, brothers and sons. But the rolling sea had given up all the living beings it would for that morning. Many were led away sobbing as the *Carpathia* gave up the search and headed for New York. Some 1500 partially frozen bodies remained behind bobbing lifelessly in their life jackets, encased in the tomb of the ship, or consigned alone to the depths of the Atlantic Ocean.

Madeleine, Rosalie, and nurse Caroline were rescued. Madeleine and two other ladies, now widows, traveling in first class, were given the use of the captain's quarters.

Maggie began organizing lists of survivors, and helping out as soon as she was on board the rescue ship.

Harold Bride and Jack Phillips were together when Captain Smith released them from their duties.

"Go along now, lads. The ship is going down. Do what you can to save yourselves!" shouted the captain above the noise and confusion reigning on the deck.

"Come on, Jack," called Harold, as he hurried out on to the deck.

Harold did not hear an answer from his friend. He did not have time to think of Jack any further. There was a collapsible lifeboat being launched. Harold ran to help. Just then, a great wave crashed over the deck and swept everyone off into the sea.

Harold found himself in the water underneath the overturned lifeboat. He dove under the edge of the boat and swam to the surface. He grasped the side of the boat and hung on with all of his strength. Men were sitting on top of the boat.

"Help me! Help me!" he called out. His pleas were drowned by the voices of many others making the same cry. The water seemed to be boiling with humanity. Some men on top of the boat turned away from him. There were so many others wanting to be rescued.

But Harold did not give up. He cried out again and again, until he felt a hand reach out for his, and he was pulled to the safety of the bottom of the overturned boat. In the days ahead, Harold suffered much with frozen feet. He eventually made a good recovery and lived to see many other days.

Jack Phillips was not so lucky. He stayed at his post tapping out SOS a little too long. He did not survive.

Captain Edward Smith, who had determined to retire following this trip, went down with his ship.

Second Officer Charles Lightoller was the last person rescued by the *Carpathia*.

First Officer William Murdoch did not survive.

J. Bruce Ismay, president of the White Star Line, was criticized for surviving. He insisted he entered one of the last lifeboats when no women were present. Even so, his reputation was ruined for the rest of his life.

Thomas Andrews, who designed the ship, was last seen staring vacantly into space in the lounge. He did not survive.

Victor Robbins, valet to Astor, did not survive.

Most ladies in first-class were saved. An exception was Mrs. Ida Straus. Her husband, Isidor, was the owner of Macy's Department Store. She was about to enter a lifeboat, but changed her mind at the last minute. She chose to stay with her husband. They both were lost.

Sir Cosmo and Lady Duff-Gordon made it to safety in an almost empty lifeboat with only three other passengers and seven crewmen. They were accused of ordering the crewmen to row away from people who were drowning, and could possibly have been saved. The charges were never proven, and although Sir Cosmo and Lady Duff vehemently stated their innocence, their reputations suffered permanent damage.

J. P. Morgan, who had financed the *Titanic*, was forever thankful that, although he had booked passage on the ship, business concerns had caused him to cancel. He was not on board.

When the *Carpathia* docked in New York, Madeleine was among the first down the gangway. She was met by Vincent, her stepson. Madeleine, Rosalie, and Caroline, were quickly ushered into a waiting car.

Madeleine rarely spoke of that terrible night. Once she did mention that one of the last things she remembered was seeing Kitty frantically running back and forth on the deck.

The White Star Line engaged the ship MacKay-Bennett to recover bodies from the sea. The ship set out on its grim mission from Halifax, Nova Scotia on April 17.

On Monday, April 22, seven days after the sinking, the crewmen were working in stunned silence. Looking out over the sea of bodies swaying in a macabre dance with the swells of the water, they were reminded of their own mortality. There were no words to express their emotions as they grasped, pulled, and hauled bodies out of the sea with nets and winches.

They had recovered over 100 bodies, when they saw one partially crushed and covered with soot. He had light hair and a moustache. He looked to be about 50 years old. Later, he was easy to identify. He had the initials J.J.A. sewn in the back of his shirt collar. His watch, cuff links, and rings, were of gold and diamonds. His wallet held a large sum of American and European money. His blue handkerchief was still in the breast pocket of his suit.

The body of John Jacob Astor IV was sent to New York City. He was buried at Trinity Cemetery in Manhattan.

Changes were made on the *Titanic's* sister ship, the *Olympic,* after the disaster. The hull was reinforced inside, bulkheads dividing the watertight compartments were raised, and the number of lifeboats was changed from forty-eight to sixty-eight. The *Olympic* served throughout the first World War as a troopship and, although damaged by submarine attacks, she became known by the nickname "Old Reliable." She served as a passenger ship following the war until 1935. The Great Depression of the 1930s resulted in the Cunard and the White Star lines merging. The *Olympic* was retired and its glamorous accouterments sold at auction. The lounge furnishings are preserved in a hotel in England.

The ship which had been planned to be named the *Gigantic*, instead, was named the *Britannic*. It was the third of the trio of great ships brought to life by the meeting of the minds of Lord Pirrie and J. Bruce Ismay on that fateful night in London in 1907.

The *Britannic* entered service in December, 1915. It was during the time of the first World War. The *Britannic* was never used for a passenger ship. She was converted to a hospital ship for the War. Alas, the *Britannic*, which originally was to have been even grander than the *Titanic*, with an even more spectacular grand staircase and a pipe organ, survived less than one year. In November, 1916, she was blown up off the coast of Turkey in the Aegean Sea. Some said she hit a mine. Some were convinced she was torpedoed. The ship was close to shore and all but thirty of the 1,100 on board were saved.

Chapter 23

Elsie was nursing her baby daughter whom they had named Dorothy Gladys Bryan. The baby was five days old and it was Elsie's twenty-fourth birthday.

She had survived the ether two days before the *Titanic* sank. She gradually came around as Roy stroked her face and Dr. Carter ministered over her. She felt strange. She did not remember the birth of this baby. When she first woke up, the ether made her throw up. It took a while before she realized she even *had* a baby. The room was out of focus and her brain did not register where she was.

Roy was overcome with emotion. Tears were running down his cheeks. He had been so afraid for her. Momma took over and shooed the men out of the room as soon as they carried Elsie back to the bed. She gave the baby to Elsie to hold. She washed Elsie's face and placed a fresh pillow under her head. It was so comforting to have Momma there, Elsie thought. She really did not want to move away to Montana, but she would because Roy had a good job waiting and she loved him and it was her place to go.

Now it was her twenty-fourth birthday. She wondered if she would ever feel so sure of herself like Momma did. Momma always knew what to do and say. She wondered how old she would have to be before she felt that sureness.

Dorothy was a beautiful baby. Elsie was secretly so glad to have a girl this time. She had not wanted to tempt fate and wish too hard for a girl. She had really only wished for a healthy baby. It would be such a pleasure to dress little Dorothy and curl her hair and make her look like a little princess.

Momma and Poppa, some of the girls, and Billy were coming here today to help celebrate her birthday. The others were busy working or with their own families. Elsie was proud of her brother Dee who was a St. Louis policeman. The other boys had good jobs, too. They could not always make family occasions. Anyway, Roy and Elsie's house was too small to accommodate the whole family and their families, too.

Irving came striding through the door in a purposeful manner. He looked agitated.

"The paper says a ship has been sent from Nova Scotia to look for bodies from the *Titanic*," he stated. "It seems God has taken Astor. He was not on the list of those rescued. No one could have survived in that water. I reckon they will find his body.

"I sent a telegram off to the Astor attorneys. I reminded them he planned to settle with us. They know that. They can't go back on the deal now."

"What deal was it?" Roy asked, as the rest of Elsie's family trooped into the small living room in their rented home.

"Irv, you know there wasn't any deal. It was just the report that Astor said he would settle when he arrived home," Ella said. She was tired of hearing about the whole estate affair. It consumed Irving. He had thought and talked about it night and day lately.

"You can be sure Astor knew what he was going to do. He planned to make things right with us. Now we don't know who is in charge of the fortune. Whoever it is will surely honor the wishes of Astor himself," continued Irving.

Vida and the twins, Mabel and Myrtle, took turns holding little Dorothy. She had a round face and lots of dark hair. Her little mouth worked back and forth in a sucking motion like a fish in a pond waiting for a tasty bite.

Billy, at eleven years old, was recovering from an unfortunate incident. He had received a smallpox vaccination which had given him blood poisoning and limited the use of one of his hands. He could still play the piano better than almost anyone, but it was felt that probably he would not make it as a classical pianist because of this. Billy liked jazz or ragtime better anyway and he still could play those pieces with wild abandon. He was not too worried about his future. His mother, on the other hand, could not help but be disappointed that his early promise of becoming a famous classical pianist might not be achieved.

This was to be a last get together for Elsie's family before their move to Montana. Roy and Elsie were planning to leave St. Louis as soon as Elsie felt well enough. Roy was eager to arrive in Billings to take up the job he had been promised with the Northern Pacific Railroad.

Momma brought a birthday cake, a new tan shawl for Elsie and a lacy white dress for her newest granddaughter. Momma always had a knack for picking just the right gift. They ate cake and drank lemonade and laughed and talked together until just about dark when the Emerick family went home.

"I'd like to leave next week if you're up to it, Elsie. We'll just take what we absolutely need. I'm glad they gave us train passes, but we can't ship very much. We can replace things when we get there."

"I'll be ready, Roy."

Roy had gone up to Billings just before the baby came. He had found a converted boxcar on the edge of town that was being held for them. He was hoping Elsie would like it. There was a wood cook stove in the middle of it and plenty of wood to be had nearby. He felt lucky to have found it, as housing they could afford was not plentiful.

So off they moved to Billings, traveling by train with Lynn, who was four-years-old, and baby Dorothy who was two weeks.

Elsie did like the converted boxcar. She remembered it as one of the most comfortable homes they ever had.

One of the first things they did after they were settled was to plant a large garden. There was a nice sunny spot on the west side that was just perfect. Elsie knew how to preserve foods. Momma had taught her that. She had never really had a good place for a garden before though. So she had ambitious plans to put up plenty of good vegetables for the winter. They planted radishes, carrots, onions, potatoes, beets, several kinds of squash, cucumbers, corn, peas, string beans, turnips and pumpkins. The hot Montana summer would be good garden-growing weather.

And it was hot in the early summer of 1912.

With the move and getting settled, Elsie all but lost track of what was happening with the Astor/Emerick estate. Irving wrote her long letters telling her about it. After Astor's body was found, Irving and some other relatives hired attorneys to contact the Astors and ask for a settlement.

One group of attorneys met with Madeleine, but she had no idea what they were talking about.

Madeleine was left with some access to, but not control of, the Astor fortune, as long as she remained unmarried. John had apparently listened to his cousin William and rewritten his will shortly before his marriage. He took good care of Madeleine by giving her about 1.7 million dollars. Some money was left to his son Vincent, until his majority, and to any children from his marriage to Madeleine.

A group of trustees was appointed by Astor's will. The group included James Roosevelt, Nicholas Biddle, Douglas Robinson, a Vanderbuilt and a Hughes. They would oversee the bulk of the fortune. Early in 1913, William Vincent Astor, son of John Jacob Astor IV, was appointed as an additional trustee and executor, as he had reached 21 years of age.

Irving was unable to make any headway in obtaining a settlement for the family. The courts still ruled that since there was no will, it could not be determined how the John Nicholas Emerick estate should be divided. More and more "relatives" were turning up every day. Some were legitimate; some were not. Sorting it out was going to be a problem. Valentine had married several times; so had Irving's father, Warren. Irving still believed his uncle Lynas had sold the will, left in Christopher's possession, to the Astors years ago. The Astor attorneys denied that and denied knowing what John Jacob Astor IV had in mind, if anything, to settle the estate.

Irving wrote his oldest daughter that he was not giving up.

Roy liked his job as a carman on the railroad. It had some status and a steady paycheck. Working for the railroad was the best opportunity he ever had. It did not pay much, but it was regular and not as subject to layoffs, as most of his jobs in St. Louis. Things were going well for them in Montana.

Roy was awfully tired one summer evening. The heat was fierce during the day. He worked under the railroad cars sometimes where it was a little cooler. This night he just could not seem to cool off. Elsie made him a large glass of cold tea she had kept in their ice box. His back was aching—probably from crawling around under the boxcars today, he thought. His head was feeling a little achy, too.

The next morning he was not feeling well at all, but he did not mention it to Elsie. She had her hands full tending to the children and the large garden and trying to ease into a new and different life. He could not afford to stay home even if he did not feel tip top. He kissed Elsie goodbye on the cheek and went off to work.

Late that afternoon, at about time for Roy to come home, a wagon pulled up in front of the boxcar home. Elsie started out to see who it was. Roy, who was lying in the back of the wagon, raised up and shouted at her to stay away. The man driving the wagon did the same.

"Don't come near, Missus. He's got the smallpox," shouted the driver.

"Elsie, you've got to help me. The railroad doc says I got smallpox. They're taking me to the Pest House. You got to help me. You got to bring me food and some blankets. There's nobody there to take care of us at the Pest House, only the sick ones." Roy made a great effort to talk and then fell back in the wagon.

Elsie stopped in her tracks and grabbed Lynn as he came out the door to investigate.

"Oh, Roy, oh, Roy," she gasped, feeling helpless and not knowing what to do.

"Missus, you get him some blankets and some food. Lay it on the step and I'll come and get it. I've already had the pox. I made it through. I ain't going to get it again. Then you'll need to take food everyday to the Pest House. Take a wash pan or something like that to leave it in. Don't touch anything. Leave it by the fence, near the gate. You know where the Pest House is?"

"No," said Elsie, still in shock from this unimaginable happening.

The driver explained where the Pest House was located. She had no horse, nor wagon, nor car. She would need to walk the several miles everyday, with her babies. She was not acquainted with anyone in town yet. The townsfolks would not want to help her anyway, as everyone would be afraid she might be coming down with it, too, and would avoid her company.

Elsie took Lynn with her into the house while she gathered up a loaf of bread, and some meat and cheese. She did not have extra blankets. She removed the ones on their bed. She would use the shawl she had received for her birthday to cover up with in the early morning when the air cooled down.

She laid the things on the step and called out to Roy, "Don't worry, Roy. I will come every day. I love you. You will be all right. Try to rest."

Her sentences came in short staccato gasps. She wanted to say something more meaningful, but it did not come.

Roy raised his hand from the wagon and said, "Oh, Elsie, I am just so sick. I love you, too. I hope you and the kids will be okay."

"Try not to worry, Missus. As I said, I made it. He can, too."

The driver clucked to the horse and the wagon rolled away.

Elsie leaned on the doorjamb and watched it disappear down the dusty road.

Smallpox had plagued mankind for hundreds of years. The first recorded episode had been in 1350 B.C. when Hittite warriors caught the disease from the Egyptians. There had been evidence of it in Rome in 180 A.D., when millions of Romans including Emperor Marcus Aurelieus died of it.

Through the centuries, it had continued to periodically assault mankind. It was said that smallpox kept the churchyard cemeteries full in England. There has been no disease, except the plague, that has caused more death and destruction. Some civilizations, such as the Hittites and the Aztecs, were literally wiped out by the disease.

Vaccination for the dread disease had been available in the 1700s. General George Washington had decreed that all his troops be vaccinated against it. Benjamin Franklin, whose son died of smallpox, fought to have vaccinations take place for all. In 1912, people were often vaccinated for smallpox. Sometimes there were complications, like those that had happened to Billy Emerick. Sometimes people were afraid to be vaccinated. Sometimes when they were, they contracted smallpox anyway.

Whether or not Roy had been vaccinated is unknown. Perhaps he had been and that helped him to survive. For whatever reason, Elsie and the children escaped the malady.

Smallpox is spread by infected saliva droplets. It can be contracted by face to face contact, or contact with contaminated clothing or bedding.

When initial symptoms begin they include high fever, head and back aches, vomiting and delirium. The rash starts two or three days after that. Flat, red lesions appear and become filled with pus. Scabs develop, and then fall off in about three to four weeks. There is some risk of contagion until all the scabs have dropped off.

Smallpox kills about thirty percent of its victims. The speckled monster, as it was known in eighteenth century England, is particularly lethal to the young, the old, and the weak.

The Pest House was the short name for the House of Pestilence. Pestilence, in England, was also a name for the plague. In America, the Pest House was a place where people with communicable diseases, such as cholera, scarlet fever and smallpox, could be quarantined. Hospitals refused admission to those with such diseases.

There were no medical practitioners to serve the patients in the Pest House. There was no medicine.

Standards of cleanliness were poorly observed. As people recovered, they took care of those who were extremely ill. Others would go to the fence for those who were too sick to retrieve their own food. Those who had no friends or relatives to help, depended on others in the house sharing their food with them, or they stole food from those too sick to eat.

Patients remained in the Pest House until they recovered or died. Many of them died.

These were the conditions that Roy faced as he entered the Pest House in Billings, Montana, the summer of 1912.

Elsie lay awake all night covered with her birthday shawl. It was not cold, but she was shivering from fear and worry. The rent would be due soon. There would be no paycheck, as Roy was not working. She needed meat and milk. They had a few laying hens so she would have eggs. Thank goodness Roy had cut a large pile of wood. She would need that for cooking. She knew Roy would be gone for many weeks, if he survived at all. She had to believe he would survive.

Elsie cried and prayed most of the night. She knew she must have faith that God would see them through this trouble. She recalled how more than once when she was growing up her family was without food and hungry. Irving made them all get down on their knees as he prayed. He bade each of the children to call upon the Lord for help and it happened each time. It was just like magic. The answer came. There was a knock on the door and someone delivered baskets of food. She remembered that happening. It was very convincing to Elsie as a child. She believed in prayer with a fervent and honest heart. She knew the God of her father listened when she prayed.

As dawn broke, a glimmer of an idea began in her brain. She tossed it back and forth mentally, weighed its chances, considered what it would take and how it could be accomplished. By the time Dorothy had begun to cry, waiting for her first meal of the day, the idea was beginning to congeal into a real possibility. She considered further as she sat comfortably nursing the baby. With the universal instinct of motherhood, Elsie knew she must look after the needs of these children in her care. She vowed to herself she would do her best.

In later years, Elsie referred to this time in her life as "The Miracle of the Radishes."

The garden was just coming on and the first things ready were the bright red and white radishes they had planted with such care. In the beginning, they were the only vegetables ready. She would start with the radishes.

Roy and Frank had made Lynn a little wagon to pull before they left St. Louis. They had brought it with them in the move, although it was not easy to stow on the train. Elsie pulled the radishes from the warm earth that morning. She bundled them in groups and tied them with string. She filled Lynn's little wagon with radishes. She and Lynn took turns pulling the little wagon as they walked to town. Elsie fashioned a small sling to carry baby Dorothy.

They walked to town in the early morning sunshine. They went to the best homes in town. Elsie sent Lynn to the doors to knock and offer the radishes for sale. Most of the city folks were delighted to have some fresh produce, even if it was only radishes. Either that, or they could not resist the little, four-years-old, boy who offered them with a sweet smile. They sold out quickly.

They then found the Pest House and left food for Roy by the fence with a note.

A man with scabs all over his face shouted to her, "Who's that for, Missus?"

"It's for Roy. Roy Bryan. He came yesterday," she called back.

"The young Irishman. He's too sick to eat, but I'll take it to him," replied the man.

"Thank you. Oh, thank you. What's your name?" said Elsie.

"M'name's Jim, Ma'am. Just call me Jim."

"Thank you, Jim. Please tell Roy I'll come every day. Maybe I'll see you tomorrow. Do you need anything, Jim?"

"I could use some smokes, Ma'am."

"I'll see what I can do," she answered.

Elsie quickly decided it would be money well spent to buy some cigarettes for Jim. If he would help take care of Roy, she would get whatever she could for him. And she did.

In the next few weeks, while Roy was imprisoned in the Pest House, the garden flourished like no one had ever seen. There was plenty of produce to feed her family and plenty to sell. Her regular customers could hardly wait for her deliveries each morning. The carrots were long and crisp, the tasty little peas bursting from their pods. You could not find produce any fresher unless you had your own garden and many in town did not.

Elsie was very busy in those days. The garden needed to be tended; the children did, too. The fledgling business needed to be kept afloat and provisions taken to Roy each day. Somehow she and little Lynn managed. Little as he was, Lynn never forgot the summer of 1912. Even when he grew up and owned a large house on Van Ness Avenue in San Francisco and had fine furnishings, he remembered what it was like delivering vegetables in his little wagon. It was always a humbling thought.

Roy was not well enough to come home and return to work until the produce was winding down in the garden. The garden produced as long as it was needed. Elsie's faith in God and hard work had truly produced "The Miracle of the Radishes."

By the end of the summer, Ella had decided to move to Billings with Vida, the twins, Mabel, Myrtle, and Billy. She contracted to run a boarding house and dining room in Billings. The dining room was known as the Cottage Inn.

Irving did not come with them. He had his preaching and his job on the streetcar line. Part of the reason Ella decided to take the opportunity in Billings was that she wanted to get the children away from Irving for a while as he was very hard on them. There was much friction between him and Billy as Billy grew older and had his own ideas about things.

They received a letter from Elsie in which she mentioned selling vegetables to the Cottage Inn, which was going to close for lack of someone to run it. One thing led to another in Ella's mind. She sent an inquiry off to find out about the terms.

"Irving, I think it will be a good opportunity," Ella said when she received information about the job. "Elsie says it is a good place to live. Now that Roy is over the smallpox, maybe they can get on their feet. Anyway, I would like to see the babies and get our youngsters out of the city."

By this time of life, Irving was not so inclined to argue with his wife. She had shown herself to be an independent woman. But he would be darned if he would give up his jobs and position in St Louis to follow her whim.

"Well, Ellie, you're going to do what you're going to do. I'm not ready to leave St. Louis. I have my preaching and the streetcar job. People know me in this town. I don't know what I could find there. You all go ahead. If it works out, then maybe I'll feel like coming. I'm still hoping that we can make a settlement with the Astors. We were so close. If it just hadn't been for the *Titanic* sinking we would all be on easy street right now and you would not have to work ever again."

"Yes, Irv. I know. I am sorry things have not turned out like you expected. We just have to go on in life and see what comes next. We have always been all right and we will be still."

She patted his shoulder. She did truly feel sorry his dreams of wealth had not come true. She felt sorry for *him*, but not for the lack of money.

Ella and the children moved on to Montana. Elsie was pleased to have her mother nearby again. She helped out with the cooking and the work of the boarding house and dining room whenever she could.

The following year, Vida, who was sixteen, married Roy's nephew, Harry Bryan. The huge family that Ella once had was gradually becoming smaller and smaller. She noticed the lack of Vida's help with the work, but the child was entitled to her own life.

"My, but the girls married young though," she thought. She hoped it was a good choice for Vida.

By 1915, Irving had decided to join the family in Billings. He wasn't there long before he found a church in which to preach. He insisted that fourteen-year-old Billy come along to play the piano. That worked out for several Sundays. Then one Sunday, instead of playing the assigned hymn, Billy broke into some impromptu jazz. Right in church. The preacher's son. Irving was so angry when they went home he threw Billy into the burning fireplace. Billy left home on that day and made his own way ever after. He never spoke to his father again. He did send money to Irving over the years, however.

As the 1920s began to roar in, Roy had the chance to move to Tacoma to continue his job with the railroad in the South Tacoma Shops. By 1922, all the family— Roy and Elsie, Vida and Harry, Ella and Irving and the twins—had moved to Tacoma. Billy was living in the same area, but was on his own.

Roy and Elsie bought a small house on South Wapato Street. Irving and Ella found a place nearby. Vida and Harry moved on to Longview before long and then later to Vancouver, Washington, where they owned the Bryan Piano store on Main Street for many years.

Ella, unfortunately, did not live long after that move. She died of a cerebral hemorrhage in the same month she was born, July, 1922. She was 59 years old. She was right about the Astor money being pie in the sky, at least as far as her life was concerned.

Ella's children, especially the girls, were devastated to lose their mother. It was not expected. Elsie had not yet found out from Momma just when and how the sureness and confidence came. Momma always knew the right words to say and the right things to do for her family. It would be so hard to go on without her. Elsie was glad her children had at least known their grandmother for a few years. Maybe they would remember her love and good spirit when they were older. Momma did love her grandchildren so and she had been there when they were born. Elsie vowed to herself she would take flowers to her mother's grave, especially on Decoration Day, as Memorial Day was called then, every year she could. And she did.

Irving did not let much time go by before he married a Scandinavian woman named Anna. She did not speak much English. Irving spoke only English. Anna was short, squat, elderly and crabby. The family, all rather shocked at the rapidity of Irving's remarriage, always called her "the old woman." She was never really accepted, although in her good Christian way Elsie took care to be kind and friendly to her new stepmother, as much as she could be when they did not speak the same language. Anna smiled and nodded a lot. Some of her teeth were bad in front. No one really understood why he chose Anna. Perhaps she was a good cook, Irving's daughters thought. Whatever the reason, the marriage lasted the rest of Irving's life, which was about twenty years.

Chapter 24

On August 14, 1912, Madeleine gave birth to a son. She named him John Jacob Astor V.

Madeleine went into a period of depression following the sinking of the *Titanic*. She had been rescued, which was a miracle in itself, when so many had lost their lives. She felt some guilt about that.

She read the reports of other women in second and third classes. Some were with child also and had not survived. She remembered her fear that night of being thrown into the terrible icy water. It must have been so horrible for John. She was sure he would make it into a later boat or some other boat would pick him up if he was swept into the sea. He was John Jacob Astor. He was known around the world. He deserved to be saved if anyone did.

She had found John to be a good, kind companion in their year together. She had soon tired of the traveling, as interesting and exciting as it was. She longed for home. However, John had known the places to go and he had been eager to share them with his young wife, who had never seen such wonderful old world sights. He had been so enthusiastic as a tour guide—able to make himself understood in any country. Madeleine looked back fondly on their travels together and always remembered that rather magical time when he had loved her so and she had been the princess of the world.

He had wanted her to be able to hold her own with the ladies of his set at home. She would have experienced some of the same places and the type of life they were used to by the time their trip was over. She would have common experiences to talk about with them. He hoped the passing of time would allow Madeleine to be accepted in his upper-class society at home. It would be easier for both of them if that were the case. If not, he would find other friends for them—friends like Maggie Brown, who was not so persnickety about position and age differences. The quality of the person was what counted with Maggie.

It seemed odd to Madeleine: now that John was dead, his friends were more tolerant of her. The horrifying experience in the night on April 15 had somehow given her status she had previously lacked. She gained, through no action of her own, the sympathy vote.

The ladies of the 400 set began to sing a bit of a different tune.

"The poor child. Imagine losing your husband like that, expecting and all…"

"Such a shame. He was the best catch she could ever have found…"

"John was a good man. Whatever he saw in her must be of some value…"

While they were not so rejecting of her upon her return, they were not exactly accepting either. She found herself in a gray area betwixt and between social sets.

With the birth of her son her status was heightened further. She was the legitimate mother of the son of the man who had not only had impeccable credentials, but had been the richest man in the world. No one could ever deny her that. She had access to the Astor homes and enough money to live very comfortably.

Why then, was she not happy? The events of the past year had taken a great toll on her life. It would take some time to recover.

Mrs. Force was thrilled with her new grandchild.

"Oh, Maddy, he really is the most beautiful baby. Of course, he would be with you as his mother, darling. What else could he be, hum? With such good breeding and two of the finest parents ever…"

Mrs. Force was trying to raise her daughter's spirits. Her sentence trailed off as she realized she only had reminded Madeleine of her loss.

Although still depressed, Madeleine could not help but smile when she looked at her new little son. He was so active, thrashing about with his tiny arms and legs like he had a Mexican jumping bean inside of him. How glad she was that he was in fine condition, seemingly unaffected by his mother's night of fright and subsequent grief.

Gradually, she came back from the edge of her withdrawal and depression. She found she slipped easily back into the social circle of her parents and her sister Katherine. It was comfortable and warm there. She felt accepted and loved.

Some months after the sinking of the *Titanic*, Madeleine was visited in her home by two attorneys hired by the Emerick family. She agreed to see them out of curiosity.

The attorneys had been unsuccessful in their efforts to work with the Astor attorneys regarding a settlement of the Emerick estate. They knew control of the fortune was in the hands of the trustees. Their pleas to those men were ignored. Irving pressed them to contact the widow.

Visiting Madeleine was recognized as a long shot at best. Not having had success elsewhere they had nothing to lose. Perhaps her influence with the board controlling the fortune would make some difference.

Madeleine met with them in the elegant living room of her home on Fifth Avenue in New York City.

"We are so sorry about the loss of your husband, Mrs. Astor," began one of the attorneys. "However, congratulations on the recent birth of your son."

"Thank you, thank you," murmured Madeleine. "What can I do for you gentlemen?"

"Well, ma'am, we represent the family of John Nicholas Emerick who was partner to your husband's great grandfather. Ah..., your husband decided to settle a long-standing suit against his estate by the Emerick family. He agreed to make settlement when he returned to the U.S. We are here to see about honoring his agreement to do that," stated the Emerick attorney.

It was an awkward situation. Why had they allowed Irving and the others to prevail upon them to do this? It was clear this young woman was still grieving and was so young she probably did not know about her late husband's business.

Madeleine was thinking about the little she did know about John's business. She recalled that morning they were sitting in a small cafe beside their hotel in Paris. They were sipping coffee near the window enjoying the winter sun. Victor found them to deliver a telegram which had just arrived. John read it and tucked it in his pocket.

"Will there be an answer, sir?" asked Victor.

"No, not now. Thank you, Victor."

"What is it, John?" she asked expectantly, as soon as Victor had gone.

"Just some business, dearie. Nothing you need concern yourself about. I will take care of it later. Right now I want to sit here in the sun with you and enjoy our coffee. You are the most important thing to me at this moment. I shall not let business spoil our time together."

That night he made passionate love to her in the luxurious suite of rooms he engaged for their stay in Paris. She always believed that may have been the night she conceived their son.

There were many other times on their year's journey when John did tend to business. Messages would arrive or sometimes he would have meetings with men who came to him for discussion or decisions. She never really paid that much attention. She had never heard of the Emerick suit or of any agreement.

She, therefore, answered the Emerick attorneys, "What agreement?"

The attorneys recognized a lost cause when they met one. They thanked her for her time and made their exit. For the moment things were stalled regarding this case. They did not look forward to discussing this with Irving again.

Madeleine kept a low social profile for the next few years. She devoted much of her time to raising her son. After four years of widowhood, in 1916, she began to see her former beau, Willie Dick. He continued to be a successful and wealthy importer. She had been quite fascinated by him before her meeting and marrying Astor. Dick was still unattached and he began to romance the still startlingly attractive Mrs. Astor.

She talked things over with her mother.

"I will have to renounce any claim on the Astor moneys for myself if I marry Willie. That is really not a problem, as Willie has the means to take care of us both. Of course, Johnny will continue to receive his trust fund at his majority. It is so dreary to think of these things, Mother."

"My dear, Madeleine, you have always had your head in the clouds about practical matters. I felt years ago Mr. Dick would make you a fine husband. You probably would have married him and been living happily if you had not met Astor. Oh, he was a lovely man as well. Just not quite as suitable a match for you, although he did nicely by you. Your family has no complaints there. Do choose wisely this time is all I ask. Do you truly love Mr. Dick?"

"He is such fun to be with. He makes me laugh and we seem to like the same things. I have been lonely these past years. Oh, I know you and Father have made such an effort for me, and little Johnny is my treasure. Still, I want to have someone to be with again."

Mrs. Force sighed. It was not the answer she was looking for. She guessed it would have to do as Madeleine seemed to have made up her mind.

When Willie and Madeleine applied for a marriage license in Bar Harbor, Maine, they were told there was a five day waiting period. They were both annoyed at this interference with their plans. The license clerk remembered how irritated they were.

However, Madeleine was again the star of the day when her second wedding, to the heir of the Dick sugar fortune, took place. This time she felt a little more relaxed and not like such an interloper. She hoped this alliance would assuage the emptiness she felt in her heart. Only time would tell.

Chapter 25

The summer of 1924, Elsie's favorite uncle, Dr. Lynn R. Emerick, was practicing medicine out of his and Olivia's home on Somers Street in Easton, Ohio. His letterhead billed him as a specialist in diabetes. It also stated his office hours of 7 to 9 am, 12 to 2 pm and 6 to 7:30 pm. In his letter to Irving of June 3 that year, he recounted how he had contracted malarial fever in the swamps of Missouri years before and how because of that he had lost his health.

"Well I do not know whither(sic) I would have made a better sheep or cattle raiser than Dr. or not. I sometimes think I could not have made worse.

"However through my malarial condition I received my bad liver and in turn and time it culminated in a Diabetic condition then considered incurable. But I got cured and am now curing others. Just took on my 49 case today. Have them from all over the country. Am treating by mail. And most of them I do not see. I have 6 patients in Newark, Ohio, one in Huntington, Nebraska, 1 in Parsons, Kansas. Some is doing almost unbelievable well. The after effects of my Diabetes was that I lost all my teeth, and here at 51 only have not a tooth in my head. But get along good with my store teeth."

Before 1922, when insulin became available to treat diabetes, the condition was a slow death sentence.

Dr. Lynn did not identify how he was cured or how he was treating patients by mail. By 1924, when he wrote this, doctors were giving insulin for diabetes.

The following year, Dr. Lynn became interested in the fight for the Emerick money. He wrote to Irving in November 1925 that he had discovered proof that George Emerick was their grandfather. He had been unable to secure proof of their relationship to Christopher yet. He knew Irving had the family papers from their father, which should prove their relationship. He still wanted to secure additional proof for the fight ahead.

"Have you given the lawyers all of this information? And did you write to brother Bert? He and I are the only ones that are interested. Well let them turn up their noses, who cares. We'll go on just the same.

"Well I am tired and sleepy. Been up some nights. Had two very severe cases, but both better."

In 1924 and 1925, Roy was active in Tacoma politics and attended the Eagle Lodge regularly. Elsie had been writing to Emericks to find relatives, to see who was interested in participating in the fight for the Emerick money. She wrote to some who answered her with the wrong information, indicating they were not related to either Christopher or Valentine.

In March 1925, attorney Calvin I. Hoy was hired by the Mississippi Valley Association of Emerick Heirs. He was involved in the fight for many years. He pursued the case with a dogged determination that outlasted most of the many, many other attorneys who worked on or dabbled in this suit. He worked closely with Elsie and with Dr. Lynn. And Irving? Well, that part of the story is yet to unfold.

In 1926 Roy, who was popular and well-liked, ran for constable in Tacoma on the Republican ticket. He did not win. He and Elsie began to think about moving out of the city into the county and having a little more property.

That same year Billy, who was living in the Seattle area and performing on his own radio show on station KOMO, decided to try his luck in Hollywood. He was a very popular musical artist on the radio. He sang songs of the day and played and sang his own "ditties," with light chatter interspersed between songs. The radio listeners loved it. His always sweet spirit shone through on the airwaves. He had had an earlier marriage which did not work out. It seemed like a good time to try the big time in California. The station manager at KOMO expected that the time would come when he would be off to greener pastures and possible greater fame. They assured him his job with the station would always be available if he should decide to come back.

Billy had some contacts in California with people he had met in the music business. Hollywood was the place to be, they told him. "Come on down. We'll see you meet the right people."

He was introduced to a young singer named Bing Crosby, who was also from Washington state. Bing was part of Paul Whiteman's Rhythm Boys. He was also seeking his musical fortune in Los Angeles. Bing thought Billy's piano stylings were terrific. The following year Bing's solo recording "My Blue Heaven" soared to number one on the charts. He was off on his way to a lifetime career as a singer extraordinaire.

Billy, for whatever reason, was not that successful. He had no trouble finding jobs at small nightclubs and bookings for parties. He had some glamour pictures taken and sent one to Elsie and Roy. He looked resplendent in a tuxedo and black tie. His light hair combed in its natural waves, his handsome slightly pouty face and clear eyes staring right at the camera showed an impressive young man. He used his given name of Arthur when he signed the picture in beautiful flowing script.

Billy had a habit that was beginning to become a problem for him, even at such a young age. He was quite a heavy drinker. He could play piano all night, drunk or sober. In fact, he often played better after several drinks. Well, what of it? Everybody in the Hollywood set drank. Although Prohibition began in 1920 and would last until 1933, bootleg liquor continued to flow freely at Hollywood parties.

It was at one of these parties one evening that he met the Countess, well, Viscountess, to be technical. But Americans, not being schooled in royal protocol, tended to call her, "the Countess."

Nancy Witcher Langhorne was born in Greenwood, Virginia in 1879, so she would have been about forty-seven years old in 1926. After her divorce from her first husband in 1903, she moved to England. Three years later, she married Waldorf Astor.

Waldorf was a great grandson of John Jacob Astor I. Part of the Astor fortune had departed American shores with Waldorf's father. It seemed there was plenty for all. The English Astors lived in Hever Castle, a grand estate with sumptuous formal gardens surrounding it. Waldorf's father became a member of the House of Lords and later a Viscount. Waldorf himself was elected to the House of Commons in 1917. When his father died, Waldorf resigned his seat to take over duties as the second Viscount Astor and entered the House of Lords.

Lady Nancy Astor assumed her husband's seat in the House of Commons and was subsequently elected in 1919. She was the first woman to win a seat in the House of Commons. She retained her Conservative seat until she retired in 1945.

Nancy Astor was known as a fiery champion of women's and children's rights, and was a strong advocate for the Temperance movement. She was able to hold her own with such a verbal deftness that some of her remarks remain well-known quotes.

She was often annoyed by the political positions and personality of Winston Churchill. They engaged in verbal sparing matches in the House of Commons and on social occasions. Because of Lady Astor's strong opinions about the use of alcoholic drinks, and Churchill's love of such stimuli, harsh words passed between them in that regard.

In her salad days, Nancy had been a beautiful young woman as the famous painting of her by John Singer Sargent showed. However, she had a way of thinking and speaking her mind freely, that belied the delicate, gentle soul looking over her shoulder at the world in the painting. She once admitted she would not want a woman like herself for a friend.

Lady Astor and Churchill were both Conservatives in the House of Commons, but that did not mean that they agreed. Neither gave an inch when a position was taken. Partly because of her gender, she was known as emotional, headstrong and cocky. Churchill, while a great leader of his time, had many more annoying personality quirks than that. It did seem, sometimes, that there was very little they could agree upon at all.

Billy was playing piano tunes in his inimitable style at a party of Hollywood elites. He was sipping drinks and playing and talking at the same time. It was something he did so well.

He was seated at a white grand piano at one end of a large white carpeted living room. Pale green draperies were swooped back from the windows by braided golden ropes with glossy tassels slightly waving in the breeze from the open French doors. To his right, Billy could look out on a small expanse of green lawn and a swimming pool with a gently percolating waterfall at the far end. Tall palm trees and blooming roses completed the outdoor picture.

Inside, the room was filling with people from the movie and entertainment colony. Billy knew some of them. The host was a major studio owner. No expense was spared for this catered evening. The food looked delicious. It was spread on a long table at the opposite end of the room. It was mostly finger foods; tiny sandwiches with watercress and cucumber, delicate pastries, cheeses, cold meats and a variety of crackers, and rare chocolates from Belgium. A large floral display sat majestically in the midst of the culinary delights. Later, Billy might partake. Right now he was not hungry and he had a job to do. Billy had been engaged to play background music for the affair.

She came over and leaned slightly on the piano.

"They tell me your name is Arthur Emerick. Do you know who *I* am?" she asked.

"Well, of course, I know who you are, my Lady. You are the Queen of the evening. You are the Most Favored Guest. You are the nearest many of us here will ever get to royal sho-society. Have you come to slum with the peasants?" he answered laughing.

She laughed, too, and leaned a little harder on the piano.

"If only all the Emericks were as talented and clever as you, Arthur. Your family would have no need to pursue these continuous lawsuits against us."

With her animated response she spilled some of her drink down the front of her peach colored chiffon gown.

"Come, it's time for me to take a little breaky anyhow. Let us go into the kitchen in searsh of, in search of...Well, let's go into the kitchen and see what we can find." Billy took her arm and they strolled toward the kitchen.

Billy waved his hand at the guests. "Back in a jiff. The lady needs some sopping up."

No one paid much attention as the two people made their way into the kitchen.

Billy found a towel and began to pat the front of her dress as if he had known her for years and had the right to do it.

"Really, Arthur, dear, thank you. If you only had an idea of how much trouble it is to keep up the estate. The family has advertised for Emerick heirs for years. It is *so* expensive. We know, will or no will, the Emerick lawsuits will probably have to be settled eventually. We really *want* to settle. We have spent thousands of dollars dealing with the whole affair."

"Well, it's only money, isn't it, my dear Lady Astor? What do we care? Here let me freshen your drink. Look, someone has left a bottle of booze right here in plain sight. What if the little lady with her hatchet should show up and whittle us all down to size?"

"No, thank you Arthur, I am drinking plain orange juice. One reason I do not drink is because I wish to know when I am having a good time. Perhaps you are not aware that Temperance is one of my pet projects," answered her Ladyship.

"Well, I think you had better discush that with the person who has been pouring your drinks then. Becaush I'm sure I smell liquor on your breath er...dress."

"What! Ah, oh, my Lord. The underhanded nerve of that fellow! Churchill must never hear about this."

"My lips are sealed, dear Lady. Next time I have tea with Winston, I will not mention so mush as one word of your carousaling in California. Carousaling? Is that the right word?"

Billy roared with the laughter of too much liquor and Lady Astor joined in. She had drunk just enough of the grape to be loosened up.

"If it were up to me you could have the money tomorrow," she said, laughing and hiccupping at the same time.

"You are a pied piper, Arthur. But no, the solicitors, oh, everything is handled by solicitors, you know. We aren't allowed to make a move without consulting them. It is such a bore. One truly cannot do what one wishes when so much money is involved," said Lady Nancy Astor.

Billy put his arm around her shoulders as if to comfort her for this terrible indignity.

"There, there, my poor pretty Prinshess," he cooed.

They both burst into another laughing fit at the absurdity of it all.

Chapter 26

Nineteen twenty-seven was a banner year for the cause of the Emerick estate.

When Irving went to bed that night he was not thinking about the whereabouts of the remaining copy of John Nicholas Emerick's will. He was thinking about his next sermon as he often did. Irving's life was so attuned to the things of the Lord that they consumed almost his every thought.

Irving stated through out his life that he had seen the Lord Jesus when he was young and that he had been commissioned to preach the Gospel. This vision took a powerful hold of Irving early on and never let loose.

Irving was compiling a list of scriptures dealing with slander. He located thirteen references from the Old Testament and one from Romans in the New Testament. He often stayed up after Anna had gone to bed to work on his sermons and do scriptural research.

He thought afterwards that perhaps the research about slander in the Bible had tweaked his brain to experience the dream it did that night. He felt the Astors had in a way been slandering the Emericks for years, saying there was no proof the Emericks were entitled to anything.

If only J.J. the Fourth would have lived, Irving thought many times. He was a good man. He would have done the right thing.

But when he went to bed he was not thinking of that at all.

Irving had seen John Nicholas Emerick's sea chest when he was a teenager and visited his Aunt Lucinda in Eau Claire, Wisconsin. He asked about the story. Aunt Lucinda said the trunk was upstairs in the attic and he could go look at it but must not bother the trunk. So he only looked at the outside of the old leather chest.

This night Irving had a dream. He dreamed of John Nicholas Emerick's trunk. It was clear to him because he had seen it in the attic almost fifty years before. He dreamed that the will of John Nicholas Emerick was hidden under the lining in the top of the trunk.

The next day Irving made plans to travel to Eau Claire where he knew the trunk was still in the attic of his cousin, Edna Carnahan. He went to see Elsie before he left.

"I've got to go, daughter. I am sure the will is hidden in the top of that trunk. Now that I think of it, Aunt Lucinda might have even said she knew, or suspected, something was hidden there. I was in my teens. It did not mean so much to me at the time. My whole life was ahead of me. Now I'm 63 years old. I would like to see this settled before I die. The Lord is leading me to go to Wisconsin. I have my train ticket."

Elsie was surprised.

"Poppa, do you really think the will is there?"

Irving always threw himself wholeheartedly into any enterprise in which he was engaged. His excitement and enthusiasm did not necessarily convince Elsie. She knew him too well.

"Daughter, I am sure. The Lord would not have given me that dream if it were not so. I will write you as soon as I know."

"All right, Poppa. We will wait to hear from you. Make sure you take a warm coat for the train. It gets cold at night."

Elsie kissed him goodbye. Whatever he was, he was her father and she had always believed in him and loved him. She knew he was extraordinary and eccentric. That did not matter. He was Poppa and he was the only parent she had left. She wished him well on his trip.

Irving's arrival at his cousin Edna's house in Eau Claire was met with some surprise and consternation. Irving was known as the family member who was a bit peculiar. His relatives in the east knew of his fanatical bent and singular nature. From the time he was a teenager and lived with his Aunt Martha after his mother died, his personality was often a topic of conversation among the more distant relatives. Yet, there was a certain amount of respect that must be given to a parson who had published several books and was sought after for his preaching ability. He had to be given his due. Somehow, though, it seemed easier for the general public to revere Rev. Irving Grant Emerick than it was for his own relatives.

Never one to beat around the bush, Irving stated his intention when he had greeted family members at cousin Edna's.

"I tell you the Lord gave me a dream and I know the will of John Nicholas is hidden in the top of the trunk," stated Irving firmly. "Edna, I believe your grandmother knew something was there. She almost told me so."

"That was a long time ago, Irving. You know that trunk has been searched and nothing has been found," countered his cousin.

Edna remembered the stories her mother and grandparents had told about the fortune and her relationship to John Nicholas Emerick. The trunk in the attic was a source of interest as an old relic which belonged to John Nicholas. She would not have thought of ripping it apart to see what it might contain. It would be a sort of sacrilege to desecrate such an old item. She thought the will and his papers might have been left in Germany with his family there. That avenue had been investigated, though, and nothing was found.

Edna's great grandmother, Nancy Emerick, wife of Christopher's son George, had brought the trunk to Eau Claire when she moved there after her husband's death in 1849. Nancy's daughter Lucinda had married Henry Jones. They had had a daughter, Ann Emerick Jones. Ann had married Ben Castle, a Civil War veteran, who had the distinction of being one of the few survivors of the cavalry unit that captured Jefferson Davis. Ann and Ben Castle were the parents of Edna Carnahan, Irving's cousin.

So John Nicholas Emerick's old sea chest made its way to Edna's attic when her parents came to live with her. After her mother died, Edna found a note which was in her grandmother's possessions. It was a note from Christopher.

"Here, Irving, you might be interested in this," Edna said as she passed the note to him during their discussion. It read:

"My 80th birthday. Time takes its toll. My youngest son and I are looking at my mother's Bible, our family chronicle, and also at the suitcase of my brother John Nicholas. John Jacob is the most worthless and darkest crook who ever lived. They do not shy away from anything to get his possessions into their hands, and they have no scruples to hold it. My brother, Valentine, never had experience with them as I had.

Now I am an old man, and would like to know whether my children will see the day for sure when pay-out will come, or whether this remains for another world."

Christopher Emerick

Irving was very interested. He did not know of the note's existence.

"Edna, this is good evidence. Have you showed this to anyone?" said Irving after he had read the note.

"Only to family members."

Edna's daughter arrived then. The family listened to Irving's plea to cut the lining of the lid of the old trunk.

It was discussed, re-discussed and considered every way from Sunday. Someone brought up that it would ruin any antique value of the chest if it were tampered with in that way. Of course, any antique value could never approach the value of the present day holdings of John Nicholas Emerick's estate, as Irving was quick to point out.

At last it was decided to slit open the top of the trunk. It was important to have proper witnesses to this act for future claims of the validity of anything that might be there. Edna made an appointment with their attorney for the following morning.

Edna and Irving carried the old trunk into the lawyer's office. Other legal personnel came into the room in order to be witnesses to the opening. Irving's heart was pounding hard in his chest as the attorney took a pen knife and slit the top lining of the trunk.

One hundred and twelve years after Jonathan, the cabin boy, had fearfully carried the trunk to the dead body of John Nicholas Emerick, the old trunk finally gave up its secrets.

To the astonishment of all present, except Irving, who believed in his dream, there were papers and documents secreted in the top of the old leather trunk. The documents there included the original partnership agreement between John Nicholas Emerick and John Jacob Astor, dated 1787 and signed by both. There was the will setting out the terms of the 90 year trust agreement and naming as heirs the descendants of his brothers Christopher and Valentine.

There were two notebooks that told the story of John Nicholas coming to America. In them were recorded the important happenings of his life and of his business. They told about his cousin Andrew, who lost his life from wounds he received in battle. The journals told how he met John Jacob Astor and how he took him into the fur-trading business.

One excerpt from his diary was this statement:

"Thirty-one years have passed since I brought John Jacob Astor from Baltimore and then to Bowen in New

York with his flutes and without any money. He worked good and in 1787 I made him my partner with one third." March 1815

Also found in the trunk was John Nicholas' Bible and the old hymn book.

Irving picked up the fragile yellowed papers. The ink had faded and the documents were hard to read. Irving asked for a magnifying glass and one was located for him. He read over the will as others chattered and projected opinions about the value of what they had found and how it might affect their lives.

Irving read:

"This is to certify that I, John Nicholas Emerick two-thirds joint partner of John Jacob Astor have left in trust with said partner my estate for a period of 90 years after which time said estate together with the accumulations therefrom shall be given to and divided between the descendants of my two brothers Christopher and Valentine that said heirs shall be advertised for every ten years until found and due settlement made.

"I farther(sic) state John Astor was a poor boy I loaned him money and taught him the business.

"Farther state I value One million dollars and I own ships, and 35 acres of land at New York City, partly inside the present city limits.

"4000 acres of land in the coal belt Berks County, Pennsylvania adjoining Stephen Girard with whom I was once associated in business 300 acres partly in the city of Germantown and other small acreage.

"I have made other legal papers, but fearing Astor as he is not the man I thought when I made him my partner I am leaving papers in my trunk to safeguard my estate.
(Seal)
JOHN NICHOLAS EMERICK
October 24, 1815
Germantown, Penn."

There was a legal description of the 35 acres of land located in New York City. It was described as follows:

"Beginning at the corner formed by the intersection of the East side of Broadway formerly Bloomingdale Road and the North side of West 42nd Street; then running North and along the East side of Broadway, One hundred and four feet three inches; then running East and parallel with West 42nd Street and along the center line of the block between West 43rd and West 42nd Streets. One hundred forty feet nine and three-fourths inches; then running South and parallel with Sixth Avenue and part of the distance through a party wall. One hundred feet five inches to the North side of West 42nd Street; then running West along the said North side of West 42nd Street One hundred and

Twelve feet ten and one-half inches to the corner of intersection or place of beginning."

The documents were written in brown ink, which was later tested for proof of authenticity. The paper and ink were authenticated as being the type used at that time. The signatures of John Nicholas Emerick and John Jacob Astor also were identified as being genuine signatures of those two men.

What a find! Irving telegraphed the discovery of the will to Elsie and Dr. Lynn.

Edna's attorney proceeded with immediate action against the Astors. Now that the will was found, there could be no doubt that the Emericks were entitled to their share of the Astor estate.

The suit that Edna's attorney filed told where the Emerick/Astor money went and to whom it was left since the death of John Jacob Astor I. He had died in 1849, leaving the bulk of his estate to his son William B. Astor, who increased the fortune.

William B. Astor's will was probated in 1875. In it he bequeathed the bulk of the estate to his two sons: John Jacob Astor and William Astor.

William Astor, who married Caroline Schermerhorn, increased the fortune left to him. When he died in 1892 he left his estate to his son John Jacob Astor IV, who married Madeleine Force.

John Jacob Astor IV, when he died in 1912 in the *Titanic* disaster, left the greater part of his fortune to his son William Vincent Astor, when he reached twenty-one years of age in 1913. Vincent was one of the defendants named in the Edna Carnahan lawsuit filed on behalf of the Emericks. Also named was Farmer's Bank and Trust.

The Carnahan suit further proclaimed that in court proceedings in 1902 the Trust of John Nicholas Emerick amounted to $39,000,000 in cash, stocks, bonds, personal and real property and that it has not been accounted for by the Astors.

The suit requested a full and complete accounting of all assets assigned to the Emerick trust, including property and items which they may have disposed of.

Word of the finding of the will spread throughout the land. Newspapers ran front page stories with pictures of the old trunk and the documents contained in it.

By this time, in the fall of 1927, many groups of relatives were organized for this fight. Some were better organized than others. Some of the names were:

The Mississippi Valley Association of John Nicholas Emerick Heirs
Southwestern Ohio Association
Portland, Oregon Association

301

West Coast Association
Northwest Association
Pittsburgh Association—this was the largest and the strongest.
Northeastern Ohio Association

There may have been others. Dr. Lynn belonged to the Mississippi Valley group. Irving, Elsie and their families were active in the West Coast organizations, as well as the Mississippi Valley Group. They conferred regularly with Calvin Hoy, the primary attorney for the Mississippi Valley Association, in which many close relatives in Ohio, Wisconsin and Missouri were active.

Dr. Lynn Emerick, of Ohio, was chairman of the Executive Committee of the Mississippi Valley Association. The letterhead of August 1928 for that group lists fourteen other officers, including William H. Wehking, president, Edna Carnahan, secretary, and three attorneys. The attorneys were: Evan Lewis, Philadelphia, PA; Calvin I. Hoy, St. Louis, MO; and Charles W. Letzgus, Camden, NJ.

Lawyers for the various groups prepared to file lawsuits for their members. Some of them consulted each other and tried to gain the best information for themselves. Others refused to share what information they had. There was a mad scramble among the Emericks and their legal representatives to get in on this treasure which was finally found. The end of the rainbow was in sight. Relatives and would-be relatives suddenly found this fight worth joining.

An article, in a St. Louis newspaper, tells about some of the suits. The article states the heirs of John Nicholas Emerick are seeking a half billion dollars from the Astors. It tells of the finding of the will and mentions 250 heirs who are meeting to plan their strategy.

Calvin Hoy notified the Emerick heirs that he would be starting legal action in the Surrogate Court of Pennsylvania and in the Court of New York by the spring of 1928.

Another article, also in 1927, from a local paper in Elsie's hometown, upped the ante. It stated the Tacoma heirs were seeking $2,500,000,000. Irving, Elsie, Vida and Mabel were all mentioned by name and address.

The article goes on to tell the story of John Nicholas and states that 490 heirs are in planning to have a share of this estate.

In May, 1928, newspapers all over the country carried stories on the legal fight. There were front page headlines in the prominent New York and Philadelphia newspapers, as well as many other papers. Headlines cited the finding of the old will and the suits filed by the Emerick heirs against the Astors.

Several newspapers printed a picture of the old sea chest. Some pictures showed a U.S. Marshall reviewing the contents and pointing to the slit in the lining of the lid. Some were of the sea chest alone and the contents. The old German Bible is pictured along with John Nicholas Emerick's notebooks and hymnal.

Various newspaper articles over the years assign different amounts of value to the John Nicholas estate. The number of heirs also changes drastically in the stories, too. As the stories made their way out in the magazines and newspapers more and more "Emericks" turned up. By the nineteen thirties some newspapers were citing as many as fifteen hundred heirs.

In December 1927, Dr. Lynn stated he was receiving fifteen to twenty-five letters a day regarding the case.

As 1928 dawned Dr. Lynn wrote Brother Irving an optimistic letter, January 14, 1928. In it he talks about lawyers fees.

"I am told it is up to the court to fix his (Hoy's) and the other attorneys remuneration in this. But do not know for sure whither that will hold or not as laws differ in different states. However, Hoy, I believe is honest enough if he can get the other attorneys that are necessary in the case in order to bring it to a successful termination to consent for less remuneration he will gladly do so. Your attorney out there talks like he would take it for 5%. In the wind up, the chances are Hoy will get much less than that. He said if he got 1/2 of 1% out of it he would be tickled most out of his shoes.

"But we must have some other attorneys and some of the best that can be had and they demand big returns. This is no little affair. And big propositions are not cheap propositions."

He went on to mention cousin Vernon, or V.J. as he was known. V.J. was not able to make it to the last meeting of the Association. Dr. Lynn felt not enough notice was given to allow some from the West to arrive in Chicago. This is the first mention of V.J. Perhaps cousin V.J. felt he was not treated fairly by the Association. Later his actions become a trouble for the heirs. A few of the Emerick family members chose to go it alone and ended up possibly fouling the porridge for all.

About this time, Irving became disenchanted with Calvin Hoy. Mr. Hoy had not filed the claims in the courts as he promised to do in September. Irving became impatient and hired an attorney named Oscar Zabel who had offices in the Dexter Horton Building in Seattle.

Dr. Lynn reported in a letter of January 27, 1928, that Hoy had been on a fact-finding trip in the east. He was finding out many things that had not been known in the past. Some of the other attorneys entered faulty

information about who was related to John Nicholas
Emerick and who was not. Mr. Hoy reported he had
between twelve and fifteen hundred letters that were
demanding an immediate answer. On his trip he
found interest very high. He had written and asked
five heirs to meet him in Philadelphia and seventy-five
people had shown up.

Hoy was organizing all the Associations and trying "to
get the largest law firm in New York to take a hold of
our proposition. A firm that handles the Rockefeller
interests."

While on his trip in the east Hoy found "many of the
(court) clerks nauseated at the method a lot of people,
some of them attorneys, had used into order to get or
try to get data from records. And that Vincent Astor
had become so thoroughly disgusted that he had gone
to Europe. There seem to be so many who want to
take things in their own hands...a group of heirs in
New York...not willing to affiliate with us, but boast big
they are going to see this estate is settled at once...It
is enough to disgust the best of people."

In addition, Hoy reported he had found evidence that
Valentine had been married three times and had
twenty children.

Dr. Lynn also mentioned that he had been told that
Irving had started a lawsuit against Hoy for not
proceeding fast enough. Ever loyal, Dr. Lynn told the

person that he was misinformed—his brother would not do that.

By March Dr. Lynn received solid information from a German Bible, that Konrad was not John Nicholas's father, John Daniel was. He thought the case was in good shape and that the evidence shows the family's relationship and "we are sitting pretty."

He advised Irving to say as little as possible. There are many wild goose chases going on. The attorneys are continually being sent information and when they or Hoy trace it down it is not true. Dr. Lynn thought the opposition was setting up these scenarios in order to exhaust the patience and the money of the rightful heirs.

Dr. Lynn was sure his family was the correct one. Otherwise, why would "our grandfather hold the trunk and will of John Nicholas." He advised Irving to go easy on the attorneys and not be in such a hurry.

He wondered if Irving was living with Elsie and Roy because the newspaper article they sent listed him at the same address, and what had become of the Norwegian frowling (Anna)? He expected Lynn liked his big bank job and wanted to know how Arthur was doing?

Arthur was back at KOMO radio in Seattle. He eased back into his old time slot and again garnered a large radio audience who loved his songs and patter. He was known as Billy Emerick on his radio show. His adventure in California was just that. He decided he would remain in the Seattle area for a few more years at least until after the Emerick/Astor suit was settled. Then the world might be his oyster. He did like the sunny climate in southern California. He decided it was better for him to be a big fish in a small pond in Seattle, than to be a tiny, unnoticed fish in the rough and tumble world of the Hollywood entertainment industry.

A Seattle newspaper ran an article about Billy being an Emerick heir.

The headline read: "Who Wouldn't Sing in a Case Like This."

The article called him "the man with the million-dollar voice." The story claimed Billy had been advised his share of the Emerick fortune would be two million dollars. Billy maintained he would not leave his radio program even if he obtained the money.

He said, "It wouldn't be justice to the fans or myself to drop my radio work at all because I like to sing, and if I can provide a little happiness for others with my songs and novelty numbers, I'll keep on doing it." Billy said he would not give up his radio program even if he receives the money. "Besides, I haven't gotten the two million yet."

The article went on to say Billy stated emphatically Seattle will always be his home and that may mean "Seattle will not lose one of its favorite radio artists even though he becomes a millionaire."

No doubt Billy meant his statement at the time.

Another newspaper article, from a Tacoma paper, announced Billy would be entertaining at the Tacoma Advertising Club's luncheon meeting at the Winthrop Hotel. It called him a "popular pianist."

While in Hollywood, Arthur/Billy Emerick had some glamour pictures taken and sent one to Elsie and Roy. He signed it in a beautiful flowing script.

John Nicholas Emerick's will was discovered hidden in the lining of his old trunk. Illustration by Angie Rose.

Eaton O. Oct 4th. 28

2,

Arthur told Mrs. when we was out there about meeting Lady Astor in Calif. two years ago and about her stating they wanted to settle, that it was so expensive to keep up the estate. That that they had spent thousands of dollars advertising for the heirs.

That would be very valuable evidence for Hoy and us. I wrote to Arthur to give me a statement of what she stated to him. And he never answered me at to that. Hoy & Weakling have both tried to get a statement from him, but he would not give it.

When he was in Calif this last time the Mr Teraft he stopped with finally got why he would not tell. They were all drunk. Drunk or not drunk. it is very valuable information to us. And I would have written to him long ago but did not know his address. If he wants to help the Emericks out and not the Astor

In this letter of October 6, 1928, Dr. Lynn discusses Arthur and Lady Astor.

However you may tell your group or read this letter to them. If all knew what we do there would be a great shout go up from camp and some even would cry for joy. We are going to win. We may have to carry it to the supreme court, But if that is necessary then to the supreme court we go.

But rest assured we who are carrying on this fight know now, we are not fighting a lost cause. Of course we have all made mistakes, But experience is a great teacher and our case is getting stronger all the time. We will go into next court twice as strong as in the one just gone through. Every thing humanly possible is being done on both sides, But we have the data, the information the goods on them, and they are fighting a losing fight and we know it, I do not believe they have one chance in a million.

On April 17, 1929, Dr. Lynn wrote this positive letter to his brother, Irving. He states, "We are going to win." He does not think the Astors "have one chance in a million."

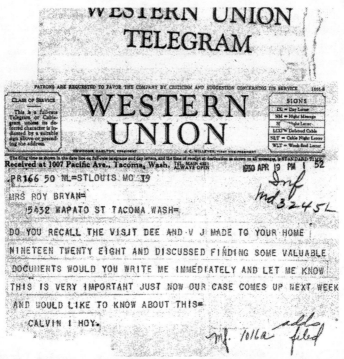

This is a copy of a telegram to Elsie from Calvin Hoy, attorney, regarding Dee and V. J. It was sent on April 19, 1930.

THROUGH AN AGREEMENT, A STRIFE FOR INHERITANCE WHICH HAS LASTED FOR A NUMBER OF YEARS HAS BEEN SETTLED BETWEEN THE ASTOR FAMILY AND THE HEIRS TO THE FOUNDER OF THE ASTOR DYNASTY, JOHAN JAKOB ASTORS PARTNER EMERICK. HE HAS TEN HEIRS IN DORPAT AND NOT LESS THAN THREE HUNDRED FIFTY HEIRS IN GERMANY WHO HAVE EACH RECEIVED A SUM OF $120,000.

Irving's second wife, Anna, saw this article in the Seattle Swedish newspaper, April 24, 1930. Irving had it translated and typed it on a card.

Dorothy Bryan Morris and Harold Morris, 1931.

5432 SOUTH WAPATO   PHONE MAD. 3245-L.

ROY BRYAN
CANDIDATE FOR
CONSTABLE

SUBJECT TO THE REPUBLICAN PRIMARIES SEPT. 14, 1926

Roy ran for constable in Tacoma in 1926.

Roy and Elsie Bryan, circa 1932.

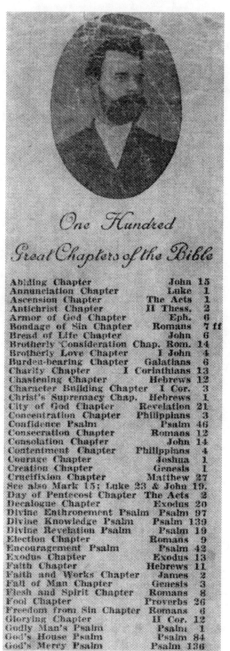

One Hundred
Great Chapters of the Bible

Abiding Chapter	John 15
Annunciation Chapter	Luke 1
Ascension Chapter	The Acts 1
Antichrist Chapter	II Thess. 2
Armor of God Chapter	Eph. 6
Bondage of Sin Chapter	Romans 7 ff
Bread of Life Chapter	John 6
Brotherly Consideration Chap.	Rom. 14
Brotherly Love Chapter	I John 4
Burden-bearing Chapter	Galatians 6
Charity Chapter	I Corinthians 13
Chastening Chapter	Hebrews 12
Character Building Chapter	I Cor. 3
Christ's Supremacy Chap.	Hebrews 1
City of God Chapter	Revelation 21
Concentration Chapter	Philippians 3
Confidence Psalm	Psalm 46
Consecration Chapter	Romans 12
Consolation Chapter	John 14
Contentment Chapter	Philippians 4
Courage Chapter	Joshua 1
Creation Chapter	Genesis 1
Crucifixion Chapter	Matthew 27
See also Mark 15; Luke 23 & John 19.	
Day of Pentecost Chapter	The Acts 2
Decalogue Chapter	Exodus 20
Divine Enthronement Psalm	Psalm 97
Divine Knowledge Psalm	Psalm 139
Divine Revelation Psalm	Psalm 19
Election Chapter	Romans 9
Encouragement Psalm	Psalm 42
Exodus Chapter	Exodus 13
Faith Chapter	Hebrews 11
Faith and Works Chapter	James 2
Fall of Man Chapter	Genesis 3
Flesh and Spirit Chapter	Romans 8
Fool Chapter	Proverbs 26
Freedom from Sin Chapter	Romans 6
Glorying Chapter	II Cor. 12
Godly Man's Psalm	Psalm 1
God's House Psalm	Psalm 84
God's Mercy Psalm	Psalm 136

Irving's Bible Bookmark

Irving Emerick, in his back yard in Tacoma, circa 1940.

Harry Bryan, left, and Roy Bryan on a downtown Tacoma street, circa 1950. The Republican and the Democrat.

Dr. Lynn and his second wife, Loveda, in Elsie and Roy's yard. The white picket fence and whitewashed rocks line the driveway in the background. Circa 1952.

Chapter 27

Irving and his wife, Anna, were living near Elsie and Roy in South Tacoma. He used Elsie's address for estate information purposes. He was just not sure what Anna would do with the mail. She did not read English and she was getting forgetful.

He dropped by to see Elsie one morning. She had received some mail for him from Mr. Hoy. She handed it to him.

"It's the heir ship papers, Poppa. I received mine and have been working on filling them out. I think we have all the information. We have to send proof," said Elsie.

Irving tore open the letter from Dr. Lynn which accompanied the heir ship papers.

"He says there is nothing new on the estate. All are working as rapidly as possible. I don't think Hoy is working as rapidly as he could and what's more I think he may be in cahoots with the Astors."

"Why, Poppa, how could you think that? Mr. Hoy has worked harder than anyone. He is the one who verified things in Germany and in the east. We are lucky to have someone so interested in this case. He believes in it."

"Humph. Well, maybe he does and maybe he doesn't. Maybe we are all being taken for a ride. It should not take this long. The will is available. It has been ruled to be the actual will of John Nicholas. Why should it take so long? These attorneys want it to take a long time. That is why and nothing else."

Elsie did not answer as she knew it was futile to try to change his mind. He had made it up and was determined not to let her or anyone else change his opinion.

As a part of the verification they must provide, they had made affidavits before a notary giving their lineage and listing all the places they had ever lived and for how long.

In addition, Irving had papers from his father. There were originals of birth and marriage records of his parents and a listing of how they were related to Christopher and where they had lived, signed by his father. Irving had persuaded his father years before his death to entrust this important material to him. Irving had always been the one most interested in the story and the possible fortune. He was now very glad he had these papers. They would be needed later on. The originals were what would count if this ever had to go to court.

"Elsie, I'm going to leave these papers here with you. I am not sure about Anna. She might just throw them in the fire," said Irving as he handed her a large, old, torn envelope with the family papers.

"All right, Poppa, I'll take care of them." Elsie put the papers where she kept important things—in her little brown leather suitcase.

Elsie received a letter from Dee. She was still so fond of her younger brother. He wanted to move to the Northwest like some of the rest of his family. He had quit his job on the police force in St. Louis and come west to seek his fortune. The letter was from Medford, Oregon. He said he had a good job doing long-distance hauling to Portland and San Francisco. He was looking for something better, as he thought long-haul trucking was too hard.

Dee heard that Elsie might be making a trip to St. Louis. He expressed the hope that she would go there. Then she could bring information back to him direct. Dee asked something special of Elsie. He wanted her to talk to his wife, Grace, while she was in St. Louis. Grace did not want to come west. Elsie thought Grace put on airs above her station in life, but she would never have said that to Dee. Grace absolutely refused to leave St. Louis. Dee felt sure they could do much better in the Northwest. His job in St. Louis had not been good enough for Grace and he was trying to make life better for both of them. He was considering a job on the new Southern Pacific bus line or possibly, he said, he might buy a good filling station.

"Let me know what Grace tells you right away through mail from St. Louis, so I will know, as I sure am lonesome as these are all old people but they have been good to me. Will close with Love to all.

Your Bro Dee"

Around the same time, Elsie received a handwritten letter from attorney Calvin Hoy from Philadelphia. He shared with her his disappointment that some information they had counted on had not worked out. He was fearful about the case, but cautioned her not to let the Astors know that.

Elsie and Irving completed their papers a few days later and mailed them to Dr. Lynn as instructed.

He replied with a letter requesting they sign notarized powers of attorney for him to vote for them in Chicago at the coming meeting of the Mississippi Valley Association.

Roy, Elsie and Irving talked it over and decided Elsie needed to attend the meeting herself. She was planning a trip to St. Louis to see her remaining family there anyway. Dr. Lynn responded in a letter, July 30, 1928, and said he was glad Elsie was coming. He assured them they did not need to be concerned about the estate.

"Don't need to worry over the outcome of the estate. Think it is about over except the shout. As soon as the Court approves of claims. I think Astors will be ready to settle. Mrs. joins in sending love and best wishes to all.

"L.R.E.

"P.S. Another thing you stated in that letter…that father said he did not believe the estate could be settled. You did not carry that far enough. Father said "till the time come or the trust agreement run out." He told Oris that he would not live to get it, but that Oris should. And I think he told we children that also. So you better explain that. You see these few things dropped here and there if we are not careful will be damaging. And on the witness stand might be a little embarrassing to explain. We hope this whole thing won't have to be thrashed out in court. But if necessary to win it must. There has been too much money spent on this already to stop short of going clear to the bottom.

"Sincerely, L.R.E.*"*

In this letter, Dr. Lynn gently scolded his brother for his actions. It was the beginning of a continuing dialogue along the same lines.
s
Dr. Lynn and Olivia had just come in from an October afternoon of squirrel hunting. It was a favorite pastime. It got them out into the woods for a

refreshing stroll. Today Olivia shot one and Dr. Lynn shot two. There would be squirrel stew for dinner tonight.

They took off their boots and sat down for a few minutes. Later Olivia would tend the squirrels and Dr. Lynn would clean their twenty-two caliber rifles. The mail had come through the slot and was lying on the floor next to the front door. Dr. Lynn picked it up, opened a letter from Irving and read it.

He shook his head back and forth.

"Livy, sometimes that older brother of mine makes me so mad. What is wrong with him? Ever since I remember, he was always in a disagreement with somebody. He seems to be getting worse."

"What is it now, Lynn. You have been so patient with him."

"First off, he's upset because Jack Emerick is getting paid by the Association. Why, Jack has been working full time on the estate for months. A man has to have money to take care of his family. The Association is only paying him $150 a month and out of that he pays about $60 to his stenographer. Jack's letter yesterday said he was 400 letters behind and has been in the hospital for two weeks from exhaustion. I, for one, am glad he is willing to do it. I can't do it. Can't spare anymore time from my practice and keep it going. I can barely keep up with all the letters from heirs, and having them show up at the door takes so much time. I know Hoy has shortened his life by years working for us so hard. No, I could not do it."

"Of course not, dear. You know how Irving is. He was born with a burr under his saddle for sure. I often wondered how Ella put up with him. Oh, he's smart enough. But he has never been easy. Is he still with that Norwegian woman?"

"He doesn't mention her anymore. Makes me wonder. He thinks I'm keeping things back from him. Now why would I do that, Livy?"

"Well, you wouldn't, dear. Don't let him get you all worked up."

"He either can't or won't get Arthur to do his duty by the family."

"As I said before, Arthur looked me in the eye and told me he had met Lady Nancy Astor at a party in Hollywood and she told him the Astors wanted to settle the case. It was becoming too expensive and they had spent thousands of dollars dealing with it," said Olivia.

"I know. It's a shame Arthur wants to stick up for the Astors instead of his own family. Well, at least we know his reason now. That friend he stayed with in California said Arthur told him they were both drunk and he could not testify to anything that went on between him and the Countess. It would sure help our case if he would testify. I wrote Irving before to get Arthur to a notary and get a statement from him. Drunk or not drunk, it is very valuable information to us. If I had his address, I would have written to Arthur by now. Irving washes his hands of the whole thing. I know they haven't spoken for years, but this is important. We can't have too much evidence."

"I am so surprised that sweet little Arthur would do this. I *know* he was telling me the truth. I have never known him to lie and I looked into his eyes. Do you think there might be another reason? Arthur is a very handsome man." Olivia said.

"You are daft, Livy. Lady Astor is old enough to be his mother and from all I've heard she is one tough woman. You may be right though. There may be another reason.

"We may end up having to go to the Supreme Court after this next go around. Our attorneys had that hearing on September 25th and the Astors was to have a hearing yesterday. It looks like it may end up being a close shave. I've told Irving everything I know. He just does not understand how these things are played out. Brother Bert won't even answer Irving's letters anymore, he is so tired of the religious harangues."

It was three-thirty in the afternoon and the doorbell rang. They looked through the sheer curtains on the window of the door.

They were a little apprehensive of strangers at the door since their good friends, another doctor and his wife, were shot dead by a burglar recently.

"Oh dear, now who is that? Is it anyone you know?" asked Olivia.

"Can't say it is."

"I'll go see what he wants. Office hours don't start until six. Now you remember that, Lynn."

Olivia opened the door and asked, "Are you a patient or an heir?"

The middle-aged man at the door looked puzzled.

"I'm not either one that I know of yet," he said.

"Oh, I am sorry. It has been so hectic around here lately," she smiled. "How can we help you?"

"I know it's not office hours, but I have to catch a train at six. I heard Dr. Emerick treats diabetics," said the stranger.

"Well, I'm sorry, but the doctor is not available just now," said Olivia.

"Nonsense, my dear, show the gentleman in. How are you, sir?" said Dr. Lynn coming up beside her still in his hunting clothes and slippers.

Olivia left in a bit of a huff to go take care of the squirrels. They would be easier to deal with than her overworked husband.

Following a meeting in Chicago with Mr. Hoy and other attorneys Dr. Lynn wrote a strong plea to his brother Irving about Arthur in a letter dated October 22, 1928.

"We have won two big fights so far and two smaller ones with the Astor attorneys. They tried to have our first bill of complaint thrown out. That was two big victories. Then they tried to make it appear we had been neglectful, not only for us, but that our forefathers were. Since they and we knew this estate existed.

"But we can come back at them and claim they have never advertised as the will and contract both stipulated, i.e., the contract of the articles of the trust. They were to have advertised every 10 years at the end of the trust period and every ten years thereafter till the heirs were found.

"We have failed to find a single instance when they have advertised…They have five attorneys of high standing to fight us. And they are bringing ever jot and tittle of evidence they have against us and we are in very great danger of losing our case. Now we must have all the evidence in every way, shape and form we can against them.

"Arthur's conversation with Countess Astor is some evidence which is very weighty in so much as she admitted the estate belonged to us. And stated they wanted to settle. Now listen, you have him go before a Notary and make an affidavit to every word that passed between them. The exact circumstances and all. This is a fight of life and death with us. If we lose, we have lost a fortune…And we must not let a speck of evidence we have against them go by default. So regardless of what they might do to Arthur and his job we must have that conversation in black and white. And have Arthur forward me same by airmail. He must not hesitate. He must line himself and his evidence with us. We, i.e., Hoy and our attorneys, are very hopeful of winning the case. But we are just beginning to realize the hard fight we have. And we cannot afford to lose at any cost.

"I am sorry I do not have Arthur's address. So you get this letter off to him with an earnest appeal to him to make out affidavit of the conversation between them. Mr. Hoy said it would have lots of weight with the judge. And he agreed to show it to the judge without ever making it public or giving the Astors or their attorneys any chance to see it. Just like a lot of evidence he is giving the judge to help influence his decision in our favor. He has had a number of conferences with the judge and has access to him at any time. Says he is a man of very high type and wants to see us win.

"But we must get all our facts and all our evidence before him. Some, of course, will be public property, but some will not. So Arthur you do not need to worry a minute about this getting in their hands. Now do this at your very earliest possible. And get to me.

"Please do not delay and please do not desert us. You have hundreds to gain and nothing to lose. And you can trust Hoy to the limit. I think more of him every time I see him. Love and best wishes to all. We are fine, not much sickness. Mrs. joins with lots of love to all.

"L.R.E"

Irving had read Dr. Lynn's letter to Elsie and Roy.

"He needn't think I am going to contact Arthur over this. I have told him how I feel about Arthur. He is practically dead to me. The idea that I would encourage a son of mine to testify that he was drunk with a member of the British Parliament! Satan has his clutches on Arthur and I'll not advertise it. He has been a willful child all of his life. He would not listen to me in any case," said Irving.

"If he's dead to you, how come you take the money he sends, Parson?" said Roy.

"It's only his duty. Children should take care of their parents. You know that, Roy. You helped to care for your mother for years."

"Yes, I did and I would do it again. It's a little different situation though, if you ask me. You and Arthur ought to patch things up and not just because of the estate. You ain't getting any younger," said Roy.

"Poppa, I could write to Arthur. This is important. Let me send Uncle Lynn's letter on to him. Then he can decide," said Elsie.

"You'd best stay out of it, daughter. If the Lord means for us to have the estate money, and I believe he does, then we will prevail despite Arthur's behavior. No, you just let it ride."

Dr. Lynn tried again in November and December to get Arthur's address or cooperation in letters to Brother Irving. He and Olivia had been in a car wreck. They were broad sided at a stoplight by another car. It was not his fault, Dr. Lynn reported. He had the right of way, but the other fellow ran the light. Olivia had broken her ankle in two places. She was "lying in bed singing and whistling as if she had a good leg. She laughed and said, 'Well, why not?' Taking care of the Mrs. and doing the housework and cooking and my practice all keeps me pretty busy and I don't mean maybe."

He was also still busy with estate business and hoped it would not mean going to trial with the Astors. In addition, he was running for county coroner.

By December, Judge Thatcher had "passed the buck" and sent the case on up to Federal Circuit Court. Dr. Lynn thought the judge was like Arthur: afraid. He would be very much ashamed of his nephew if "he does not stand by our guns."

Throughout 1927 and 1928, newspapers across the country had many stories concerning the fight for the estate. Articles with large headlines appeared in several New York and Philadelphia newspapers as well as in papers in Portland, Oregon, Seattle and Tacoma, Washington, St. Louis, Missouri, and in Wisconsin and other states. Some of the stories sounded very favorable toward the Emerick cause. Some reflected an attitude that the upstart Emericks were trying to cheat the most worthy Astor family out of their rightful fortune. Something for everyone. Take your pick.

An item in a well-known magazine of the time, proclaimed the millions of the Astor family might disappear. The article stated that documents recently discovered seemed to show conclusively that two-thirds of the Astor millions belonged to the heirs of John Nicholas Emerick. According to the article, the legal charges were that Astor not only had taken the third which belonged to him but, also, the two-thirds which belonged to Emerick. While the article recognized the rights of the Emerick family to reclaim their part of the estate, the writer stated doubt that this would happen.

Chapter 28

Calvin I. Hoy, attorney at law, first heard of the Emerick case in March 1925. Little did he realize how his eventual obsession with the case would alter his life over the next seven years.

A client of his mentioned the case to him in the course of discussing another matter. She kept referring to the Emerick case. He realized he had never heard a story just like this. Oh, he had heard of other old cases that may have been similar, but he had never given them any consideration. However, there was something about this case that fascinated him.

He decided to look into the story. After some investigation on his part, he determined the case appeared to have merit. Not only that, but Hoy was a breed of attorney that some fear may be nearly extinct. He sensed an injustice had been done to the Emerick family. He attacked the injustice with the zeal of a crusader. It was a classic David and Goliath scenario. It was so appealing to fight on the side of right. It made the heart swell and the palms sweat just thinking about a possible victory.

Hoy was not immune to an ultimate fat payoff at the end of this quest. In 1925, he was married and had three young children. Like any husband and father he aspired to provide the best living he could for his family. His office in the Commercial Building at Sixth and Olive in St. Louis did not lack for clients. But this case excited his imagination like no other. While his motivation was not pure altruism, it was something close. He believed in the cause. He loved the mystery. He salivated to solve it.

The fact that most of the events important to this case took place over 100 years ago added a challenge which Hoy found irresistible. The Emericks were fortunate to have had a man of his dedication to lead their fight for so many years with so little remuneration. Over the years, he had struggled with this case. He had agonized over it. At times, he was not sure whether he could or should continue. Yet, like one of those punching bags that is knocked down and comes right back up in your face, Hoy rebounded, time and time again.

When he first began on this case, he had not seen any documentation to verify any of the story. The will had not been found or the journals or the Bible. He quickly discovered an attorney named Thompsen had worked on this case off and on for a number of years, beginning in 1903. He used some of that information to build on.

He undertook travel to the east coast to search for the whereabouts of John Nicholas Emerick's grave and to verify where he may have lived. He visited many, many courthouses, cemeteries and county seats in his tireless research. During his search, he received some documents from Edna Carnahan. With these, he was able to locate John Nicholas's burial place. He spoke with the grandson of the first undertaker in Philadelphia, and discussed the records he had received from Edna with the grandson. Hoy satisfied himself the documents Edna sent were in keeping with the kind used in those days and were authentic.

He uncovered letters and city records testifying to the truth of the Emerick story. Then the will and other papers were found in the trunk. Things began to look even more hopeful. As a wave of euphoria passed through the Emerick ranks, Hoy rode the crest.

As time passed, more and more Emericks joined the various associations. Each had their own lawyers. Hoy met with and spoke to many of the groups. He filed motions and prepared briefs. By early 1929, he had been away from home nine months out of twelve. One of his children was now in high school. He sold the family car to meet expenses. The Mississippi Valley Association chipped in with extra money to help him meet financial obligations. Dr. Lynn was instrumental in arranging for this. He asked members to send from one to ten dollars a month. Not all of the members were pleased. Irving particularly had a hard time accepting the need to contribute even more money for Hoy.

It was about this time that Hoy was contacted from Germany by a man named Koerber, who purported to be representing a group of relatives of John Nicholas Emerick from Germany.

These were relatives of John Nicholas's half brother, Solomon. No where were they mentioned in John Nicholas's will or trust agreement. Regardless, they filed to claim part of the fortune. They were to play a much larger part than Calvin Hoy ever imagined in the Astor-Emerick saga.

Koerber provided some additional letters, which were found in Germany. He willingly sent these to Hoy. They were very helpful to the case. Hoy, therefore, saw Koerber as an ally in this endeavor.

Hoy wanted to have a look at the documents mentioned in John Nicholas's letter of November 1816, which said he had left papers at The Hague, Holland, for safekeeping. The last court decision had cited numerous laches, or omissions, in the Emerick brief. Hoy was hoping the documents at The Hague would help illuminate some of the unanswered questions in this case.

On March 20, 1929, Hoy sent a cable to Koerber in Germany asking if he could go to The Hague and get the documents.

Koerber answered in a cable the following day saying he would go to The Hague and send certified copies to Hoy immediately.

What happened next was nothing. Hoy sent cables and cables, but no papers arrived. Finally, Hoy went to Washington, D.C. and spoke with the Ambassador from Holland and the United States Assistant Secretary of State. The Ambassador, who happened to be a woman, advised him someone should go to Holland and take care of the matter as to try to obtain the papers from the United States would require a great deal of red tape.

Hoy knew he must file an appeal to the latest court decision. He had only 90 days to file an appeal and many of those days had already passed. The Ambassador from Holland gave him the name of the Keeper of the State Archives and said it was likely some information could be obtained from him.

There was nothing to do but go himself. He lost no time. As soon as he could, after going home and attending to a few matters, he booked passage on a ship. He went to New York and sailed for Holland on the first of April 1929. The ship was a slow boat to Holland. He did not arrive until the middle of April. He immediately contacted the Consul, who put him in touch with the Dutch Secretary of State.

Hoy wired Koerber to meet him at The Hague. To his surprise, Hoy received a wire back stating Koerber could not meet him on that day because of his religion. Hoy was astounded to realize Koerber was Jewish. He was not aware that John Nicholas's father had remarried a Jewish woman and that his half-brother, Solomon, and his relatives were Jewish.

Now, Hoy had no more prejudice than many others did in those times. As much as we may not like to admit it today, it was common at that time for people in the United States to call those of a different nationality by a slang name, such as, Wops for Italians, Degos for Mexicans, Krauts for Germans, Niggers for Blacks, Japs for Japanese, Chinx for Chinese, Poleskis or Pollocks for Polish people, Jarheads for Swedes and Kikes for Jews.

In the United States at that time, there was not the dangerous backlash against Jews that there was in Europe, especially in Germany, where the Jewish businessmen had a strangle hold on much of the German economy. Relations between the Jewish people and the Germans were becoming very strained. While prejudice was not so rampant against Jews in the United States, there was a definite distance between Jews and non-Jews.

It meant something to Hoy when he found out he was dealing with an Orthodox Jew. It brought him up short and made him consider their relationship in a little different light. This man was not exactly like him. He was considered different enough for Hoy to adjust his thinking. Suddenly the man's motives became suspect. It was well known that Jews always had a money motive. Or that is what passed through Hoy's mind.

The Consul kidded him about the time he would have dealing with an Orthodox Jew. The implication was that if a Jew and money were involved Hoy had better look out. He now wondered if he could trust this man who had been so helpful.

Hoy wired Koerber to come to The Hague. He would not come, nor would he say what had happened to the John Nicholas Emerick papers, which were missing from the file and no longer kept safe at The Hague, as John Nicholas had hoped. Someone had removed the papers recently, according to the Keeper of the State Archives. He could not account for how they had gone missing. They simply were no longer where they had been kept for over 100 years.

Hoy could get no satisfaction from Koerber. He decided he must go to Cologne, Germany and try to see Koerber from there.

The Consul at Cologne assigned an interpreter to go with him. They tried to make an appointment for Hoy to see him, but Koerber was evasive.

Hoy told the Consul, "I am going to his town and see him if I get killed. I did not come 4,000 miles to be sidetracked like this."

The Consul reminded him, "race prejudices run higher in Europe than they do in the United States."

"I understand. I have been warned time and time again. I am determined to go regardless of the consequences," replied Hoy.

Finally, it was agreed that Hoy and Koerber would meet at the office of an attorney, Hildebrand, in Essen. When they arrived Koerber tried to keep the interpreter out of the conference. He said one of the attorneys could speak English and the interpreter was not needed.

The interpreter answered adamantly that the American Consul had sent him to look after the interests of Hoy, who was an American citizen, and he was going wherever Hoy went.

As it turned out, it was a very good thing the interpreter stayed. Although Koerber tried one more time to exclude him as they entered the conference room, the young man would not be deterred from his duty.

The discussion centered around the documents each group had. It was agreed to put both parties' documents out on the table. Hoy was prepared to allow them to look at the documents he had with him. However, the Jews presented nothing and then a hot argument in German ensued. The interpreter was able to explain they did not actually have the documents in question. They had already been shipped to New York.

The interpreter said to Hoy, "The documents are with a man named Snitzler in New York. Do you know him?"

"I know of him," answered Hoy.

"Well, that is where your documents are and you might as well go home. You will not get anything further along these lines here," advised the interpreter.

Hoy's mind was whirling. He had come all this way to track down documents that were at this moment in New York City, whence he had just come. He had put up with two weeks of travel on a slow boat, days of jockeying back and forth with Koerber and more travel just to get an audience, and now it was all for naught. He put his head in his hands and wondered if he could keep his sanity. Why would Koerber do this to him? What was his motive? Were the Jews, as well as the Astors, sending him on wild-goose chases to use up the Emerick heirs' money and patience? Well, his patience was certainly being tested and as for money, he had not seen much of that lately. The Emerick heirs had helped finance this trip. They would want to see results. He knew he could look forward to another angry letter from Irving when this became known.

Riding back on the train, the young interpreter, who had by now developed a sense of curiosity about the case, asked Hoy, "What do you know about this Snitzler? Who is he?"

Hoy sighed, "This is the strangest thing. Before I left home I went to see the German Consul in New York City. I told him about the case and how I was trying to obtain information from Koerber and could receive no reply. He sent me to see his attorney. And who do you suppose that was? His name was Mr. Snitzler. That is not a name one would forget, is it?

"When I met with Snitzler he seemed quite interested and said, 'Oh yes, there was a decree entered a number of years ago in this matter.' I pressed him for further details of the decree he was talking about. He called it an Emerick decree. He became very short with me after that and ended the interview."

When they arrived back at the Consulate in Cologne, both Hoy and the interpreter signed affidavits attesting to what had happened on their trip.

Early the next morning, Hoy received a call at the hotel asking him to return to Essen for further talks.

He said, "Nothing doing!"

So Koerber came to him. They met at Hoy's hotel. Koerber said they had decided to throw in with Hoy and his constituents. They had decided it was the best thing they could do. Koerber said he would prepare a letter which would help Hoy get the papers when he arrived back in New York. So Hoy carried the letter and his high hopes across the ocean and back to New York.

But it was not to be. When Hoy reached New York, there was a cable from Koerber stating they had changed their minds. They planned to settle with the documents they had independently of Hoy. They were making a deal with the Astors.

The gall rose in Hoy's throat.

"Why, those Jews have no more claim to this inheritance than I do. They got into this fuss just to bargain and see what else they could claim for themselves. They betrayed me. Their game was to drive a hard bargain," thought Hoy.

Hoy did what he was trained to do. He went back to work to answer the omissions in the court decision which had been appealed. He spent long hard days in the law library. He cited 168 cases and he read about twice that many to find them. The brief was ready by the agreed time.

Koerber contacted Hoy again. They both accused the other of duplicity. Letters and cables flew back and forth. Hoy was incensed at Koerber's betrayal. Then their relationship ceased for several weeks. In fact Hoy hardly heard from anyone. He had already had his scolding letter from Irving. If only that man could understand the intricacies of working out such a tremendous settlement. Taking away a fortune that had been in the hands of the Astor family for over one hundred years was a neat trick if one could pull it off. He still believed in the rightness of the cause—and by damn he was going to keep trying.

Chapter 29

Elsie was at home alone in the house on Wapato Street in Tacoma. She had just taken two apple pies out of the oven when she heard a knock at the door. She could see familiar shapes through the glass. She wiped her hands on her apron and quickly opened the door.

"Why, Dee, V.J., what a surprise!" Elsie gave her younger brother a big hug.

"What are you fellas doing in Tacoma?" she asked as she ushered them into the living room and invited them to take a seat.

"We just thought we'd drop by and see you, Sis. How's Roy and the children?" said Dee.

When she thought about it later, Elsie remembered he looked a little nervous. And V.J. was very quiet. After the initial greetings, V.J. sat and picked at his pants leg and adjusted his tie. They both wore dark suits, vests and ties, as men did in those days when they went out visiting.

"We are all fine. Just fine. Did you hear Billy is married again?" asked Elsie, eager to share family news.

"Yes, yes, I heard," said Dee. "Have you met her?"

346

"We did. Her name is Noreen. A pretty name for a pretty woman. She seems nice, too."

"Well, let's hope she's better than that last one he had. Grace is out here with me now, Sis. I think the talk you had with her that time you were back there helped convince her to give it a try. She doesn't like it out here like I do though. She misses her ma."

"Well, give her time, Dee."

"Thing is, I'd like to get into something where I could make more money. Grace, she's a good spender, if you know what I mean.

"Me and V.J. we got a line on something."

Elsie turned to V.J. becoming aware of his silence. "How's your family, V.J.? I know Poppa would love to see you. Can you stay a while? He often comes over in the afternoon."

"Well, we cain't stay too long, Elsie. My folks is all fine. Don't see 'em much though." V.J. shifted his position on the couch.

"See, I was wonderin' what sort of papers you or your Poppa got on the estate. You know, on the claim against the Astors. I got something I think would help settle it. We, Dee and me, we was wondering what those papers were my granddad gave to your Poppa. That might be some of the best evidence we have."

Elsie picked up on the part about V.J. having something that would settle the claim. "What do you have, V.J.?"

"Well, you remember when old Astor died and they had that hearing in 1849?"

"Yes," said Elsie, "I've heard that story all my life. The decision of the court was that nothing could be touched until the 90 years was up in 1906. It was to be settled in 1906 according to that court decision. Then the courthouse with all those records in it was burned to the ground by arsonists. The records were lost, except for the decree the family got and it was sold back to the Astors for $50,000 by Lynas Emerick. Then he felt he had done wrong and offered $25,000 to get a copy back. Lynas left the country and nobody knows what happened to that copy he got back or if he even did get it back. Or if any of it is true. Maybe it's all just a story."

"What would you think if I told you I know where the box is that holds that decree?"

"Why, I would think you better tell someone quickly, if that is the case. We have been working on this settlement for years and it still seems just out of reach. You must tell the attorneys immediately and turn it over if you have it."

"I didn't say I had it, Elsie," said V.J. holding up his hands. "I said I know where it is and me and Dee are going to go get it."

Dee shot V.J. a look that said he had said too much already.

"Elsie," said Dee, "I'd really like to see those papers of Poppa's. You have them don't you?"

"Yes, I have them. I am trying to take in what I just heard. V.J., this is a very important piece of information. You must contact Mr. Hoy right away."

"Sure, sure, we'll do that. We just wondered what you had. It would make a nice package altogether. Maybe we could get something for it."

"If anyone gets anything, it is to be shared by all. You both signed the contract with the Association," said Elsie firmly.

"Of, course, of course," both men said together.

"What exactly are those papers that Poppa gave you?" said Dee. "I'd like to get a look at them."

He was her younger brother. She had helped to raise him. If he could not be trusted, who could?

"I'll get them," said Elsie.

She went into the bedroom and brought the little brown suitcase out from under the bed. She carried it into the living room and set it on an end table next to the couch. The two men moved closer as she opened the lid. Irving's papers were under some newspapers and pictures. She brought out the large torn envelope and carefully removed the documents.

They sat together, V.J. and Elsie, on the couch. Dee pulled a chair up on the other side of Elsie. The three of them examined the documents that verified for certain their relationship to Christopher. They were fragile and needed to be handled with great care.

"These look like the real thing all right," said V.J. as he passed a look to Dee over Elsie's head. Their eyes met for an instant in a look that bore into each of their souls.

When they had finished perusing the papers, Elsie slipped them back into the little brown suitcase, under the newspapers and pictures.

As she was closing the lid, Dee said, "Is that apple pie I smell, Sis? I'm tellin' you, V.J., my sister makes the best apple pie in the world. Better even than Momma's used to be and that was fantastic. How about a piece for your favorite brother?" he said, as he grabbed her around the waist and swung her around in a sort of dance.

Elsie smiled and enjoyed the moment. Dee followed her into the kitchen.

She started to turn back, "I better put the suitcase away first," she said.

But Dee put his arm around her and said, "Oh, that can wait, but my stomach can't. You remember how you used to bring us a treat when we were little?"

"You always had a good appetite and that's no lie. I swear to goodness, I never saw a boy eat more or enjoy it more. Course, all you boys were good eaters," said Elsie as she set pie plates out for two. She would wait until later when Roy was home to have some.

"I sure do wish Grace could bake a pie like you do, Sis. She's never been much on cookin'. But she's great on lookin'!" he joked.

They reminisced together as she cut the pie into good-sized pieces. She had made it from King apples which were a favorite of hers for pies and applesauce.

She called to V.J., "We'll be right back, V.J. Don't mean to be rude leaving you there all alone."

"Oh, don't worry about me, Elsie. I'm doing fine. That pie sure sounds good."

The two men enjoyed their pie. Dee looked nervous and kept glancing at V.J. As soon as they were finished, they said their goodbyes and left. Dee said he needed to get going, as Grace would be worried if he was not back to Medford by tomorrow.

After the men left, Elsie snapped the locks on the little brown suitcase, picked it up and slipped it back under her side of the bed where she knew it was safe.

Irving arrived about an hour later.

"Oh, Poppa, you just missed Dee and V.J. They stopped by and had a piece of pie."

"What are they doing in Tacoma?" asked Irving.

"Oh, I don't know. They just stopped by to catch up on family news and they wanted to look at what we have on the estate business. V.J. says he has some scheme. He says he knows where that old decree is that would really help the case. I'm not sure he was telling the truth. You know how he sometimes exaggerates. I wouldn't worry. I told him anything he finds he is to share with the Association. He's signed the contract just like the rest of us."

"Hum," said Irving.

"Would you like a piece of apple pie, Poppa?"

"Elsie, I would love a piece. The house still smells like pie just came out of the oven. I'm still not used to Anna's cooking. I get tired of all that fish and smelly cheese. The cheese she likes smells like something the cat did on the floor."

They both laughed.

"She is not a bad cook. She puts the meals on the table and I thank the Lord for that. We remember some lean times, don't we? But the Lord always took care of us."

"Yes, Poppa, the Lord always took care of us."

"Say, Elsie, I'd like to look at the things we have on the estate myself. You have most of it now."

"Sure, Poppa. I'll get the suitcase and you can look while I dish up the pie and get the meat loaf going for dinner."

Elsie returned with the little brown suitcase. She again set it on the end table by the couch. Irving scooted over and placed the suitcase on his lap.

"You take your time, Elsie. I'll just look through these things. One of these days, your old Poppa may be right and we will settle with those scoundrel Astors."

"I'm sure we will, Poppa. Uncle Lynn writes so positively about how things are going. I'll just leave you a bit while I start the meat loaf and then I'll get that pie for you. I could give Anna the recipe..." Elsie's voice trailed off as she realized Anna could not read one of her recipes or listen to her tell it and understand. It did not require a response from Irving. Anyway he was already looking into the suitcase.

As he thumbed through the contents of the little brown suitcase, he moved aside a newspaper Elsie had placed there a few years ago. It told about Charles A. Lindbergh flying solo across the Atlantic in May of 1927. He never believed he would have lived to see such a thing. Elsie must have thought so, too, because she had saved the paper.

Irving wanted to look again at the papers he had left with Elsie. He knew she kept them in the suitcase. He moved some other old newspapers. Here was the one from 1908 about Billy. My, that boy could play the piano. If only he had used his talents for the Lord.

He was searching for the large old torn envelope with those papers verifying their relationship to John Nicholas Emerick and showing the family line. He knew he had given them to Elsie. He thought he knew. He had been confused sometimes lately. He knew he was not crazy, no matter what Harry said. He did not get much respect sometimes from some of the family.

What if he only thought he had given Elsie the papers? If he asked her, she might mention it to Vida and Harry. After that episode last time they were in town, he did not want that to happen.

Elsie and Roy and Vida and Harry were especially close. After all, Elsie and Vida were sisters and Roy and Harry were uncle and nephew. It made for a doubly close family connection. Not that they always got along smoothly.

After losing the election for constable on the Republican ticket in 1926, Roy had joined the Democratic Party. Harry, a small businessman, voted Republican every time. It made for some hot discussions around the pinochle table. They would pound the table and call each other, "You horse's patoot" or "You dad blasted buzzard" or "Gol dern your crazy hide, you so and so."

They would not dare to use real cuss words in front of the minister's daughters. So they invented a repertoire of colorful substitutes which they trotted out on a regular basis. Their spates of anger and argument never lasted very long. Soon they would be laughing and bidding way too high in the card game trying to outdo each other.

Harry Bryan had an Irish gift for dishing the blarney in buckets. He had a contagious and irrepressible sense or humor and eyes that really did twinkle. When he told a funny story he would laugh the loudest and slap his knee with rollicking good humor. His face would crinkle up with mirth.

He often kept a cigar tucked in the corner of his mouth. It was not always lit. He kept it there for effect and used it from time to time to hold in his hand and punctuate the air in concert with expressing his opinions or telling slightly bawdy jokes.

That last Sunday Harry and Vida had been in town, they were all about to have dinner at Elsie's. Anna did not come and was not missed by the assembled family.

Irving could not remember now how the subject came up, but he had told the story of how he had saved a man from hanging in Mukeltio many years ago. He did not want the community to bear the wrath of the Lord for hanging a man without trial. Irving helped the man to escape and then some of the people in the community tried to poison Irving with arsenic and carbolic acid and he saved himself by eating 100 eggs and the fat of five chickens and quarts of buttermilk and how he hid out with his rifle and the Lord sent a young Indian to save him and...

That was when Harry cut in. "Gol dern, Parson, you know those things aren't true. You keep talking like that and one day they'll be carting you off to the asylum."

"Now, Harry," said Vida.

"Well, we all know those things aren't true. His wild stories are getting out of hand."

Irving looked puzzled. He thought it was true. It was a story that came into his head. It seemed like it had happened to him. But the children were saying it had never happened. Sometimes the thoughts came into his head so fast. He determined to be more careful about what he said in the future.

"Never mind, Poppa. Dinner's ready. Come to the table," said Elsie patting his shoulders, as if to pour soothing oil on the troubled waters.

They all came to the dining room table. Elsie set a feast before them of juicy browned roast beef smothered with onions and carrots, the meat so tender it was falling apart, mashed potatoes, rich brown gravy, green beans canned from the garden, hot biscuits, fresh creamery butter and blackberry jam.

"Well, Parson, you gonna talk to the plate?" said Harry.

They all bowed their heads. Irving began to pray. He thanked the Lord for the food and for the family and for the church and the land and the country and the country's leaders and for peace. It was a long prayer.

Harry looked up and rolled his eyes at Vida who was peeking out at him across the table. She made a frowny face and mouthed, "Shush."

The steam had stopped rising from the potatoes. A skin was forming on top of the gravy. When Irving took a breath, Harry said, "Amen, pass the spuds."

So, as Irving was sitting on Elsie's couch, looking through the little brown suitcase for the papers he had given her, he decided not to mention he could not find them. He would ask Anna and look at home first. And he would think. Sometimes if he thought for a while he would remember the information he was seeking. That was the best tack to take. He did not want that son-in-law of his trying to put him in an asylum. He was not that crazy. Not yet.

His family did not want to recognize it, or could not recognize it because of Irving's eccentric personality, but as early as 1930 he was beginning a very gradual decent into senility. In 1930, he was mentally alert and coherent most of the time. But there would be these bizarre tangents that would overcome him. He began to believe he could prophesy just like Elijah from the Old Testament. Never one to hold his feelings back, he spewed out what ever elements were trundling through his brain at any given moment. If no one was there to listen, he wrote letters.

V.J. and Dee were driving back toward Oregon in V.J.'s Model T Ford.

"I don't like doing that to my sister, V.J."

"We were lucky she had them papers. We never could have convinced your pa to even let us see them. We have as much right to them as anybody in the family. Just because your pa had them doesn't mean they are any more his than ours. The way that Association is going, they ain't never going to settle this case. You and me, we might just as well get what we can for them from the Astors. It's all we're going to get, I tell you. We won't live long enough to collect, if the Association handles this. Besides, more and more "relatives" are showing up sniffing for money. It will be split so many ways, none of us will get enough to amount to anything. I think this is the best way to go," said V.J.

"I still don't like doing it. It isn't right. I feel like I am cheating my own family."

"Your own family is Grace and your little girl, Violet, cuz. Keep your priorities in mind."

While V.J. drove, Dee looked out the window at the miles and miles of tall fir trees lining the road. Well, V.J. was right about one thing. Grace was a priority, and Violet, too. But Grace. Ah, Grace. His life had never been the same since he had seen her that first day.

He was pounding the beat on his job as a policeman in St. Louis. He was proud to put on a uniform and help keep the city safe. It was an interesting job. There was always something new happening on the streets. He liked talking with the people and he liked the way they looked at him, as if he was somebody important. He was good with the people, too. He had a calm way of speaking and he could run like the wind to catch the feisty young toughs who tried to grab and run at the shops. They mostly were not bad lads. There were some real serious problems in the city, but not often on his beat. He felt good to be a part of upholding the law.

One day, he saw her as he walked by the Five and Dime. She was the new salesclerk at the candy counter just inside the window. She had long red hair, tied back with a bright-green bow. It was a brighter shade of green than the store smock which all the clerks wore. He had not seen her there before when he had walked by this store twice a day checking to make sure all was well inside. He noticed she carried herself proudly in a special way, which made her stand out from all the other clerks. She noticed he was looking at her and gave him a quick smile as she counted out change to an old man and handed him his small paper sack of candy.

Dee suddenly had a hankering for something sweet. He walked through the door and acted as if he was in the store just to keep an eye on things. Then he sauntered casually up to the candy counter.

"Good morning, Officer. May I help you?" she said in a soft southern drawl.

Dee looked up from surveying the candy in the glass case into her lovely gray-green eyes. For a moment, he was so drawn under the spell of looking into those eyes that he could not come up with something to say.

Then he recovered and blurted out, "Horehound."

"Why sure, we have horehound. How much would you like?"

"Oh, just a few pieces. My pa used to bring horehound home sometimes when he had been away and give it to all us kids," Dee said awkwardly. It was all he could think of to say.

"Well, horehound has never been my favorite, but lots of people like it. I'll get you some. No charge."

"Thank you, Miss, er, Miss…"

"It's Grace. That's my name. This is my first day."

"Well, thank you, Grace."

As he turned to leave she called after him, "What's your name?"

"I'm Dee Emerick. I come by here everyday, twice a day most times."

"Well, maybe I'll see you again then, Dee Emerick."

They did see each other again. He made the Five and Dime a regular stop twice a day. The other salesclerks began to take notice that the handsome young policeman was very interested in the pretty new candy clerk. The store manager had no complaints. His store was getting more police protection than any other store on the block.

Everyday, Dee noticed, Grace prettied herself up just a little differently. She wore different bows in her hair or tucked a flower behind her ear. It did not matter that the flower was wilted by afternoon. It was just the fact that she did it. She cared enough to make herself stand out in little ways that she could. Dee thought you could tell a girl like that knew what she wanted and would go places in life. Just by looking at her, you could tell.

By this time he had learned that her folks had moved to St. Louis recently from Alabama. They had lived in Alabama four years and before that they had lived up north in Pennsylvania. Grace had adopted the southern speech of her neighbors and schoolmates in Alabama. She liked to drag her words out in a slow honey-sweet way. He believed she knew it added to her charm to speak in that slow lazy manner, which was not so prevalent in Missouri.

Dee asked her if she would like to go to the Sunday band concert in the park with him. She said she would like that "evah so much."

As they walked to the park on Sunday, Dee thought she looked a great deal nicer without her usual green Five and Dime smock. Her flowered dress was of plain cotton material. But Grace had swept her long hair up in a large pouf and topped it with a bright blue bow. Around her neck, she had a narrow black satin ribbon which held a small gold locket. She stood straight and tall and walked with that confidant air that attracted him so much.

When they arrived at the park, they chose a spot far enough away from the bandstand they could hear the music and also hear themselves talk. Dee took off his light jacket and spread it on the ground for her to sit on.

"Don't you just love to heah such music?" said Grace. "It makes me just fill up with dreams."

"Why, sure, I like the music a lot. My younger brother, Billy, can play anything you ask him on the piano if he has heard it once. He was in the newspapers..., of course, that was before you came here.

"What kind of dreams do you have, Grace? Tell me what is filling up your mind."

"I dream of fine things. I'm not going to work behind the candy countah for long. I want something bettah. I want silk clothes than shimmah on your skin and a couch that feels like a cloud when you sit down and a scullery girl to do the housework. I do hate doing the dishes at home. My mother does all the cooking and she says I should not complain about doing the cleaning up. I want a house with lots of room on a nice street with rows of shade trees. I'm not going to settle for less. I have my dreams," she said in her soft voice which became less southern as she talked.

He could see her dreams in her eyes. She had a far off look as she gazed beyond him up toward large maple leaves that made a canopy of shade over them.

There was something so simple and unpretentious about Grace. She did not hide her aspirations. They were right out in the open. She was like a cat. Cats know what they want and they set out to get it. If they want you to pet them, they demand it by rubbing your leg or jumping on your lap. They know how to ask for food by persistent meows. If a cat is not pleased, it shows its teeth and claws. A cat knows how to state its demands clearly. It comes with the breed. Grace was like a cat.

Chapter 30

Judge Harlan Grantham was walking down the street toward his Chicago office on a crisp January morning. The limbs of the bare trees that lined the street were outlined in icy white frost. His breath blew a fog bank before him as he walked. He was over six feet tall which in 1930 made him stand out in a crowd. He had thick dark brown hair, which, refused to remain calm and contained all day, in spite of treatments by Vitalis and various other hair preparations used by gentlemen to slick their hair to their scalp. As the day progressed, so did his hirsute bushiness. As if it had a delinquent life of its own, his hair resisted containment and gradually escaped into freedom as the day progressed. He was not able to keep from running his hands through it in times of concentration or worry. That did not help. His office staff could tell what kind of a day he was having by the volume of his hair, but he did not know that.

His hair and height were not Judge Grantham's only identifying characteristics. He had a prominent, rather hooked nose and when he smiled his mouth went crooked, pulling down on the right and up on the left. None of these detracted from his looks. There was a rakish handsomeness about his face. He looked kind and a little dangerous at the same time.

He took great satisfaction in his job. At forty-five, he had achieved his career goal. He had been a bright student in school and had considered going into medicine. He chose the field of law instead because he loved the mental gymnastics required and was not attracted to the sometimes gruesome and bloody details which must be dealt with in the medical profession. He could deal with those details mentally in court. That suited his nature better.

He had done well in his chosen profession and been appointed to the bench four years before. There was some talk among his colleagues that politics might come next, but he was not seriously interested. In fact, Judge Grantham was not seriously interested in anything much these days. Oh, he still focused intently while at work. It was after hours when time hung heavy for him.

Harlan Grantham was an only child. His had been a remarkably pleasant childhood. His parents encouraged him in all his endeavors. They were very proud of their only son. There were only the three of them. Relatives had been left behind in Germany. Harlan's father had changed their name from Goldenstein when the couple had arrived in America. They had left their Jewish heritage behind and had begun to attend the Methodist church in order to assimilate. Harlan was simply an American. He had known nothing else.

Unfortunately, the flu epidemic had taken both of his parents in 1918. He had missed them ever since. He and Lily had only been married a few months when they had died, and now Lily was gone, too.

He knew she was frail when he married her. She was lovely and gentle and needed someone to care for her. Her heart was weak. She hoped to have children, regardless, but it had not happened. So when her weary heart had given out a year previously, it had left Harlan alone for the first time in his life.

He still had not totally adjusted. He tried hard not to let it affect his work and, indeed, when he was involved in the variety of life that paraded before his bench each day it was easy to forget the emptiness of the morning, evening and weekend hours.

As he walked into his office that morning he greeted his clerk.

"Good morning, Martha."

"Good morning, Judge. That Mr. Hoy cabled. He would like to meet with you next week. He is one of the lawyers for the Emerick family. You are hearing that case next month on their suit against the Astors. What should I answer him? You are going to be in New York next week for that conference."

"Let me see," Judge Grantham said as he ran his right hand through his plastered locks, giving them their first lift of the day.

"I am meeting with the Astor attorneys in New York on Wednesday. Tell him if he cares to come to New York I will see him on Tuesday evening."

"Judge, you need not press yourself. See him when you get back," said Martha.

"It's all right, Martha. I know he is anxious to see me. It will give me something to do one evening. Besides, this Emerick-Astor suit has been going on for years. If I can help to get it settled, well, that is what I would like to do. The Emerick's have a good case. Tell him I will meet him in New York."

Hoy traveled by train and arrived in New York City at the Pennsylvania Station at 11 am Tuesday. He walked into the gigantic building and as always, his heart filled with American pride as he gazed at the great ornate expanse with its domed skylight letting the morning sun through in brilliant rays that seemed almost touchable. His footsteps clicked decisively on the marble floor. Tap, tap, tap as he made his way out to the street. It made one feel important to experience such a building and to hear each step resounding as progress was made.

He hailed a taxi for a ride to the Biltmore Hotel. That was where Judge Grantham's conference was being held. It was good enough for Hoy, too. Sometime, though, he would like to stay at the Waldorf-Astoria, the classiest hotel in the city. Or he would at least like to have a look inside. He could not do that right now.

Not when this case was not settled. It would be disloyal and the prices were higher than at the Biltmore. All he needed was for Irving to find out if he ever did stay at the Waldorf-Astoria. Then there would be hell to pay as well as a high hotel bill. Someday, when this case was settled and everyone had received their share, he would bring his wife and they would stay at the hotel built by the Astors on land which John Nicholas Emerick had bought for a shilling an acre and they would order a bottle of good champagne from room service, he and his wife, and they would toast old John Nicholas Emerick.

Just then the taxi arrived at the Biltmore, interrupting his reverie.

He checked in and then had some lunch at the hotel cafe. Afterwards he went to his room and reviewed the materials he had brought with him in preparation for his meeting with Judge Grantham at 7 pm. About four, he was getting sleepy so he went out for a cold, but refreshing walk on the streets of New York. It was always exciting to walk these streets which radiated energy as if it came up through the sidewalks. He knew the energy really came from the multitudes of people swarming the streets like busy ants, each with a predetermined destination that pulled them swiftly in many directions. The walk woke him up and after an hour gave him an appetite. He stopped in a deli for a hot meatball sandwich. They really know how to make meatball sandwiches in New York, he thought.

By seven, Hoy was at the door of Judge Grantham's hotel room. He had showered and changed his shirt. He had only brought with him the suit he had on. He felt ready. He knocked on the door.

Judge Grantham was ready, too. He welcomed Hoy into the room. After some brief preliminary small talk they got down to business. Hoy presented the Emerick story and told of the verifications he had of the family's claim. Judge Grantham listened intently, asking a few questions which Hoy tried to answer succinctly. The meeting went well.

"I do not mind telling you I am very partial to your claim, Hoy. The Emericks have been wronged. They deserve recompense. The point, though, is proof. I would like to see a copy of that 1849 decree," said Judge Grantham.

"I would, too, Judge," responded Hoy. "There are rumors, as I said, that there are two copies. We know Lynas Emerick had a copy and there may be another copy. The original decree, of course, was burned up in that fire that destroyed the courthouse in 1849."

"If you could just get a copy of that decree, no one could deny the claim," said Judge Grantham. "I will have to consider all the facts as they are presented before me in court. If you can produce the documents you have spoken of, I will be glad if I can rule for you. This case has gone on too long. I am meeting with the Astor attorneys at lunch tomorrow."

"How about I drop by tomorrow evening around the same time to see how that meeting went?" said Hoy.

"Well, I see nothing wrong in that. I cannot discuss their strategy, of course, if they should reveal that to me, but we can have one more chat if you like."

"Good. I will see you here tomorrow evening around seven. Goodnight, Judge and thank you for your time."

"Goodnight, Hoy."

Hoy spent the day visiting some museums and enjoying the feel of the city. He cabled Dr. Lynn and Bill Wehking, Mississippi Valley Association President:

"Met with Judge Grantham. He is definitely in our camp. Expect to have more news after final meeting tonight.

C. I. Hoy, Biltmore Hotel, New York City"

At 7 pm, Hoy went to Judge Grantham's room again and knocked on the door. There was no answer. Perhaps he was not back from dinner yet. Hoy left and came back in half an hour. Still no one answered the door. He returned every half hour until 9 pm. Then he went to the front desk.

"Has Judge Grantham checked out?" asked Hoy.

The desk clerk consulted his records. "No, sir. He has booked the room through Friday and has not checked out."

Hoy asked to speak to the hotel manager. He explained the situation and asked the manager to open the room in case the judge was in there and unable to come to the door.

"We had an appointment two hours ago. The judge would not have changed his plans without letting me know. We must see if he is all right," Hoy pleaded.

"Such an action is highly irregular, sir. Our guests are free to make or change their own plans without interference from hotel staff. Chances are something came up and he did not get word to you," said the manager.

"No! No!" insisted Hoy in an agitated manner. "We must check. I have a feeling…Please."

"All right, all right," said the manager finally relenting. "I will unlock the door. If he is not in there you may not enter his room."

"Yes, yes. That is fine," said Hoy.

The manager and Hoy went to Judge Grantham's room. The manager knocked. There was no response. He took out his master key and unlocked the door. The manager stepped inside.

"See, his things are still here," he said. "He will be back."

Hoy could see into the room. Despite the instructions, he took a step inside.

Grantham's valise lay open on the bed. His night clothes and slippers were there. His razor and toothbrush were on the sink in the bathroom. Hoy felt a cold, sinking feeling. He did not believe Grantham would be back. Something had caused him to leave in such a hurry he had left his things behind.

The hotel manager refused to intervene until Friday. On Friday, the room looked just the same as it had on Wednesday evening. Judge Grantham had disappeared. Vanished into thin air. No one had seen him leave. His colleagues at the conference were polled. They knew nothing. They had not seen him since Wednesday morning. He said he was taking lunch at the Waldorf-Astoria. No one had seen him since.

The newspapers in Chicago and elsewhere were filled with stories of his disappearance, but only for a short time. There was no family to press for the search. Hoy tried to tell the police about Judge Grantham's meeting with the Astor attorneys, but he did not know their names. The police were not convinced a crime had occurred. People run away from their lives all the time, they reasoned. They had more important matters on which to spend their time. Soon the case of the missing judge from Chicago made its way to a bottom drawer at the police precinct. Like words written in the sand and washed away by rushing ocean waves, the case disappeared from mind and sight as the world of the New York policemen moved on through the crimes and misdemeanors of every day life in a large city.

"They have murdered him! That's what they have done!" Hoy stated vehemently.

He went to Ohio to Dr. Lynn's home after leaving New York. He and Dr. Lynn were seated in the small office where the doctor did his paperwork.

Hoy was shaking with rage at the memory of what had happened.

"The police wouldn't give me the time of day. Said they didn't find evidence of a crime. He would *not* just have up and left like that. He was as fine a man as I have met. He was sympathetic to our cause. They found out about it and had him killed. I know they did."

"That is a very strong accusation to make, Calvin," said Dr. Lynn. "It will not help our case if such an accusation gets out. Let's try to keep it to ourselves."

374

Dr. Lynn, however, did not exactly follow his own advice. He had written to Irving of Hoy's favorable cable from New York. Now he had to explain why the case would be delayed and a new judge appointed. So he wrote Irving the truth. He did not mention Hoy's accusation of murder against the Astors. He might just as well have, as Irving, upon hearing the news, jumped to his own conclusion that Judge Grantham had been either bought off or murdered by the Astors. He did more than just reach his own conclusion about events. He wrote a letter telling of the incident and accusing the Astors of arranging for Judge Grantham's disappearance one way or another. He also expressed his dissatisfaction with Calvin Hoy. "We might just as well throw in with V.J. or the Jews. We would do better than sticking with Hoy," he wrote.

He sent the letter to many of the members of the Mississippi Valley Association of Emerick Heirs.

Now, the members knew about the judge disappearing and about the claims by the German Jews and they all knew V.J. Emerick, but they did not know what Irving meant by throwing in with V.J. What did V.J. have to do with it? Letters and cables began to pour in to Hoy and Dr. Lynn.

"What is this about?"

"What is being kept from us?"

"I paid good money to get this settled."

"What does Vernon J. have to do with this?"

Folks wanted to know.

Hoy was appalled when he learned of Irving's letter. "That old coot. What will he do next to undermine this case?" thought Hoy. Perhaps he should plan a trip out West to see I. G., as he called Irving, and his daughter, Elsie Bryan. He had the highest regard for Elsie and her integrity. She could be relied upon to support his position and his actions because she said she would. One thing she could not do was rein in her crackpot of a father.

Hoy wrote to Dr. Lynn requesting his interpretation of what I.G. had meant. Then he sent a general mailing off to the members of the Mississippi Valley Association to advise them he was planning a trip West. He assured them he would try to find out what was going on. He had no idea what the reference to V.J. had meant. Like a dog worrying a bone, Hoy had sunk his teeth into this project and did not intend to let go until it was completed.

If Hoy was appalled, Dr. Lynn was furious at his older brother. It was getting so that he dreaded the arrival of the mail. What new calamity would be presented by the innocent looking pieces of paper lying on his living-room floor after mail delivery? It would strain the patience of Job trying to keep his brother from ruining whatever chances they had in this case. Dr.

Lynn did not know what Irving meant by his reference to V.J. either. He quickly wrote a letter to Irving asking for an explanation.

He was not pleased with the response from the West Coast. Irving wrote that V.J. and Dee said they either had a copy, or could get a copy, of the 1849 decree and they had somehow taken the family papers verifying their relationship to John Nicholas Emerick out of Elsie's suitcase. He had not told Elsie yet and he did not think she knew. He had not told her because he was afraid if he was wrong the children might try to send him to an asylum. He was sure the family papers were in that little brown suitcase where Elsie kept all the information about the estate. He could not keep those things in his own home as he was not sure what Anna would do with them. Now they were not there. They went missing right after V.J. and Dee had visited Elsie and asked to see the papers in the suitcase.

Dr. Lynn was doubly angry at his brother. This unexpected complication brought on them by V.J. and Dee seemed like it might sink the ship. He thought he and Hoy should have been notified immediately of V.J.'s boast. He thought V.J. could not possibly have found the decree. Where had it been all these years? He would like to have V.J. in his living room for just five minutes. He would tell him a thing or two. If Dee and V.J. violated their signed contract, Dr. Lynn thought they just might end up in the penitentiary for fraud and conspiracy. He also was angry at the slurs against Calvin Hoy who was a good man and was trying so hard to settle this matter.

Dr. Lynn sent a scorching letter back to Irving. In addition to the items above, he also asked him again to leave the "religious stuff" out of his letters to Hoy and the other members. Hoy was not interested in reading it and neither was anyone else. Hoy had even said to Dr. Lynn when they met last, "I.G. is crazy over religion." Sometimes Dr. Lynn thought his brother was just plain crazy.

Anna plopped a copy of a Seattle Scandanavian newspaper on the table in front of Irving along with his breakfast. The newspaper was dated April 24, 1930.

"Huh, look, dares da money, all gone," said Anna tapping her finger on a short item on the front page.

"What are you saying, woman?" answered Irving. He could not read the Swedish article, but he could recognize the names Johan Jakob Astor and Emerick in the story.

"All gone," said Anna again shaking her head.

Irving finished his breakfast, donned his suit jacket and fedora hat and left the house with the Swedish newspaper tucked under his arm. He had better find out what this story was about. He knew where he could get a translation. He walked the mile to the Scandinavian market where Anna shopped. The owner knew how to read and write English as well as Swedish. He needed to for his business. He had helped Irving before when he and Anna could not negotiate the language differences and needed some means of clarification.

The shop owner was only too eager to help the husband of one of his good customers. He translated the short article. Irving wrote it down on the back of an envelope. He thanked the man, went home and typed it up on his typewriter. It read:

"Through an agreement, a strife for inheritance which has lasted for a number of years has been settled between the Astor family and the heirs to the founder of the Astor dynasty, Johan Jakob Astors (sic) partner Emerick. He has 10 heirs in Dorpat and not less than three hundred fifty heirs in Germany who have each received a sum of #120,000."

He took the typewritten article over to Elsie's. They pondered over what it could possibly mean. Elsie sent it off to Calvin Hoy to see if he could figure out what it meant.

Hoy answered in a letter of May 15, 1930. He said he was "tremendously interested" in the Swedish clipping. He said the papers are full of stories about the case. It is hard to believe all one sees, but he would like to see what is being written on the matter and that he was trying to follow every clue.

He discussed his recent trip to the West Coast and thanked Elsie for the pleasant visit to her home and the chat with her and the other parties. He would very much like to know if any party has that court decree. It would "shorten and solve a great mystery and go far toward ending this litigation that so many Emerick people are interested in...I do not expect to do that which is not right, and do not want to cause any grief in any family but if wrongs have been committed, I would like to see them righted and all done that can be done to see justice meeted (sic) out," he wrote.

Hoy's trip to the West Coast had at least served to quiet Irving for a time. They met at Elsie's and each was warily courteous to the other. The family was not sure yet just what V.J. and Dee had or what they planned to do. Harry and Vida were in on the meeting, too. Until V.J. and Dee made a move, the rest of them were taking a wait-and-see attitude.

Dr. Lynn chimed with his opinion about a month later in a letter to Irving. He met with V.J. in Chicago and was sure V.J. did not have the court decree. He may have a metal box, but not the decree. Dr. Lynn was sure. He told Irving to get that notion out of his head. He cautioned Irving against making wild statements. "They just delay the case."

Dr. Lynn, who had no children of his own, also wondered why Irving could not just have a heart-to-heart talk with his son Dee and straighten this whole thing out.

"I've made up my mind to offer the decree to the Association first. If they want it, they are going to have to pay for it. I'm the one who found it. You helped with the family papers. If the Association doesn't want to settle, I'll offer it and the family papers to the Jews or the Astors," V.J. said to Dee. "I'm going to ask at least $100,000. You'll get your share, cuz. Either way we will be set for life."

They were sitting in a coffee shop in Portland, Oregon. Dee, who was still living in Medford, was on a long-haul trucking run and they had arranged to meet there. Dee did not want Grace to know just what was being planned. He would tell her when the time was right. If she knew they had money coming in soon, it would all be spent before they got it. Grace never seemed satisfied with the living he could earn. Well, she had never made a secret of the fact she expected fine things. He knew that going into the marriage. It was as though he was bewitched. She had held such a power over him. And still did.

Maybe if he got this money and doled it out to her a little at a time she would be able to have the things she wanted. She sure could get angry when she was crossed. He would have to be careful. He, also, did not trust her to keep her mouth shut about the plans or the money they might get. He was not anxious to have his family find out about his perfidy. Nor did he want to listen to Grace's continual financial demands. He felt he had to do it...be a party to stealing those papers. What other chance did he have to better their situation in life? Grace was talking about going back to St. Louis with or without him. He could not let that happen. He could not be separated from either Grace or Violet. His little daughter was very precious to him and he would do whatever necessary to give her, and Grace, the best life he could. No, he had done the right thing throwing in with V.J. It was his only hope.

"Oh, Elsie, I am sorry," he thought.

"Okay," said Dee back to his cousin. "Go ahead with your plan, but leave my name out of it if you can."

Chapter 31

Clickety-clack, clickety-clack, clickety-clack. The Southern Pacific train was heading south through the flatlands of western Oregon. By nightfall it would reach the mountains and take on an extra engine. The rhythm of the wheels would change to a slower pace as it pulled uphill.

Elsie sat facing forward, looking out the window, watching the pastoral fields and trees, just ready to leaf out in their spring finery, come into view. Her head, resting on the back of the seat, swayed back and forth gently with the motion of the train, as if she were continually disapproving or voting no. The bench seats were arranged to accommodate four people: two facing forward and two facing backward. The seats were ramrod straight, like church pews. They were slightly padded and covered with a sturdy green felt-like, well-worn material.

The sound of the wheels on the tracks was hypnotic, but Elsie was not sleepy. Her mind was active with thoughts.

The four of them, Elsie, Roy, Dorothy and Irving, were traveling to visit Frank and Etta in Marysville, California. Roy and Irving were going to help Frank build a new house there. Because he worked for the railroad, Roy could get free passes for his family to travel on the train. On the way, they were stopping over at Medford to visit with Dee and Grace for one night.

Roy went forward to swap stories with the conductor. Dorothy, now almost 19 years old, was visiting with a young woman across the aisle who had a tiny baby. The woman, a girl really, with waist-length caramel-colored hair and a sweet face, was traveling to California to meet her husband who had found work there. Dorothy was sitting with the young woman helping with the baby and sharing talk. Irving sat across from Elsie. He was traveling backwards. He had been watching the scenery disappear until his eyes closed and his head dropped on his chest. It was hard to sleep traveling coach class on the train. There was no place to put your feet and there was an arm rest in the middle of the bench, so reclining was not an option. Still, the steady cadence of the train on the tracks and the late afternoon lured Irving into a sleeping, if not restful, state. Elsie was alone with her thoughts.

Paramount on her mind was what she would say to her younger brother and his fiery wife. Grace was one for speaking her mind no matter what the consequences. Elsie avoided confrontation whenever possible. She had instructions from Mr. Hoy to find out all she could about what Dee and V.J. actually had, if they had anything, and what they might be going to do with it.

My, it seems this estate case has caused so much grief and dissension in the family, thought Elsie. So many times she believed it was close to being settled and then more and more roadblocks appeared. She did not like quizzing her brother or trying to manipulate him into talking. She was not good at deceptive behavior.

She had determined that she would try to talk to Dee alone and maybe try with Grace alone, too. She instinctively knew that one-on-one talk was likely to reveal more than if others were present. Grace and Dee's house was small, so it would be difficult to talk to anyone alone in the short time they would be there.

Roy said it was her family and it was up to her to ferret out any information she could. As much as he would like to see the estate settled, he felt it was up to Elsie to figure it out. There was no dealing with the Parson, Roy said. He had mucked things up plenty of times already. Roy thought maybe Harry was right and they should consider putting Irving out at Western State Hospital for the mentally ill. When he brought that up, Elsie would not hear of it. He was still Poppa and she was proud of all the good things he had accomplished in his life. She wished Anna was more help with him. He spent more time at their house than he did at his own. Anna just did not seem to notice.

She ran little scenarios through her mind. "Dee, you and V.J. said you were going to get that copy of the 1849 decree. Did you ever get it?"

Or, "Dee, you know, if anyone who signed the contract with the Association keeps evidence to themselves they could be charged with fraud and conspiracy."

No, no. She could not say that to her younger brother. She did not know if that were true. Maybe she could ask Grace if she and Dee were still active in the Association. You never knew what answer you might get from Grace. She might come back with a biting remark or she might gloss over her answer using her southern voice and not answer at all. Elsie did not think Grace and Dee got along very well together. She also thought that was not her business.

It was good to think about seeing Frank and Etta. Their house was always a happy turmoil and Etta was so cheery. Elsie was looking forward to time away from the concerns of the Emerick estate. Frank and Etta were disinterested parties in the whole affair. Elsie felt she could talk to Etta and not have to worry about being careful of who said what to whom. Etta would listen and empathize and let it pass through her brain without stopping for long. Elsie also thought it was going to be a nice change for Dorothy.

Dorothy had tried working at a retail store in downtown Tacoma. They accused her of pocketing money when the cash register came up short. She was so insulted she walked right out of the store, not even going back to collect her pay. They were not going to treat her that way and get away with it, she thought.

Elsie worried that her daughter needed more to do. She had not yet met anyone who was special to her. Elsie thought, "At her age I was married and had given birth to two babies." She thought about how old Little Frank would have been if he had lived. She had not known her second baby, but Little Frank remained an ever-present, never forgotten part of her life. She kept his little overalls and the black socks with the bright red toes and heels at the bottom of the little brown suitcase. They were still dirty from the last day he had worn them and had crawled around on the floor. She must put those thoughts out of her mind for now. For now she had a job to do. She had to find out what was going on with her brother and cousin.

Elsie's mental plans died aborning. When they arrived at Grace and Dee's, they exchanged preliminary pleasantries.

"So good to see you."

"My how that little Violet has grown."

"Nice place you have here."

"Well, is that my little niece, Dorothy? All grown up!"

Those things that families say to each other tumbled out of their lips almost without thought.

Then Irving spoke out, "What's all this about you and V.J. having that decree, Dee? By the Lord, you cannot keep something like that to yourselves. What's the matter with you, son? You gave your word to the Association."

"Now just wait a minute, Pa. Where did you get an idea like that?"

"Well, that's what you told Elsie when you were at her house."

"I don't think that is exactly what was said. Elsie, really, you didn't believe that did you?" said Dee.

Elsie was still trying to recover from her father's blunt attack. So much for family harmony.

"Dee, it's what V.J. said. Is it true or not? Do you and V.J. have the decree?" asked Elsie.

"I don't know where you got such an idea in your head, Sis. We never said anything like that."

Elsie was stunned. Her own brother whom she loved and helped to raise had just called her a liar. She could not think what to say.

"Son, you had best tell the truth. It is an abomination unto the Lord to lie like this," said Irving. "The Lord will smite those who do not obey Him. The Lord can tell, if man cannot, when lies are told. Blessed are those who follow the Lord. Damned are those who put forth false prophesies. Tell the truth, Son."

"I'm not lying!" insisted Dee.

"Why the verah idee-ah," said Grace in her most southern voice. She faced her father-in-law. "You will not come intah our home and accuse my husband of these things, you crazy old man."

Dorothy took six-year-old Violet by the hand and said, "Come on, honey, let's go take a look at your room. Would you like me to read you a story?"

Violet was rooted to the floorboards. Her eyes were as big as cow pies. She did not want to go to her room. She wanted to stay right there and listen to what was going to happen.

Dorothy, on the other hand, did not want to stay and listen to her grandfather rave on and on as he sometimes did. She had heard it all before. Once he got going, it was hard to stop him. Pretty soon, it would turn into one of his sermons and he would not even know he had made the transition.

"Poppa, can't you do something," said Dorothy to Roy looking at him with an urgent plea in her eyes.

Roy had determined he would stay out of this. However, Elsie seemed struck dumb by her brother's words and she would not go against her father in any case. Dorothy was too young to intervene. He knew if Irving got going on a toot it would be hard to stop him.

Roy stepped forward and took Irving by the arm, "Come on there, Parson. The boy is as stubborn as you are. Let's you and me take a walk outside."

He propelled Irving out the door.

Everyone fell silent for a moment then Grace recovered her composure and offered a cup of tea. Elsie and Dorothy gratefully accepted. The rest of their visit there, the subject of the court decree and what Dee and V.J. had or were going to do was not broached again. Families have a way of closing over subjects which are too painful to consider. It is as if by tacit agreement the slate is wiped temporarily clean. No one really forgets the elephant in the room. The subject hovers in every mind, just pushed back. Conversation tiptoes around any reference to the painful subject. But ruffled feathers calm and family interaction goes on. Even Irving avoided further reference. Perhaps it was something Roy had said to him outside, or perhaps his mind, deflected away from the concern, temporarily forgot it.

Dee, Grace and little Violet took the family to the train station the next morning. Goodbyes and hugs were given all around. Elsie was the last to board the train. She was on the bottom step. Dee was a few feet away. He was holding Violet up and looking for the others to appear in the window of the train.

Grace leaned over to Elsie and said quietly, "Don't you worry about your brother. Dee has already got his share of the estate."

Elsie had no time to answer. The conductor removed the little stool he had put out to help folks reach the steps up into the train. He placed it inside the train and said, "Bo-ard. All Aboard," as he stepped up beside Elsie.

Elsie looked back at Grace who had a mischievous sparkle in her Cheshire cat's eyes and a slight smile on her lips.

"Etta, I just don't know what she meant saying Dee had already gotten his share. I don't know what to do with that information. I surely did not accomplish much in finding out what Dee and V.J. are up to. I've got to let Mr. Hoy know, but I don't know what to tell him for sure."

Elsie and Etta were sitting at the kitchen table lingering over a cup of black coffee. Etta had pushed aside the dirty dishes and scattered newspapers and other deleterious materials to make a small place for them to set their cups. Elsie, normally so fastidious about housekeeping as Momma had taught her, forgave Etta for her messy disorganized house. Anyway, this was not really a house. It was a little two room shack on the property they had bought. There were big gaps between the boards on the walls. "Good thing it is warm weather," thought Elsie.

There was a tent up in the backyard for overflow. The men had set to work helping with building the new house as soon as they arrived. Irving liked to work with his hands, was a good builder and needed the money Frank offered. Roy had two weeks off from the railroad and was willing to help his brother.

"Now, honey, it will all work out. Don't you worry," said Etta. "Let's go next door when we finish our coffee. I want you to meet my neighbor, Nancy Morris. They have five young'uns all still at home. Oldest boy, Harold, is about Dorothy's age. A real handsome boy, too."

Elsie sighed. Etta was such a comforting presence. It was good to be here. She would relax today and enjoy whatever came. Tomorrow she would write to Mr. Hoy and tell him what happened.

When Hoy received Elsie's letter he determined he must make a trip to Medford and talk with Grace and Dee himself. V.J. denied everything when Dr. Lynn and the Association officers spoke with him in Chicago. So they were both denying they said anything about the decree to Mrs. Bryan.

Hoy knew one thing. He knew Elsie Bryan would not make the story up. He had to get to the bottom of this.

He still believed in the cause, although sometimes lately it seemed a hopeless one. He believed Mrs. Bryan and her family deserved to have their inheritance. He would continue fighting and trying to unravel this tangled web of information. He did not know who the enemy was—the Astors or the Emericks themselves.

Mrs. Bryan did not even know about her father's letters to V.J. offering to go in with him and suggesting he (Hoy) be cut out. Dr. Lynn assured Hoy that Irving was just trying V.J. out to catch him. Hoy was heartsick to read the things Irving had written about him. The letter, which was sent to many people, made its way to him eventually. Dr. Lynn was much more forgiving of his brother than his brother deserved, thought Hoy. V.J. admitted nothing. If it was a test by Irving it had not worked.

Sometimes he wondered what force compelled him to continue with this case. Many of the lawyers hired by various Emerick groups had long ago dropped by the wayside. The Appeals Court judge who replaced Judge Grantham had ruled against them in February. It was enough to make a fellow lose heart. Then he remembered that he continued for people like Mrs. Bryan who would not be able to navigate the legal system without a competent guide. He had given her and Dr. Lynn, as well as many others, his word. If a man did not stick by his word, what good was he?

That was a funny business about Koerber, too. After months of nothing from the German Jewish side, Koerber turned up again. Again, he was willing to share information. Just what information exactly, was never made clear. Ever hopeful, Hoy met him at the dock when his ship arrived in New York. They went to Koerber's hotel and had several meetings over the next three days. Koerber was secretive, but kept hinting and mentioning the names of others who would help Hoy.

Koerber said he had papers at a bank in New York that he would retrieve and share with Hoy. They had breakfast together and Koerber planned to move to Hoy's hotel later in the day. That was the last Hoy saw of him. He disappeared, just like Judge Grantham, except in this case Koerber checked out of the hotel and left word at the desk he was taking a noon ship to Germany. Hoy had not seen or heard from him again, and that was last year.

Hoy thought, add that to his trip to view the original will of John Jacob Astor I, and you have some pretty shady goings on. The will, which was kept in the Hall of Records in the Surrogate Court in New York, was missing. He was able to see only a copy. He wanted to check the signatures on the will for himself. Who knew he was going there and arranged for the will to go missing after all these years? He had not made a secret of his trip and the purpose. Many in the Association knew. There was a Judas Iscariot in the Emerick clan for sure. Who would have the power to arrange for something like that but the Astors and their kind? V.J. did not have that kind of influence, surely.

He was not sure just yet what the item in the Swedish newspaper meant. He was unable to verify that story.

In addition, there was that nurse in Germany who was convicted and jailed for 10 months for an attempt to get some of the Astor millions for a group German Jews. Her name was Bertha Kirchner. She must be quite a con artist. She promised the group she could settle the estate and they paid her to do so.

Well, the law caught up with her, thought Hoy. Just like it did with that plot the Astors tried a few months back. Thought they would settle with a few heirs and call it even. Well, Hoy fixed their wagon by exposing them and bringing them into court. That had stopped them. Or had it?

Dr. Lynn tried to cover for Irving with Hoy, saying his brother was just testing V.J. to see if he would confess. To Irving, Dr. Lynn wrote an angry letter reminding him he had promised Elsie he would quit writing letters. Dr. Lynn reminded him that he had signed the contract whereby he promised to do all in his power to help adjudicate the estate. He accused Irving of turning traitor against his own children. He said he was deeply ashamed of him for sending so many letters. If he does not stop, Dr. Lynn said, he would disown him as a brother. He told Irving, "My God, be sensible. Please don't write a single soul."

Dr. Lynn stated he did not need the money from the estate because his medical practice brought in between $300 and $400 a month, which was plenty for anyone. But Irving's family needed the money and Dr. Lynn wanted them to have it.

"Now listen to me for once," wrote Dr. Lynn.

Chapter 32

"V.J. and I have as much right to that decree and the family papers as any one of you!" shouted Dee.

Hoy took reinforcements on his trip to Medford to visit Grace and Dee. Vida and Harry and Elsie were with him. Hoy confronted Dee about the missing family papers and court decree.

Elsie keyed in on the words "family papers." She did not yet know the papers were missing from the little brown suitcase.

"Dee, what family papers are you talking about?" she asked.

"He does not have to answer your rude questions," said Grace.

"Yes, Grace, he does," said Harry. "He needs to speak for himself and you need to sit down and zip your lip."

Grace batted her eyelashes rapidly and began to breathe heavily.

"That's right," said Hoy. "No one means to offend you, Grace, but Dee must answer for himself."

Grace sat down and zipped her lip. She had known something was up with Dee. She could read him so easily. She had wheedled it out of him. He told her of the plan with V.J. He could not help himself. She could not help herself either when she told Elsie that Dee had gotten his share of the estate. She had relished the surprised look she saw on Elsie's face as the train pulled out. Well, she had stretched it just a little. They were *going* to get a good chunk of $100,000. It was a sure thing. And why shouldn't they? The lawsuits by the Association were going nowhere. There were too many heirs involved anyway. This way at least they would get a nice settlement. If the Association bought the papers, then they would have a good chance to settle for all the members. If the Astors bought them, they would get the means to stall the suit indefinitely. "Either way," Grace thought, "we will come out ahead. Way ahead. Better *some* of the Emericks get paid than no one getting a dime from those hoity-toity Astors."

"Dee, what family papers are you talking about?" Elsie repeated.

"You know, Sis. The papers Pa had about the family line," answered Dee.

"The ones in my little brown suitcase? What do those have to do with this? They are at home in the suitcase under my bed."

The Story in the Little Brown Suitcase

"Well, actually, V.J. has them now," said Dee with his head down and his eyes on the floor.

"Why you horse's neck, you double-crossing, four flushing traitor!" shouted Harry as he roared up out of his chair.

"Let's all calm down," said Hoy. "Let's just take this one step at a time."

Harry was red in the face and was pacing back and forth by the window trying to remain calm. It was hard. He knew his wife and her sister to be as honest as anyone he had ever known. Yet their parents had spawned a son who was a viper with no conscience. How could they be from the same family?

"You mean you and V.J. took those papers out of my suitcase that day you were there?" said Elsie quietly.

"V.J. took 'em," said Dee.

Not only did his brother-in-law not have a conscience, he was a weasel, too, thought Harry.

"What do you and V.J. plan to do, son?" asked Hoy.

"Well, now you would have to talk to V.J. about that," said Dee.

"V.J. is not here. It is time that you told your family what you plan to do. This affects all your family. It particularly affects the ones that are here who have worked so hard to get this settled for everyone who is entitled. Now, son, you tell us what is going on," Hoy said firmly.

"Oh, all right, all right. He's planning to sell the decree and the papers to the Association if they want to buy. If they don't, he will sell it to the highest bidder," said Dee, not looking toward either of his sisters.

"And what's in it for you?" asked Harry, his eyes still flashing with anger, but his voice steady.

"We are going to get some of the money. He didn't say exactly how much. He's asking $100,000, so there should be plenty for Grace and me," Dee answered defiantly.

"Oh, Dee. How could you do that?" said Elsie sadly.

"Shame on you! You have betrayed us all!" said Vida.

"Well, I'm sorry," said Dee sarcastically looking at his sisters. "I'm sorry, Mr. Hoy, here, can't get this case worked out. I think Pa is probably right. He is just letting this go on and on to keep collecting fees from all of you. There isn't going to be any settlement. He probably knows that," continued Dee turning to look at Hoy. "Why shouldn't Grace and I have a chance? We deserve it as much as any of us here in this room. Better some of us get something than none of us get anything."

The room was silent. They all had their own thoughts.

Hoy was again hurt and surprised at the animosity coming his way. He had tried his level best for years for these people and this was the thanks he was receiving.

Elsie was thinking she did not really blame Dee. She knew Grace. She knew how Grace manipulated her brother. What he said made some sense. She believed in Mr. Hoy, but sometimes lately, she did not know if the case would ever get settled. Still, it hurt to know Dee had betrayed them all. Roy would probably write Dee and Grace off for this.

Vida was not feeling as forgiving as Elsie was toward Dee and his grasping wife. Dee knew better than this, she thought. She and Elsie and all the family deserved his loyalty, not his betrayal.

Harry was having trouble keeping his hands off Dee's throat. The little pip-squeak. Gawd Almighty, what kind of a person would go behind his family's back like that? He knew Grace thought she was too good for Dee. He always liked Dee and felt a little sorry for him having a wife like Grace. It was hard to feel sorry for him now. He was a man and was responsible for his own actions.

"I have to inform you that your actions may result in legal action being taken against you," said Hoy with a sigh. For the moment he felt deflated and tired. "Tomorrow I will want you to sign a statement as to what you just told us. I, for one, have had enough for one night and it is late. We will see you both in the morning."

The others gathered up their things and prepared to leave for their hotel. Elsie gave Dee a quick hug. Not much was said by anyone.

Elsie caught an early train home the next morning. When the others went back for further discussion, Dee denied all he had told them the night before. He refused to put anything in writing and actually said they must have all heard wrong. He knew nothing about the decree and the papers.

Met with such stonewalling, there was not much they could do. Hoy had Harry and Vida prepare and sign affidavits as to what went on the night before. He wrote Elsie post haste and requested that she sign a similar document. They all knew what they had heard. Dee could not get off that easily.

Meanwhile, V.J. contacted the Association and offered to sell them the copy of the 1849 court decree and the papers from Warren Emerick establishing their relationship to Christopher for $100,000.

Dr. Lynn wrote to Irving that the other officers of the Association were furious. They absolutely rejected V.J.'s offer. Dr. Lynn disagreed. He thought the price was cheap to get the estate settled. Why, if they could settle with that they would be farther ahead just to pay V.J. the money and get on with it. They would be receiving much more than that when they settled with the Astors. They could all afford it.

Dr, Lynn wrote he was surprised to hear little Dorothy was getting married. He hoped she was getting a good man.

Chapter 33

Harold Morris had just turned 20 years old when he met the girl visiting the new people on the property next to his parents rented home. His parents, Walter and Nancy Morris, had, like the Joads in Steinbeck's *Grapes of Wrath*, migrated west during the dust storms in the Midwest. Walter was working in the fruit orchards. There was work to do all year round tending the trees and irrigating. It did not pay much, but it was a job.

Harold graduated from high school with excellent grades. His teachers encouraged him to continue his education, but there was no money for college.

After the stock market crash of 1929, the country spiraled into The Great Depression. Fifteen million men were out of work. Harold, who had a dream of learning to fly, worked in the orchards as well, other opportunities being currently absent.

Dorothy went next door with her mother and Aunt Etta to meet the neighbor lady. Harold was working on a car in the side yard when his mother brought the visitors out to meet him. His hands were greasy and his hair had fallen down over his eyes. He brushed it back with one hand and left a dark smudge on his forehead. He thought she was the prettiest girl he had ever seen with that beautiful, sparkling smile and her way of tossing her head and flashing her eyes.

For her part, Dorothy hardly noticed the smudge on his forehead. She was captivated by his handsome face and warm, kind, blue eyes. It was love at first meeting, although neither of them admitted it at first. The two beautiful people were drawn together with high hopes of making a life together in lean economic times.

Dorothy, who had heard the story of the great fortune all her life, wanted to believe there would be money coming to her family soon when the Astors finally settled. In spite of Uncle Dee, she had hopes it would be settled in their favor. Then there would be enough money to take care of them all. Harold could go to college or start his own business or take flying lessons or do whatever he wanted. She would be able to have her hair done regularly, buy the prettiest clothes, and have a housekeeper, and they could go dancing whenever they wanted. She loved to go dancing.

They were married in October 1931. An outdoor picture of them shows Dorothy seated on the grass with her white organdy dress spread out around her like a Christmas-tree skirt while Harold sits behind her encircling her with his arms. They look like Hollywood movie stars.

Dee finally admitted in a letter to Elsie that V.J. said he had the court decree, but he (Dee) had never actually seen it. He felt he had been jumped on all of a sudden and he had not had time to think, when she,

Harry and Vida had come to Medford with Mr. Hoy. He said he would go the limit to get this straightened out and that Grace and Violet had gone back to St. Louis.

In anticipation of V.J. peddling the papers to the Astors or the Jews, Hoy obtained an injunction forbidding the Astors from making a settlement with V.J.

Irving continued to write more letters with fanciful ideas about the estate, religious opinions and criticisms of Hoy. Dr. Lynn continued to scold and threaten to disown him as a brother if he did not cease.

And so,1931 came to an end with no settlement in sight.

Early the following year, a trial was scheduled in Portland, Oregon regarding the estate. Depositions were taken. The plan was to get V.J. on the stand and get him to confess where he had obtained the decree and what he had done with it. Dee agreed with this plan and was prepared to testify as to what he and V.J. had concocted.

Then suddenly the trial was called off.

Chapter 34

Madeleine Force Astor Dick was not laughing anymore. By the end of 1932, her sixteen-year marriage to Willy Dick had run its course. The things that used to amuse her no longer did. She was tired of his jokes and innuendoes. They quarreled occasionally in public. She was sorry about that, as she aspired to be a very private person. She was sorry they had not been able to keep their problems behind closed doors.

Although it was not generally known, except among their closest friends, they had agreed to live in separate establishments. She resided in a luxurious apartment overlooking the East River, and he lived in a similar apartment not far away.

So when Mrs. Dick set up temporary residence in Reno, Nevada, near the Washoe County Courthouse, where divorce takes only six weeks, their society set gave each other knowing looks, nodded and said they were not surprised. They had seen it coming. It was only a matter of time now.

John Jacob Astor, Jr. was twenty years old. A slim, handsome young man, he was becoming known as a wealthy playboy, some said just like his father. Young Willy and John H., Madeleine's children of this marriage were off at school much of the time.

Madeleine suspected her husband was seeing other women. The sad part was she did not care. The years had not been kind to Madeleine. At 38 years old, her fragile, girlish beauty looked strained and tired around the eyes and the mouth. She was still a very attractive woman and was always dressed in the latest fashions. She liked the stylish long brimmed hats of the day which provided blinders of a sort, so that part of her face was shielded from prying eyes.

There was one thing she had not lost since that terrible *Titanic* night in 1912. That was her celebrity status. She had never enjoyed being photographed by ambush or having her activities charted or her wardrobe critiqued. Why were people endlessly fascinated by her comings and goings? John had never been bothered by it. He had been born to it and so accepted it with such grace.

She had lived long enough now to know the golden time with John Astor would not have lasted forever. He would have grown tired of her eventually when her naivety had gone and her figure had thickened. She had seen it happen too many times. She was not as clever as John had been. Her beauty had been her greatest asset. It had brought her good fortune, but not happiness. Now, even that dependable asset, her beauty, was eroded.

She knew the passionate love with John Astor would have cooled in time. Still, she turned her mind back over the years, like flipping pages in a favorite book, and savoring the reading of a certain section over again. It did not matter that it had been read before.

She reviewed the memories of that wonderful year with John. The moments seemed to have halos around them. She wanted to remember the very best parts and forget the travails of traveling and the almost unendurable end of her year with John Astor.

She knew it was fantasy to imagine how things would have been. She indulged in it anyway. Her mind was a private place for her alone where no one else could come. So she thought of how things might have been if he had not died. She imagined him behaving in the very best manner, always. He would never correct her cruelly or belittle her in public. They would not argue over money or which school to send the boys.

John had good breeding. He would not allow himself, or her, to make a scene in public. And even though she knew his ardor for her would have dimmed, he would never, never have had mistresses.

It was hard for the flesh and blood Mr. Dick to compete with such a memory. The memories of John were cast in stone. Willie Dick went fluidly from day to day piling up more and more offenses on the mental list that Madeleine kept.

Oh, she knew it was wrong to compare them. She knew.

By 1933 Madeleine's marriage to Willy Dick was over.

It was not long before she married again. This time to prize fighter, Enzo Fiermonte. She sought a divorce from him in 1938. Again, happiness eluded her.

Madeleine lived until 1940. She died in Palm Beach, Florida at 47 years of age, the same age that John Jacob Astor IV was at his death.

Chapter 35

Grace was sitting on a beige sofa in their new house on a tree-lined street in St Louis. She liked the way she sank way down into the sofa. It felt as soft as a cloud. She was wearing a pale silk dress printed with delicate bunches of purple lilacs. The dress had capped sleeves and, a heart-shaped neckline and was nipped in tightly at the waist. She liked the way the fabric swished and clung to her when she moved. She liked the feel of fine silk on her skin.

Dee was sitting across the room.

"Any one of your family would have done the same thing, Dee darlin'," she purred in her honey sweet voice. "V.J. knows how to take advantage of an opportunity. It would have been stupid to refuse money like that. I expected more from V.J. though. I do not think he split fairly with you."

"Well, it doesn't really matter now, does it, Grace? We got enough for you to get some of the things you wanted. That was the whole point. I don't feel any happier. I hope you do."

"There is no reason on this earth why your family should ever find out. You know V.J. is not going to tell them whether he gave you anything or not," said Grace forgetting her southern purr.

"They will figure it out. Me refusing to testify and us getting a new place. You can bet Elsie knows."

But Elsie did not know for sure. She had fought long and hard along side her father until she watched the fight for their rightful share of the Astor millions wind down and cease altogether.

Elsie could not put a finger on it—on what had been the single most important factor preventing settlement.

Was it the Astors continually sending the Emericks on wild goose chases, or hiding documents, or making judges and witnesses disappear, or burning courthouses, or using all the stalling techniques the legal profession had at its disposal? Plus they were using the Emericks' money which they still controlled to fight the Emericks. They had seemingly unlimited funds.

Was it the German Jews, who really had no legal claim whatsoever? Did they somehow make a settlement with the Astors, as the article in the Swedish paper indicated?

Was it the Emericks themselves? Was it V.J.? Did he really have something? If he did, where did he get it? Did he sell it to the Astors even though there was an injunction? Or to the Jews? Was Dee involved? Did dissension in the Emerick ranks cause all to fail?

Was it that so much time had passed that the Emericks just could not get the upper hand?

Was it a combination of all of the above? And then some?

Hoy gave it seven years of his life. He fought the good fight. He felt he had gone around in circles. Thousands of dollars were spent on trying to unravel the Emerick family tree. He searched every record in America: cemetery records, church records, and Bibles, and followed every conceivable clue to uncover the real facts in this twisted and complex situation. He felt he had tried to keep a trust which was given to him as an attorney. He faced battles fearlessly and did not spare anyone when they came between him and his line of duty as he saw it. To say he was tired was a very small part of it. He thought he had aged 10 years from carrying such a load.

He still believed the Emerick family was right and deserved to have their inheritance. He did his best, at great sacrifice to his family and his business. His own children grew up while their father was off on Emerick family business.

And yet, even with all that considered, Hoy told the Mississippi Valley Association members that if they decided to go on, he would go on with them.

But the Associations were disbanding. It was the middle of the Depression. The people were financially tapped out. They were emotionally drained. The courts had ruled against them too many times. More and more information was required that they could not obtain. Many felt whatever information they provided would not be enough and that the Astors and their attorneys had ever more tricks up their sleeves. In addition, they had connections to highly placed people who could cause any progress on the case to be delayed. Many felt they had given enough money, time and energy to the cause.

Success had seemed so close.

After 1933, no more records regarding the Emerick-Astor fortune are found in the little brown suitcase.

Dr. Lynn's letters, at times so confident and hopeful of a favorable settlement with the Astors, arrived no more.

Newspapers no longer covered the story.

Letters and telegrams from Calvin Hoy dried up.

Irving's letters ceased to discuss the case.

In 1933, Franklin Roosevelt was inaugurated as President of the United States. The same year Adolph Hitler became dictator of Germany. The Emerick claims to their share of the Astors' wealth faded into obscurity as the world stage was set for a conflict of much greater magnitude...World War II.

Epilogue

Irving Emerick, my great grandfather, lived until 1943 and died at 78 years of age. The immediate cause of death is listed as "Senility" on the death certificate found in the little brown suitcase.

He died when I was five years old. I remember him as smelling musty, fusty when I would sit on his lap. He always wore a dark suit with vest and jacket and often a hat. I remember him speaking of the things of the Lord. I do not remember that he was senile. I just remember he was a very old man and my grandmother called him Poppa and treated him with a special reverence.

He kept writing many, many letters almost up until his death. They were filled with stories of Biblical times, interpretations of scripture, and advice on how to live one's life. He often recounted his vision of God at sixteen, wherein he was told to go and preach the Gospel. He wrote about Franklin Roosevelt, whom he admired, and Henry Ford and Dwight L. Moody, a well-known Evangelist of the time.

He scolded the American people for not getting out and spending money. He believed the country could be brought back from the Depression if everyone pitched in and kept the money flowing. He said people who hoarded money in these times were on the side of Satan. He worried about poor men and women and children striving to exist. God and the poor—they were ever his concerns.

While there is a strident air and sometimes a loss of focus in his writings, if he was crazy it does not come across as that. He was certainly eccentric and single minded and in his last years lost his grip on reality at times. I did not expect him to play such an important role in this story. I did not know him that well. If I had I might have realized his need to jump to the front and be heard. I guess, most of all what Irving was, was a true American original.

Billy/Arthur, who never reached the musical expectations of his youth, eventually left Seattle and his fans there. He migrated down the coast, first, to San Francisco, then finally settling in San Diego where he and Noreen raised two children. He had steady work playing in nightclubs and lounges where he was a popular entertainer.

I stopped in San Diego to visit him when I was in college in 1957. He and Noreen were living in a small second-floor apartment. His hands were shaky. His spirit was welcoming and sweet. He died the following year. His musical genius was appreciated, although on a smaller scale than his family imagined in early days.

Following his own code of honor, Billy never agreed to testify about his encounter with Nancy Astor.

Vincent Astor, who inherited control of the family fortune in 1913 when he reached age twenty-one, married three times. He had no children. The last twenty years of his life, he headed the corporation which published *Newsweek* magazine. He died in February 1959. Vincent arranged for the disposal of much of the Astor fortune before his death, selling some of his properties for housing projects. It is no longer considered to be among the great fortunes.

The Astor family home in Newport, is a kind of working museum. It can be rented for parties, conferences, receptions and weddings. One can look out the windows in the ballroom at the manicured green lawn sweeping down to the sea and imagine how life might have been for the people who lived there. Of course, part of the reason they could live in such an elegant home and enjoy such a lavish lifestyle was that, according to the information in the little brown suitcase, the Emerick money was never surrendered to the rightful heirs.

Calvin Hoy, the ever faithful attorney, wrote a book about the Emerick/Astor story called *John Jacob Astor, An Unwritten Chapter*. No one knew more about it than he did. It charts the story and gives particulars about the legal fight. I read parts of it on the Internet. Since I relied on the documents in the little brown suitcase I used nothing directly from his book in my story.

Dr. Lynn's wife, Olivia, died when they were in their seventies. He made a deal with his nurse, Loveda, who was a widow and much younger than he. If she would marry him and take care of him in his old age, he would leave his estate to her. She accepted. Loveda was lively and fun to be around. I am not sure the deal turned out to be a good financial one for her. Dr. Lynn, who was frail all his life and who had diabetes, lived well into his nineties. By the time he was gone, I doubt Loveda had many more years to enjoy the estate. She genuinely seemed to care for him and vice versa, so that part of the bargain was a good one.

Without Dr. Lynn's many letters in the little brown suitcase this story would have been greatly lacking. His letters gave a picture of the life of a small town medical doctor in the 1920s and 1930s.

He used to worry about his drug bills. He apparently bought the drugs he prescribed and sold them to patients. If they could not pay, that was all right. Many of them were farmers. He knew they would pay when they sold their crops. If it was a bad year for crops, it was tight times paying his drug bills. In one letter he mentioned his drug bills were over $300, which was a cause of concern for him. He wrote that in the fall his business was slow. The farmers did not have time to be sick and running to the doctor in the fall.

I remember Dr. Lynn quite well, as he and Olivia and later, he and Loveda would visit my grandparents. He was kind and pleasant. When he came he would give little hints about how to treat colds or what to do for sore feet. My grandmother trusted his medical advice above all others'.

After World War II, ended, my grandmother heard an interesting story. It may have come from Calvin Hoy. A friend traveling in France, on the Riviera, spotted a tall man with thick bushy gray hair, a rather hooked nose and a smile that went up on one side and down on the other. This friend heard the man speaking English. He looked familiar somehow. It took a while. The friend searched his mental archives. Ah, that judge that disappeared. He looked like that judge. What was his name? Grant something. Grantham. That was it. Judge Grantham. He disappeared years ago just before he was to hear that case Hoy was working on. The friend went up to him.

"Say, aren't you Judge Grantham?" he asked.

The man turned and looked him full in the face.

"Je ne parle pas anglais," he said. At that point a beautiful young woman arrived and took the arm of the man who said he did not speak English, but did. They strolled casually away down the street.

After my mother, Dorothy, legally rid herself of her second husband, the prize fighter, she married a nice man named Dick Rudow. They lived in southern California. When I would visit them in the summers they would take me to all the wonderful exotic places around Los Angeles. We were at Disneyland the year it opened. We went to radio and TV shows and Knott's Berry Farm. We strolled down Hollywood Boulevard, when it was exotic, but not the sideshow it is today. We picnicked at Big Bear Lake and Lake Arrowhead. Every weekend when Dick was not working, we would climb in their new Ford car and go make adventures. They left me with many, many wonderful memories.

Dick Rudow resembled a very popular movie star when they were both young. Once when we were at what was then Graumann's Chinese Theater, in Hollywood, some women came up and asked Dick for his autograph, thinking he was Ronald Reagan.

He sang to mother in a rich baritone voice. He liked to sing, "My prayer at the end of the day, is to linger with you..." The three of us sang together with my baritone ukulele for accompaniment. He was a kind man and it was a good marriage which lasted forty years.

Unfortunately, about twenty years into the marriage, they were in a terrible car accident on a California freeway. Mother went through the windshield. She had many surgeries on her neck after that but was never able to find relief from the pain. She began to use prescription narcotics and was hooked and in dreamland much of the time for many years.

Dick took care of her and refused offers by my sister and me to provide money or time for respite relief.

He said, "No, I will take care of Mommy." And he did until he died. By that time, she was in a wheelchair from having broken her hip. She had refused to do the rehabilitation exercises and so permanently lost her ability to walk.

My sister and I tried to do our best by her. She had not been a real part of our lives. She had not been there when the major happenings of our lives took place. She was not there at graduations, weddings or the births of our children. We loved her as a remote figure who sent us a box of gifts at Christmas when we were children or as an "Auntie Mame" who made visits to her California home exciting. I think mostly we did our best by her for Elsie, our grandmother, who *had* been there for us.

My mother spent the last ten years of her life in a nursing home. She refused to leave California to move to the Northwest to be closer to us. She said she liked the sunshine. We sent her cards and cookies and called her regularly. We traveled to see her as often as we could make the long trip. I tried to go there at least twice a year. I took my guitar and later my keyboard and played and sang for her and the other residents.   She couldn't sing with me anymore.

She had lost her short-term memory.   She could remember way back and knew my sister and me and our husband's and our children's names.   But she could not remember recent happenings for more than a few minutes.

The nursing home staff bragged about her beautiful smile.   In her eighties, her face still lit up like a 100 watt bulb when she smiled.   She always got up at 5:30 am, finagled herself into her wheelchair, cleaned up, combed her hair and dressed in fresh clothing and inexpensive jewelry.   I never let her or the nursing home know when I was coming.   She always looked well turned out.

In June of 1998, I had just arrived home from a visit to see her.   We were notified that she had been taken to the hospital with internal bleeding.   I called the hospital and spoke to the floor nurse.   The nurse said rather crossly that what my mother really needed was to see her daughters whom she had not seen for years.   I explained I had just arrived home from seeing her, but would fly down again if she were in critical condition.   We had thought she was going to die several times over the years and had made extra trips before.   The nurse assured me she was not terminal.

The doctor wanted to do a surgical test to see what was going on to make her bleed internally.   We said no; she was too frail. The doctor said then he would have to just send her back to the nursing home to bleed to death. It was such a hard choice. We gave our permission for the test. It was done in the afternoon. By early the next morning she was dead.

My beautiful, sparkling, self-centered, would-be heiress mother died all alone in a California hospital. Looking back, I wonder why I did not realize this was the final curtain for my mother. She was 86 years old. I should have known. I should have gone back, so that my grandmother's little girl did not have to die alone.

I wonder if my mother would have found greater happiness if the estate had been settled in the 1930s, when a million dollars meant much more than it does today.

Or perhaps, as was the case with Madeleine, the money could not really create the happiness my mother sought.

In a way, they seem kindred spirits, Madeleine and Dorothy. They each were beautiful, spoiled women, aware of the power that gave them.

Mother was born while the *Titanic* was on its only voyage. Madeline was rescued from the *Titanic* when it sank. They each had three husbands. They each had an unsuccessful marriage to a prize fighter.

One had comforts, security and all the things money could buy. The other, while not totally at the other end of the financial spectrum, lived a Spartan life in comparison.

It seems neither of them were able to find true happiness and contentment and that the amount of money they each had may have had very little to do with that.

I was there the day my grandmother got the call that her brother Dee had died. She was across the room at the phone, beginning to cry for her younger brother.

She did not hear Grandpa say under his breath, "Good riddance."

Grandma had been right. He had never really forgiven Grace and Dee for their betrayal.

My grandfather, Roy, passed away of a stroke in 1960. My sister and I were both there for our grandfather's funeral and stood on either side of my grandmother at the casket, supporting her as she wept and patted his face with her gloved hands and said, "Oh, Roy. Oh Roy." They had been married 56 years. My mother was not at the funeral.

It was a warm July afternoon in 1969. I was living in Tacoma. My husband, an Air Force officer, was stationed in Vietnam. Grandma came to visit and help me with our three little boys whom she enjoyed so much. She had been there for a week or so when my sister and her husband came to take her to their home near Portland, Oregon for a visit.

It was a special day, that day. We all gathered around our small portable TV to watch as Neil Armstrong became the first man in history to set foot on the moon. My grandmother could hardly believe it, that it had really happened.

It was dark when they left for Portland. The three of them sat in the front seat. Grandma sat by the window, where she could look up at the moon all the way down the relatively straight path of Interstate-5. She kept saying over and over, "I just can't believe it."

She had seen the first motor car in St. Louis. She had marveled at Charles Lindbergh's solo flight across the Atlantic and the invention of the telephone. Now she had seen a man walk on the moon. All in one lifetime.

Less than a year later, she was gone. She died in California where she and Vida had gone to help Dick take care of my mother, who was having one of her bad spells. It was probably too much for Grandma. My mother seemed to revert to childish behavior around her own mother and she could be very demanding.

My sister and I decided to dress Grandma in a bright-green dress she liked for burial. We chose her favorite hymns. Her faith never deserted her and we knew that she was now at home with the Shepherd of her life. Her son, Lynn, was there for the funeral. My mother was not.

My sister took possession of grandmother's little brown suitcase. We shared it. I had it for a short while. Then it remained in my sister's attic for over thirty years while I was moving from place to place. We occasionally spoke about it and said someday someone should write a story about the contents of the little brown suitcase.

Now as it sits before me, on the moss-green tile of my table its story having been told, I realize that the little brown suitcase holds only dreams of wealth that might have been...

The End

About the Author

A native of Washington state, Carol Lynn Caswell is a former social worker, public school teacher and college instructor. She also worked for several years in rehabilitation services for private companies and the state of Washington. She is now retired and enjoys summers in Black Diamond, Washington where she lives on ten tranquil acres in a park-like setting. Winter months are spent in Mesa, Arizona. She enjoys traveling and spending time with her three sons and their families. She has six grandchildren. This is her first published work. She is currently working on another historical fiction novel which involves the colorful, almost 100 year history of a special house on Van Ness Avenue in San Francisco.

Printed in the United States
98987LV00003B/34-60/A